PICNICS ON VESUVIUS

STEPS TOWARDS THE MILLENNIUM

Also by William Rees-Mogg with James Dale Davidson

THE GREAT RECKONING
BLOOD IN THE STREETS

WILLIAM REES-MOGG

PICNICS ON VESUVIUS

STEPS TOWARDS THE MILLENNIUM

SIDGWICK & JACKSON
LONDON

First published 1992 by Sidgwick & Jackson Limited

a division of Pan Macmillan Publishers Limited
Cavaye Place London SW10 9PG
and Basingstoke

Associated companies throughout the world

ISBN 0 283 06147 2

A CIP catalogue record for this book is available from
the British Library

9 8 7 6 5 4 3 2 1

Typeset by Cambridge Composing (UK) Ltd, Cambridge
Printed by Mackays of Chatham Plc

Dedicated to my granddaughter
Maud Craigie

ACKNOWLEDGEMENTS

The articles reprinted here first appeared in The *Independent*. I am grateful to the Editor, Andreas Whittam Smith, for inviting me to write them and for permission to republish them, and particularly to the Features editors, Features sub-editors and copy-takers who have dealt with them so helpfully over the last six years. As a weekly columnist I have scarcely experienced a single disagreement with my *Independent* colleagues over the whole time, and something close to 300 columns. I am grateful for their forbearance, their friendliness – usually over the telephone – and their professional skill.

I should also like to thank James Dale Davidson, my co-author of *Blood in the Streets* and *The Great Reckoning*, with whom I have discussed most of these ideas over the last ten years.

CONTENTS

CONTENTS

INTRODUCTION

INTRODUCTION

I n July 1986 Andreas Whittam Smith, who was launching *The Independent*, came to see me at the Arts Council. He asked me whether I would like to write a weekly column for *The Independent* which was to start in the autumn. I had written rather little since leaving *The Times* in 1981, and was delighted with an invitation to return to journalism. The column was to be of about 1,200 words, I would be free to write what I liked, and Andreas expressed the hope that I would cover a wide range of subjects. I have in fact written it now for six years, and have greatly enjoyed it, and the deserved success of *The Independent*.

At the same time I was working, as I still am, with an American colleague, James Dale Davidson, on a Washington newsletter, *Strategic Investment*, which at present has a circulation of rather over 30,000. In 1987 we produced a joint book, *Blood in the Streets*, which was followed by *The Great Reckoning*, first published in the United States in 1991 and in Britain in 1992. Both books have sold well both in the United States and Britain, *The Great Reckoning* spending several weeks on the *Sunday Times* bestseller list and reaching the top of the *Evening Standard* list for London.

Both books contain investment advice, which has proved to be only too sound. They warned about the likelihood of a property crash in the United States, Britain and Japan, and expressed alarm about the growth of debt in the 1980s and the likely liquidation of debt in the 1990s. This message was not welcome in the United States – there was a particularly ill-judged review of *The Great Reckoning* in the *Wall Street Journal* – but it has notoriously proved to be correct. The recession or depression of the early 1990s may or may not be a slump of the scale of the 1930s but it is certainly world-wide, long lasting and severe, as we said in both books that it would be.

Neither book was purely concerned with investment, nor with economic policy. Both depended on a broader political analysis, for which James Davidson coined the term 'megapolitics'. This is basically a historicist view of world development, assuming the reality of historical cycles, and the inevitability of the decline of particular forms of national power. In the middle of 1990 I came across William Playfair's *An Enquiry into the Permanent Causes of the Decline and Fall of Powerful and Wealthy Nations*, which was published in London in 1805. I wrote about it in *The Independent*, and it played an important part in the development of *The Great Reckoning*.

We came to see the world as having a series of interacting cycles of national power. The British cycle, which peaked in the nineteenth century and has been in decline in the whole of the twentieth, has been followed by the United States, which peaked in the middle of this century, and is now equally certainly in decline. We saw Japan as a rising economic power, but already near to its summit, and probably destined to enjoy only a brief predominance before being overtaken in its turn by the economic development of China and the Asian countries of the Pacific rim. This is the almost universal expectation of Japanese thinkers.

We also foresaw the collapse of the communist system, both for reasons derived from information theory and of the balance of power between a bureaucratic centre and a nationalist rim. We forecast the fall of the Berlin Wall, the reunification of Germany and the fall of Gorbachev, as natural consequences of these forces. Information theory suggests that a totalitarian state will make bad decisions because it has too little effective information to make good ones. It will therefore fail in economic competition with free market systems.

The three major ideas of these two books, and of a number of my articles in *The Independent* were therefore that debt-deflation would follow the boom of the 1980s by a crisis in the 1990s, that the inherent incompetence of socialism would destroy the communist world, and that a natural cyclical process would cause the decline of each successive economic super power in the future as it had in the past. These ideas seem more obvious now than they did when we first adopted them, but even now they are not uncontroversial.

Not surprisingly, these ideas are more resented in the United States than in Britain. The British reviewers have been divided between those who agreed with all or part of this thesis and those who did not, but they have not been shocked by it. In America there are those who regard 'declinism' as unpatriotic, and there are also still those who think an economy always needs psychological boosting. We are regarded by them as people who cause doom by forecasting its possibility. On this theory people who read *Blood in the Streets* or *The Great Reckoning* will be so alarmed that they will stop buying and this will cause the great economy of the United States to seize up. In fact people who have taken our advice have, for instance, refrained from borrowing to buy property and have been saved from loss to themselves and embarrassment to the banks.

Perhaps the British would equally have disliked an early warning of the decline of British power. It is hard to be sure. Kipling was the poet of imperialism, yet his most famous poem about the British Empire, 'Recessional', is a warning of exactly this kind. 'The tumult and the shouting dies; the Captains and the Kings depart.' That sums up the mood of what we had to write.

Both James Davidson and I became increasingly conscious during the 1980s of another aspect of decline, the deterioration of the order of society, the growth of an underclass, particularly in the big cities of the United States, themselves leading lives of poverty and desperation, with rapidly rising crime and disease. My visits to New York, Washington and Los Angeles, where one only has to watch the local television to see an urban catastrophe unfolding, increasingly alarmed me at this threat to civilization. James Davidson in Washington was living through it. The decline has been slower and has gone less far in London, though Liverpool is a bad case of a post-industrial city. Yet Britain now seems to be where the United States was in the 1960s. No one doubts that ordinary life in central London is less safe and less healthy than it was ten or twenty years ago.

As we discussed these subjects in our two books, and in *Strategic Investment*, so naturally I also wrote about them in *The Independent*. Most of the articles which are reprinted here in the sections on 'Megapolitics', 'History', and 'Economics and Business' deal with one aspect or another of the issues discussed in *The Great Reckoning*, though handled in a different way. Yet at the same time I was developing a parallel theme which we did not discuss in *The Great Reckoning*, which is the change in the religious and spiritual consciousness of the world.

Much of what we wrote is regarded as pessimistic. I am not sure that pessimism is a proper description of this type of analysis of human affairs. If one believes in historical cycles one may be described as a pessimist at the top of a boom, but may equally be an optimist at the bottom of a depression. If one expects false political systems, such as state socialism, to collapse from their own incompetence, one is optimistic about freedom. In either case, one is trying to be realistic about the phases of the human moon.

Yet my attitude to the development of religion and spirituality can undeniably be regarded as optimistic. In a rather old-fashioned way, I regard socialism and atheism as being equally in decline. I do not believe socialism has a positive future, and I do not believe that atheism has a positive future either. In each case for the simplest of reasons, that they are mistaken; they are wrong.

There was a certain stage in human history when atheism, or at least agnosticism, seemed to be plausible because it seemed to be in accord with the most modern knowledge of natural science. That plausibility reached its height rather a long time ago, shortly after the publication of Darwin's *Origin of Species* in 1859. We can well understand the crisis of faith of our great-grandfathers, just as we can understand that the intolerable industrial factory system of that period made plausible the intolerable political factory system of Marx and Engels. Yet science has moved on, and faith has moved on.

Even in the early generations after the great Victorian crisis of faith, there were thinkers who rejected the plausible arguments of scepticism which followed Darwin, just as earlier George Berkeley, the great Irish bishop, had confuted the arguments of scepticism which had followed Newton in the eighteenth century. One of the most interesting of these groups, including F. W. H. Myers and Henri Bergson, were associated with William James, the founding father of the American school of psychology, whose book *The Varieties of Religious Experience*, first published in 1902, I have been re-reading and recommending constantly since I was first introduced to it in the 1960s.

The reality of religious experience is my strongest personal conviction, and it has strengthened with each passing year. I live myself, comfortably and with reasonable orthodoxy for an Englishman, in membership of the Roman Catholic Church. I am beyond measure grateful to the Catholic Church for the gift of an orderly faith. But I am also, in the sense of the Athanasian Creed, conscious of the incomprehensibility of religion. We live in a mysterious spiritual world, which seems to be surrounded by equally mysterious but other spiritual worlds. There must I think be creatures, perhaps we should call them Angels, who are capable of consciousness of these spiritual worlds as much above ours as our consciousness of the reality of the material world is above that of the dog by our fireside.

I would not therefore reject the truth of anyone's spiritual experience. By that I do not mean that all religions are equally true, but that all religious experience, even the psychotic, has truth in it, and that the reality of religious experience is by far the most important fact about life on earth. The only people who are really without hope are those who have cauterized their religious feeling, who have deliberately deprived themselves of the openness of spiritual joy.

My feeling toward the role of human beings is very similar to that of Tennyson, 'Eternal process moving on, From state to state the spirit walks.' I cannot envisage mankind having reached the spiritual condition in which we now are, without an 'eternal process', a state of becoming which has so far reached this point, but which requires a further process to reach the ultimate point of unity with the divine which is given one aspect in Buddhism and another in Christianity. We are, all of us, half an eternity from our beginning and half an eternity from our ending, and the journey, the pilgrim's progress, is real, and involves real issues of importance. Perhaps this means that there is less difference than we commonly think between this world and the next; love and prayer are central to both.

If one believes that all religious experience is at least a reflection of the truth, one is likely to be saddened by the current state of religion in the world, and probably one always would have been. People look to the churches for sacraments, for comfort, for guidance, for education, for care. If churches are empty, there must be some failure of the churches as well as of society. In Britain there has been a thinning-out of the air of faith, it has lost its oxygen. Even in my lifetime the faith of the Church of England, which I admire though I am not a member, has weakened further as though there were a growing hole in its ozone layer.

The average English person no longer learns how to pray, how to form his soul, how to build a relationship towards God. Because the spiritual is real, that does not prevent many people from finding some religion for themselves, though perhaps far less than they might have enjoyed. But many go through life with only the faintest knowledge of what spiritual possibilities exist within them. That is a tragedy for them, often in the most practical terms. Every kind of addiction, to drink, to drugs, to money, to cruelty, to sex, is a search for the divine ecstasy in the wrong place. It is looking for the crown jewels in the broom closet, and of course they are not there.

There is therefore a link between disorder in the world of religion and disorder in the practical world. A life of prayer and love is bound to be a positive life in social terms, even in those rare cases where it is led in an enclosure of contemplation. A life of fear and desire, the natural state of the soul without God, is bound to be negative in social terms. I found once in an old scrapbook, and have had a case made for it, a fifteenth-century drawing of the crucifixion, no doubt a memorandum for religious meditation. Above it is written in a contemporary hand: 'Assit in principio Sancta Maria meo.' That translates as 'Holy Mary, be present in my soul.' I am particularly fond of the word 'assit', which is the third person singular of the present subjunctive of 'adsum', the word Charterhouse school boys still use to register their presence at roll call – the last word spoken by Major Pendennis in Thackeray's novel. Yet the word 'principio' is even more interesting. It means a 'first thing', so 'a beginning', 'a foundation', 'a principality', 'a power' or 'a soul'. The prayer asks Holy Mary to be present in the deepest and primal part of the human being, the true spirit.

The formation, education and development of this spirit is the making of any human being. Where this development is neglected or distorted, the human being will be distorted as a consequence. Bad religions make bad people; modern bad religions include such political forms as Nazism and Marxism-Leninism, but also such intellectual forms as scientific materialism.

During these six years I not only wrote about these themes, but also about art and literature – though mostly on the margin of both – about the press and broadcasting, including particularly some of the people I had known, about social variety, including cricket – where I entered into the great Botham controversy in Somerset – and Aids, on which I did some special work.

Looking back on these pieces, and on the reactions to them, I am very grateful to Andreas Whittam Smith and *The Independent* for the opportunity and the feeling of support. I have only worked for four newspapers – *The Financial Times*, *The Sunday Times*, *The Times* and *The Independent* – and I have been exceptionally lucky in all four. I was not always writing along lines that the staff of *The Independent* would have found sympathetic. It is a tolerant and friendly as well as an excellent newspaper.

I have certainly found that the readers of *The Independent* respond most, both in writing to the newspaper and in writing directly to me, when I write about religious and spiritual subjects. This is true even when politics are involved. In the middle of the last General Election it was a perceived difference between Hayek and Thring on the questions of whether a less complex mind can understand a more complex one which attracted a letter to the Editor. It is the substance that interests people most, not the accidents which flow from it.

I have not included in this selection many of the purely political articles that I wrote. In these years by far the most creative, and therefore the most interesting, political leader was Margaret Thatcher. I rather regret that no contemporary occasion led me to a full scale study of her work. I have known her from our days at Oxford together. I am not sure that I would have been called a Thatcherite when she was in power, though by some paradox I am increasingly referred to as a Thatcherite now that she has left it. In fact I always wanted her to be more Walpolean, more of a builder of coalitions, more willing to drop irredeemably unpopular policies, more concerned to build coalitions of support. If I had been advising her in her years of power I would have been trying to make her more political.

We can now see more clearly certain basic themes which she made her own. They include sound finance, hostility to inflation, British nationalism, the enterprise culture. They can fairly be called Thatcherism, because her combination of these was very personal, but I find that they are the root ideas of many of the younger Conservative politicians that I meet. Most of them admire her work; they do not choose to think in labels which belong to a particular decade, but in terms of the longer history of the British Conservative Party.

With these ideas I am in agreement. In recent years I have become more convinced of the realities which lie behind the word 'monetarism', more convinced that political affairs can only depend on natural loyalties – which makes me perfectly sympathetic to the nationalism of Scotland. From the point of view of the generation born in the 1920s and 1930s I find that I am more sympathetic to the generation which was born in the 1960s than to the one that is now in middle age.

There are cycles in all human affairs. There are cycles of morning and evening, of joy and sorrow, of conservatism and socialism, boom and slump, of puritanism and licence, of faith and doubt, of wisdom and folly. At the top of these cycles we need to fear the moment of decline; at the bottom we can hope for a happier future. But we always need to remember the uncertainties of life; even our happiest moments are picnics on the slopes of Vesuvius.

PART ONE

ECONOMICS AND SURVIVORS

My experience of business, investment and economic affairs has been dominated by inflation. When I was born, sixpence – one fortieth of a pound – would buy as much as a pound will today. In 1931, when I was three, Britain went off the gold standard. At that time a cottage could be bought for £100 which would now sell for £50,000, while government stocks could be bought for £100 which would now sell for £30. Yet in 1931 government stocks were thought a safer investment than residential property, and were the only investments allowed for most trustees.

In such an age families can very rapidly be reduced from prosperity to poverty, while other families rise from poverty to prosperity. The difference between two investments in one lifetime could easily amount to one investment rising twelve times as fast as inflation while the other fell to no more than one per cent of its original purchasing power. Affluence or ruin turned on the investment judgement of the families concerned, or their trustees, and the more prudent and patriotic the investor, the more likely their families were to be ruined.

Fortunately my father had inherited land and invested his free capital in the stock market. Farms which would have sold for £20 an acre in the 1930s did in fact sell for over £2,000 an acre after my mother died in 1978. That was not as great an increase as could have been had in some other forms of property, but it was at least two and a half times the rate of inflation. My father's stock exchange investments did even better.

Apart from inflation, taxation was extremely high during most of this period, and was confiscatory from 1940 to 1987. This applied to income tax, which hovered at a marginal rate near 100 per cent for most of the post-war period, and death duties which, as I remember, had at their worst a marginal rate of 85 per cent. Rates of taxation on capital gains tended to be relatively low and were for the first fifteen years after the war, non-existent.

The pattern of investment that this created was one of holding real assets – usually more than one could properly afford – against debt. The real assets appreciated, and resulted eventually in tax-free or low-tax capital gains. The interest on the debt could throughout be offset against profits in a company, and could, until the 1970s, be offset against earned income. Even now £30,000 of mortgate interest can be offset against personal tax.

Most of the fortunes which were made in this period followed this pattern, as did all the notorious collapses. Most of the families which protected their original assets successfully, or increased them by a moderate amount, also followed the same pattern. During the booms of the period, the late 1950s, the early 1970s and the late 1980s, this pattern of investment was spectacularly successful. During the sharper recessions, as in the mid-1970s and the early 1990s it produced general stress and some spectacular failures, such as Robert Maxwell's.

Assets matched against debt produce a very rapid increase in net worth at a time when interest rates are low and asset prices are rising. Equally when the scissors cut, they cut very hard. From the point of view of the classical rules of sound finance, as my English great-grandfather would have understood them, everyone has been forced to act as speculator in order to protect real values. His rule, which was to save half his income and put it into government stocks, made him a rich man. In the twentieth century, tax would have taken far more than half his income, and inflation would have liquidated the real value of his gilt-edged stocks. One of the weaknesses of the 1990s is that all British investors have been trained by a half century of inflation and high taxation to arrange their affairs in a speculative and risky way. Our national private capital lacks solidity.

In the newspaper world, the new proprietors, of whom in my time Roy Thomson and Rupert Murdoch were the most important, had to be great borrowers. In each case the formula was not simply one of borrowing to buy assets which rose in value because of inflation. They both had managerial skills which added value to what they bought, Rupert Murdoch mainly in rescuing unprofitable newspapers, Roy Thomson mainly in raising the profitability of existing regional newspapers, in Canada and elsewhere.

This has been the central formula, though not the only formula, of successful British business investment in the post-war period. You take a company, buying it with borrowed money, increase its profits, benefit from inflation and eventually repay the borrowed money in depreciated pounds. In the earlier phases of the post-war economy, interest rates were low, inflation was low but gradually rising, and this process could be done with only modest risk. From the early 1970s onwards, rates of inflation became more rapid, interest rates were less stable, and the risks became higher. Roy Thomson, who started his operations in the 1930s, had the best of this cycle of long-term inflation, and probably made the most money.

Inflation provided a formula for business, but it also provided one for politics. After 1945 politicians became much more aware than they had previously been that a little preparatory boom could help them to win an election. Certainly the General Elections of 1955, 1959, 1964 and 1966 were prepared for in this way, and only the election of 1964 was lost, and that narrowly.

Again things became more difficult in the 1970s. Inflation had seemed the docile servant of politicans. Now it seemed to be their savage master. In the 1950s and the 1960s a politicized version of Keynesianism had become very widespread. Both businessmen and politicians saw modest recurrent inflation as providing an answer to their problems. For businessmen it stimulated their markets, strengthened their balance sheets and helped to pay their debts. For politicians it created periods of prosperity which allowed them to win elections. In the 1970s, however, much higher rates of inflation resulted in high interest rates, rising unemployment and abuse of trade union power. It caused cash crises for businessmen and lost elections for politicians. Political Keynesianism no longer worked.

No doubt if Keynes's theories, twenty years after his death, had gone on making profits, helping investors and winning elections, they would have remained fashionable. Politicians and businessmen are pragmatic people; they are interested in the immediate consequences of theory and policy. When the politicians saw that they had lost control of inflation, they looked for means that would show them how to regain control.

Monetarism, the idea of which was largely introduced to the British audience by Peter Jay in *The Times* of the early 1970s, was the dominant economic doctrine of the period 1975 to 1985, as Keynesianism had been from 1945 to the early 1970s. Monetarism had a shorter run, probably because it imposed a more painful discipline. Since 1985 Britain has had no central doctrine; the results of that can be seen in the boom of the late 1980s and the recession of the early 1990s. Certainly monetarism would have reduced the boom and eased the recession, though the cycle itself would not have been obliterated.

I was converted to monetarism by Peter Jay at the same time as he converted many readers of *The Times*. I have not altered my view that changes in the supply of money determine the level of activity in the economy and the level of prices. Money has to be regarded as a powerful independent variable in the making of economic policy. Yet monetarism requires governments and businesses to forego the popularity and profits that inflation can produce.

During the gold standard period, the inflow and outflow of gold imposed this monetary discipline automatically. However, the First World War and the slump proved to governments that they did not need to subject themselves to this discipline, and once a discipline is lost, it may be impossible to restore it. In the mid-1970s I thought it likely that the world would experience a hyper-inflation and that gold would be the only discipline strong enough to restore monetary stability. The hyper-inflation was in fact brought back under control by monetary disciplines – particularly in the United States and Germany – which did not involve this return to gold.

Unfortunately the arithmetical monetarism of Professor Friedman has no automatic element. However successful it is, there is no guarantee that the next generation of politicians will adopt it. So it happened. The recovery of the early 1980s led on to an inflationary expansion of credit in the late 1980s, and then to a debt crisis from which the world still has to recover, though a weak recovery has been happening in the United States.

In Britain the post-1986 boom was allowed to run completely out of control. Since the Barber-boom of the early 1970s there had not been a comparable mistake of economic policy. This might have been prevented if Nigel Lawson's proposal for entering the European Exchange Rate Mechaism had been accepted in 1985. I supported British entry to the ERM even in the later stages of the boom, so disastrous was this inflation.

However the actual decison to enter the ERM did not come until October 1990, by which time Britain was in the second quarter of what had now proved the longest recesson since the 1930s. I foresaw that entering the ERM would prolong and deepen the recession, as it has, and was opposed to it. The entry was not only decided at the wrong time, but at too high a rate. The balance of trade deficit in a deep recession proves that the pound is overvalued.

Britain has therfore suffered from a badly managed inflation, followed by a badly managed recession. Few industrial countries – Italy is perhaps an exception – have had such bad economic management both in the expansion and contraction stage of this cycle. At present the need to match German interest rates in the ERM is causing a depression, particularly in the building industry, and a steady rise in unemployment to above three million. The boom and the slump could both have been avoided by normal monetary policies, and Professor Tim Congdon forecast and warned against both of them. I am certainly now in agreement with his view that Britain should leave the ERM.

The summer of 1992 has been a disastrous one for the world economy. Asset values have collapsed in Japan, where the stock market is more than 60 per cent below its peak. The recovery is weak in the United States. The European currencies are overvalued relative to the dollar and the yen, and unemployment is rising throughout the Community. The Italian financial system is hopelessly out of line with reality. Britain is passing from deep recession to the probability of a four-year depression – the second worst in a hundred years.

This is in line with what we forecast in *The Great Reckoning*, and it threatens the future of every government and every international structure. Maastricht and a single European currency already seem to be doomed. The ERM will not survive if it is a cause of 10 per cent unemployment in most of the major European countries. The European system itself is under threat. In democratic countries the public will tolerate moderate hardships for demonstrable reasons, but will not tolerate great hardships for a long time when there is no good reason to justify them.

THE OLD CITY STANDARDS
DRIVEN OUT BY COWBOYS

My grandfather was an Anglophile American of Irish descent, not a common combination, who prospered on the Wall Street of the period 1880–1920. He greatly admired old J. P. Morgan, with whom he did business, but he modelled himself on an ideal of the City of London, which he conceived as being one of old-fashioned English integrity: 'My word is my bond.'

He would come and stay at the Grosvenor Hotel in Victoria, then a fashionable new hotel, and would travel to his office in the City on the still quite modern Circle line; he would deal with top-hatted Victorian gentlemen who were punctilious in honouring their commitments. He found the atmosphere of London a pleasant contrast to that of the Wall Street of the great buccaneers.

It would be pleasant to pretend that an American visiting London would find the same contrast a hundred years later, but obviously he would not. London is now one of the big four of international financial centres. Both the dealers and the ethics have become international in character.

This does not mean that they have become dishonest. International finance cannot operate on the basis of dishonesty. But an important change has nevertheless taken place, a change in ethics not unlike the change in food. Where one used to have solid, and sometimes indigestible, old English fare of roast beef and Yorkshire pudding, one now has convenience foods, efficient but without much flavour. So the old English style of doing business has been overtaken by a mid-Atlantic style, and the old English integrity by convenience ethics.

Certainly much of the tradition has gone. Even when I first knew the City there were partners' rooms and partners' desks – those double mahogany desks which in the better houses were either Regency or at the latest early Victorian. Morgan Grenfell still has such a room, complete with grandfather clock.

There were telephones with circular dials and invariably black, often answered by those who had only recently ceased to be called lady typewriters. No one not a member of the family had yet, I think, become a partner of Rothschilds. Several of the better banks still had their original nineteenth-century houses in the City.

Now brass and mahogany have given way to plastic and leatherette. Everyone has a video screen. Admittedly the old ways were not all good. All my young years the City comfortably did business with a now dead Lord Mayor whom everybody knew to be a cheat; his shareholders' profits were regularly re-routed to his own benefit. He was somehow regarded as the City's in-house crook. But it was a tradition which valued individual character and the permanence of institutions.

There is no incentive to good conduct stronger than stability. If you have been doing profitable business with the same man for twenty-five years and hope to do it for another twenty-five, if your house has done business with his house for 150 years and hopes to do it for another 150, there is no smart short-term gain which can possibly be worth the long-term loss to the relationship.

The English tradition, which owed so much to the English-man's liking for clubs, was reinforced by the Jewish financial tradition, which had a rabbinical sense of the importance of logic and observance.

In the City of the 1950s the Jewish tradition was to be preferred because it admired intellect, where the old English tradition tended to suspect it. Undoubtedly the greatest banker of the post-war period in London was Sir Siegmund Warburg. He was a great innovator, but he also brought to London the tradition, transplanted in his case from Hamburg, of the European 'haute banque', an institution which valued both the permanence of its relationships and the quality of its own conduct.

Of course some of this remains. N. M. Rothschild has survived as a true family 'haute banque' in the old style. They replaced their old building, but New Court is still on the same site, and the atmosphere still has a traditional spaciousness and mild solemnity. Rothschild coffee is still freshly ground, not instant. There are many traditionally minded people in the City, and most City men are not only honest, but adhere scrupulously to the complex regulations of modern finance.

Yet the scale of modern financial institutions has done only too much to bureaucratize the City and most of the old stability has been lost. Control of institutions changes hands frequently, and individuals move freely from bank to bank in pursuit of ever higher salaries.

This has happened even in the house Siegmund Warburg built. At its height, in the Fifties, it was a small college of brilliant men – 'a nest of singing birds', as Dr Johnson called the Pembroke College of his time. It has now become, because of the growth Siegmund Warburg foresaw, a sort of financial supermarket.

In corporate advice quantity and quality are hard to reconcile. One wise man is worth a department of unthinking activists. Warburg's is still good, but at the end of his life Siegmund Warburg commented sadly that it had become the sort of bank 'which would not have hired me if I had applied for a job as a young man'.

Bureaucratization, short-term relationships and high job mobility inevitably make for a view of business which is short term and devoted to instant success. Because the United States is very large, and has always been more mobile, this has traditionally been the American banking ethic.

The loan officers who make the bad loans are promoted for overfulfilling their quotas and have moved to the West Coast by the time the loans default. That is now, too commonly, the London ethic as well.

In all of us General MacArthur's dictum 'in war there is no

substitute for victory' raises an echo. Yet the pressures to win have to be contained. Obviously in the Guinness take-over of Distillers they were not contained. The victory was won, but by means which the directors of Morgan Grenfell have already decided they cannot justify. A similar decision by Guinness can scarcely be long delayed.

Mr Seelig's brilliant career in the bank has been terminated. Mr Saunders's even more brilliant career in the brewery is in jeopardy. It all seems both understandable and sad. Of course those who live by the sword do perish by the sword.

That rashness was not Siegmund Warburg's style. He believed that he had a duty to help his clients to win – and they usually did – but to win in circumstances of permanent advantage. Clients who would not live by his standards were shown the door. I would be happier if I saw more signs in the modern City of the wisdom of Siegmund and fewer supporters of the corporate finance ethic of Billy the Kid.

6 January 1987

THE BISHOPS AND THE CHRISTIAN FACE OF MARKET CAPITALISM

I believe in freedom for bishops. I welcome the questions which a group of eight Anglican bishops last week posed to candidates in the general election. The bishops spoke out on behalf of the urban poor, suffering from 'long-term and grave injustices'. Their questions, as reported, leave out essential matters like inflation and crime, but invite debate on the theory behind political issues. Can the inner cities best be helped by socialism, by higher taxation, higher spending and more bureaucrats, or does a social market policy offer better solutions?

The social market philosophy believes that markets are the most efficient way of creating wealth and maintaining freedom, but that it is also necessary for government to look after those whom the market cannot provide for. The earnings market deals with buying work and skill; many of those unable to work will obviously need help beyond the market. But even in caring for them, market systems will normally be the most efficient, because they bring maximum information to bear with maximum force on decision making. There is a thrust in all free markets to increase supply, to lower costs and to meet consumer choice.

The bishops rightly start by recognizing the great change that has occurred in modern British society. As the Bishop of Liverpool observed, it has changed from being a pyramid, with masses of poor at the bottom, to a diamond shape, with a wide, reasonably affluent middle. This change for the better has been produced, though the bishop does not say so, by market capitalism.

This in itself almost disposes of the pure socialist solution. Society has always to be organized in a way acceptable to the majority. Not surprisingly, over 70 per cent of the electorate voted for non-socialist candidates at the last election.

Let me try to answer the bishops' questions from a social market point of view.

Priorities for housing and the homeless? The first priority is to increase the supply of houses to sell and to rent. We need reforms of the rent acts to enlarge the number of privately rented flats, and higher priority for new house building in a less bureaucratic planning structure. We need more, better and cheaper housing, where people want to live.

Reduction of long-term unemployment? 'What do you consider to be an acceptable level of unemployment?' Maximum valid employment always depends on the ability to adapt to changes in real economic demand. The decline in old-fashioned, mass-employment factory manufacturing should continue. Education, training, adaptability and mobility are the conditions of successful employment in new work.

The phrase 'an acceptable level of unemployment' implies that governments control the level of employment. This is true only in closed societies, which are both poor and unfree. Trade unions should co-operate in the creation of competitive labour costs. The answer to unemployment lies in raising Britain's productivity.

'A high standard of health care available to all?' The National Health Service is running out of resources even with greatly increased public funding. The NHS is an inefficient bureaucratic structure. A substantial expansion of the private sector, supported by health insurance, is the best way to improve the supply of funds for health care, to the benefit of the free public sector itself. The structure of the NHS needs to be broken down into manageable units, with market incentives to meet patients' needs.

Priorities for state education? Much higher standards are needed to train all students for the exacting work of the future. Schools should be funded according to parental choice, on a capitation fee principle, and should be free to spend their own money, both on capital development and on the pay and condition of teachers. All the existing national pay cartels should be abolished; they lower performance and increase unemployment.

The artificial creations of over-sized comprehensive schools in inner cities should be broken down, or allowed to close if they do not attract pupils. Parental choice will lead to more competitive selective examinations, and that is desirable. Teachers and students need to set their sights at Japanese levels if there are to be good jobs for British workers in the next century.

Alternative solutions to the problems of poverty? The central solution to the problem of poverty is the creation of wealth. Only a wealthy society has the resources to minimize poverty. The state has a duty to relieve involuntary poverty, and the wealthier the nation the better it will be able to do so. The creation of wealth depends on the national ability to meet the needs of the world market.

Central control of local government? Local government finance? Local government was given a large part of the welfare state to run. That has outstripped both its administrative and its financial capacity. Just as we need a reduction in the scope of central government bureaucracy, so we need a reduction in the scope of local government bureaucracy. Local government finance is grossly overloaded, and there are no obviously ideal answers. In addition, the social conditions in inner cities and the decline of the old Labour Party have resulted in some grossly oppressive and abusive local authorities being elected. In such cases, as in Liverpool, it becomes inevitable that central government should intervene.

*

Ethnic disadvantage? We must oppose apartheid in all its forms; apartheid is an artificial control on the market for labour as well as for political power. It is a racial cartel. Better race relations will come to blacks, as they came to the Jewish community, from economic and social advance and integration in society through successful work relations. This is at present happening much faster in the Asian than in the Afro-Caribbean community. Society will benefit from the natural growth of the black middle class. Separate black groups, as proposed for the Labour Party, tend to aggravage racial tension. It will damage the lives of black people if they are made a black socialist ghetto in a white market society.

I do not believe that this social market philosophy is at all incompatible with Christianity, provided that it is genuinely concerned with a broad concept of optimising human well-being and self-reliance. The distinction between a free market social policy and a socialist policy seems to be this. The market man says: 'Let us try to help you to help yourself to achieve your objectives.' The state socialist says: 'The state will do it for you, and you will do it for the state.'

19 May 1987

THE FAMILY FORTUNES OF TWENTY GENERATIONS OF INHERITORS

A modest amount of capital can make a great difference to the history of a family; over the generations, hundreds of people can benefit. One of the most beautiful medieval buildings in Wells is Bishop Bubwith's Almshouses, at the far end of Chamberlain Street, behind St Cuthbert's churchyard. The good bishop built his almshouses in 1436; he used a site which had been given to the Wells Corporation 200 years before as a house for old people.

The original gift, in 1250, was a bequest by a Wells merchant, John Mogg. It is a matter of doubt whether I am descended from him, or from the other Moggs, also called Mugges, who had settled themselves in Devon, at Buckfast Abbey. They both probably came from Wales, perhaps among the Welsh church musicians who poured into England in the first half of the thirteenth century.

At any rate, both families had established themselves as minor West Country property owners by the middle of the thirteenth century, and that, essentially, we have remained ever since. The constant theme has been the varied use of capital and opportunity. We have been merchants, clerics – seldom soldiers – land agents, teachers, surgeons, coal owners or lawyers as each generation has demanded. We have owned land, but never very much – at least by the standards of the larger estates. Our family history is by no means unusual; there are tens of thousands of similar bourgeois families. It has, however, lasted for an unusually long period – 750 years' experience of the chances of the mercantile life shows a capacity for survival.

Indeed, the Moggs are a family who did well out of the Black Death. My most distinguished forebear, William Mugge – he certainly came from Devon – was appointed the first Dean of Windsor by Edward III on the foundation of the Order of the Garter. He got the job in 1349 because the previous priest to be appointed had died of the plague. The Somerset family were able to buy the largest merchant's business in Bridgwater for the same reason. The Black Death created many openings for enterprise.

We have had many losses, but only one bankruptcy. In 1636 William Mogg of Wincanton, a great-grand-uncle of mine, went down for £1,300 in the business 'of banking in grain'. His failure was probably caused by the collapse of the tulip boom in the Netherlands, where the international markets – including that in grain – were centred and where his son died.

We did pioneer the north Somerset coalfield in the seventeenth and eighteenth centuries. On average we have produced about one good businessman a century, which has been sufficient to keep the family going. We bought no Church land when the monasteries were dissolved, perhaps because we were tenants of the Catholic family of the Cardinal Pole. We supported Charles I in the Civil War, perhaps because we were his Duchy of Cornwall agents for the north Somerset estate.

Such a bourgeois family history makes one very conscious of capital management and inheritance. Some time before 1450 a direct Mogg ancestor acquired tenure of 400 acres of land in the Somerset village of Shepton Mongagu – it is possible that the Dean of Windsor was the first Mogg actually to own that land. The moderate acreage has been the seed of both security and opportunity to some twenty generations, but each has had to remake its own position.

The opportunity has never, so far as I can tell, been seriously abused. A little of the money went on gigs and high living, much of it went on family education, a surprising amount on good works – schools, a cottage hospital, a church, clergy widows, missionary work, even food supplies to villagers in the nine-teenth century. Much of it, of course, went back into the various businesses, which must themselves have contributed to local employment and prosperity. Like many such families, the Moggs always had a puritan streak. They may have hesitated over the Reformation, but until my father married a Roman Catholic, it was evangelical piety which really suited their temperament.

Until recently there was one major objection to this way of life. Even if it made a more obvious contribution to society than that of the idle rich, bourgeois asset management was open only to a minority. Medieval society could only support a few merchants, only a few clerical civil servants could enjoy Edward III's patron-age. Seventeenth-century England could only support a few coal owners – even in the nineteenth century not every solicitor could become 'a warm man'.

What is happening now is that the world's economy is so productive that these opportunities are opening up not just for a fortunate few, but for a substantial proportion of the population of the advanced industrial countries. Capital ownership is already open to almost anyone who will work for it in California – including the new Hispanic bourgeoisie. Within a hundred years' time it will be equally open to the Russians and the Chinese. It is an enormous change in human life, and one we ought wholly to welcome.

In Britain the most powerful machinery for making every man a capitalist is the housing market, and about 60 per cent of families now own their homes. The average value of this property is hard to estimate, though in a nearby Somerset village I am told that the cheapest house to be sold in the last twelve months went for £168,000.

A competent businessman, over his lifetime, will make his assets grow – in real terms – by 5 per cent compound; a good businessman by 10 per cent, an exceptional businessman by 20 per cent. Asset values at 5 per cent double in fourteen years; at 10 per cent in seven years; at 20 per cent in three and a half years. If a business generation is taken to be twenty-eight years – from, say, thirty-seven to sixty-five years old – then £100,000 will become £400,000 in the hands of a competent businessman,

£1.6m in the hands of a good businessman, and £25.6m in the hands of an exceptional businessman. In the next twenty-five years something approaching half the families of Britain will inherit £100,000, or the capacity to borrow £100,000 against property. As Lord Beaverbrook said, it is the first £10,000 that is the real difficulty.

In an interview with Bruce Anderson in *The Sunday Telegraph* this week, Nigel Lawson observed that 'we are about to become a nation of inheritors. Inheritance which used to be the preserve of the few, will become a fact of life for the many.' Although I would not be surprised if the Labour Party were to win one of the next four elections, I do not believe this process is now reversible. Capital is always under political threat when it is in a minority. Majority capital ownership is economically favourable; it is politically irresistible.

11 October 1988

THE UNERRING ACCURACY
OF ONE MONETARIST'S
PREDICTIONS

In 1968, Peter Jay, then economics editor of *The Times*, was, I think, the first modern journalist to make the monetary figures front-page news. In 1969, he went for a year to cover the US economy in Washington. He became extremely interested in US Monetary research, and particularly in the work being done at the University of Chicago under Milton Friedman. Asking Peter Jay to go to Washington turned out to be the most influential decision I took as editor of *The Times*. There is no force changes history as much as the contagion of ideas.

When he came back he reinforced the interest in monetary theory of other influential journalists, including Sam Brittan on *The Financial Times* and Norman Macrae on *The Economist*. He certainly converted me from a loose Keynesianism to monetarism. He also influenced the Labour Party, and his ideas were apparent in Denis Healey's Leeds speech of 1975 which put the Labour Party on a prices rather than an employment standard. Monetarism dominated British financial policy from 1975 to 1985.

The monetarist view also became the orthodoxy of the new Conservative leadership. Indeed, one of the reasons why Ted Heath lost the leadership to Margaret Thatcher in 1975 was that he remained obstinately attached to an unconvincing neo-Keynesian theory of inflation, complete with incomes policies, while she believed that control of broad money was essential to the control of inflation. Her view had already been adopted by Sir Keith Joseph, her leading ideological supporter, who, at Preston in 1974, argued the simple, and correct, proposition that 'when the money supply grows too quickly, inflation results'.

By the mid-1970s, monetary theory had largely replaced neo-Keynesian theory as the dominant view of politicians and the economic press; neo-Keynesianism remained dominant in the universities, and in the official forecasting bodies. In the early 1970s, Peter Jay brought on to *The Times* a brilliant young economic journalist, Tim Congdon. Tim Congdon later decided to devote his career to the monetary analysis of the British economy. He left *The Times* – much to my regret – to join a stockbroking firm. He is now an independent economic consultant.

In 1988 Tim Congdon made economic forecasts which differed very widely from the conventional wisdom and from those given by the Chancellor, Nigel Lawson, in his Budget speech. Nigel Lawson forecast 3 per cent growth; Tim Congdon, 3.5–4 per cent; the outcome was 4.5 per cent. Nigel Lawson forecast a £4bn current account deficit; Tim Congdon, £6bn; the outcome was £14bn, though that statistic may be exaggerated. Tim Congdon forecast 6.5 per cent inflation and a 12 per cent short-term interest rate; the outcome was 7 per cent inflation and a 13 per cent interest rate.

The Congdon forecast was therefore remarkably accurate if somewhat understated; his one considerable error was to understate the likely balance of payments deficit, but in every economic factor Tim Congdon was much nearer to what happened. The monetary forecast predicted the real events when other models did not.

What was the difference between the two models? As Tim Congdon wrote in *The Spectator*: 'It is a characteristic of the standard models that financial variables such as money supply growth are seen as being *determined by* rather than *determining* spending . . . As a result, the standard models regard interest rates, credit growth and the money supply as trivial and subordinate. Our model diverged radically from that used by other forecasters. First, the financial variables drove the real variables forward, rather than the other way round. Secondly, changes in broad money were central to the economy's behaviour.'

How did the Chancellor come to abandon the monetarist approach to forecasting and to policy? He was, it is true, a Keynesian by training, and remained a Keynesian in the 1960s. But so were we all. The monetarist argument belonged to the early 1970s and Nigel Lawson played a leading role in arguing the monetarist case in the late 1970s and early 1980s. He was the main ministerial influence, as Financial Secretary to the Treasury, in developing the Medium Term Financial Strategy, a policy which did indeed bring inflation down.

He was almost certainly influenced by a desire to reduce unemployment, particularly in a pre-election period. He may have been influenced by Treasury economists. We do not know why, but we do know when he changed his mind. In the annual Mansion House speech in the autumn of 1985 he abandoned the broad monetary targets, and went from a monetary standard to a pragmatic standard of judgement, which is in fact no standard at all. This abandonment of the broad monetary targets was followed by a surge of the broad money supply, with M3 and M4 rising towards a rate of 20 per cent per annum in 1986, 1987 and the first half of 1988. We have had a massive increase of credit, which monetarists would all regard as inflationary.

Fortunately, the last nine months have seen a return to a more cautious policy, even if broad monetary targets have not yet been restored. The 13 per cent interest rate shows Nigel Lawson's willingness to use the interest rate weapon to bring inflation back under control. That seems to be working – the building societies' new mortgage credit is running about 40 per cent below what it was a year ago. The balance of payments deficit is partly structural, and there are large imports on capital account, but imports of consumer goods should be reduced if the present policy is continued. Policy is not perfect, but it is at least moving in the right direction.

The Chancellor has been a successful tax reformer, perhaps the best since the Second World War, but he must be pressed on the central monetary issues. Is he willing to go back to the old Medium Term Financial Strategy, and target the growth of broad money, in particular M4? Is he willing to resume open market operations, and use the weapon of overfunding, in order to control the growth of credit? Is he prepared to set a standard of monetary stability, or is he going to rely on the method of pragmatic guesswork which had such important results in the last three years?

These sound like esoteric technical issues. They are in fact the issues which destroyed the Heath government. They are the issues which made Margaret Thatcher Prime Minister. They are the issues which nearly lost the Richmond by-election. Abstruse as they sound, they are the issues which decide power. If Mrs Thatcher wants to win the general election of 1991, it is not Saatchi and Saatchi but Tim Congdon she should now be inviting for urgent consultations in Downing Street.

14 March 1989

THE TARGET DECISION
THAT FINISHED LAWSON

Exactly four years ago, in his Mansion House speech of
October 1985, Nigel Lawson announced that he was ceasing
to target broad money. Two years before – as Sarah Hogg
reminded us in Saturday's *Independent* – he had inherited from
Sir Geoffrey Howe an economy with a 3 per cent inflation rate,
steeply rising productivity, a £4bn current account surplus and
money supply targets which were being met.

As the author of the medium term strategy, Mr Lawson
deserved his share of credit for that. His Mansion House decision
was the error of judgement which led directly to his resignation
last week.

The explanation Mr Lawson then gave for ceasing to target
broad money was changes in international finance that made
these indicators unreliable. There were indeed technical problems, and neither the targeting nor the definitions of broad
money had been perfect. But as soon as he ceased to target broad
money, the figures began to rise very steeply.

The period since 1986 has seen a monetary explosion. That
suggests that Mr Lawson was planning an election boom, and
already knew in 1985 that he could not produce such a boom
inside broad money targets which would not be obviously
inflationary.

Between January 1986 and the end of June 1989 Britain's

various broad money measures approximately doubled. If one takes the broadest measure – M4, which includes building societies – there was a rise of about 80 per cent; bank and building society lending rose by about 100 per cent; the old measure of £M3, which concentrates on bank money, rose by about 220 per cent and has now been abolished for its impertinence. Doubling in a period of three and a half years implies a compound rate of increase of more than 20 per cent.

The Germans, who have had two wipe-out inflations this century, did not follow the same course. The Bundesbank continued to monitor and act on the broad money supply. If one turns the DM M3 broad money supply into an index, it reads: January 1986, 100; January 1987, 109; January 1988, 115; January 1989, 123; July 1989, 122. That is the path of the wise virgin.

Mr Lawson made the logical mistake of trying to track the Deutschmark without also tracking German monetary policy. The sterling money supply was allowed to increase more than three times as fast as the German money supply, at a rate of about 20 per cent to the German 6 per cent. That difference doomed the policy of aligning the pound to the Deutschmark.

Mr Lawson was right to want to join the European Monetary Regime, for that would have imposed the discipline that was lacking. Mrs Thatcher was right to see that you cannot inflate the currency three times as fast as the Germans and hope to keep the pound stable against the Deutschmark. What both failed to see was that, without a monetary rule, either of quantity or convertibility, disaster was sure to follow. Either rule would have saved Britain; Nigel Lawson would not follow the one, and Margaret Thatcher would not accept the other.

There is a strong argument that the broad money supply of any two linked currencies ought to expand at roughly the same rate. If one adjusts for the 20 per cent fall in the pound, DM M3 has risen 45 per cent in pound value since January 1986. Yet sterling broad money has gone up 100 per cent in the same period. To restore the 1986 relationship between the German and British money supply would require a rate about DM 2.25 to the pound, but that would have further inflationary effects.

The Germans have handled monetary policy much better than

us, but they do have real advantages. They have the deserved benefit of a high savings rate, as do the Japanese. They also have proper reserve ratios for the banks, and have been willing to offset the inflow of funds. The Bundesbank is an independent central bank guaranteed by the constitution; that is a much stronger position than the Bank of England's, which is subordinate to the Government. The Germans are operating in a much stronger economy. Yet the real difference is that the Bundesbank has been following a sound monetary policy, when Britain, despite high interest rates, has been following an inflationary one.

The difference can be seen in interest rates, inflation and the balance of trade. West German prime interest rates are 9 per cent. German inflation is half the British. Germany has a trade surplus of $76bn – almost as large as the $89bn of Japan, and indeed two-thirds higher than the Japanese when measured per head of population.

This crisis is not like the 1970s when there was world inflation. Britain is one of a group of only three leading industrial nations whose economies are in monetary disorder; the other two are Australia and Spain.

Each of the three has a grossly excessive increase of broad money, Australia a ridiculous 29 per cent increase over the past twelve months, Britain 17.3 per cent and Spain 14.6 per cent. Each has very high interest rates; Australia has a prime rate of 20.5 per cent – a rate which foretells bankruptcy – Britain 16 per cent and Spain 16.25 per cent. Each has a large trade deficit; Australia $4bn, Britain $42bn, Spain $27bn.

Only these countries which have inflated their broad money supply suffer from these ultra-high interest rates. The average prime rate in ten other leading countries, where the increases in broad money have been kept below 12 per cent, is only 10.5 per cent. Apart from the United States, which has a much lower trade deficit than Britain relative to population, the rest of the advanced world has balance of trade surpluses or deficits which are manageable in size. A small and exceptional inflationary group has acute symptoms of a common disease, and we belong to it.

The credit explosion of the past three and a half years has financed a number of different things. It financed a general boom in 1986 and 1987 which made doubly sure that the Conservatives would win the last election – but may also have made sure they will lose the next one. It financed a boom in the housing market which doubled house prices and resulted in the £1m country house becoming a commonplace in the Home Counties. It financed a huge increase in imports which has produced a trade deficit now running at the same rate per head as the Japanese trade surplus.

Our imports are a negative miracle. It has financed a return to inflation, partly suppressed by the growth of imports, but already producing the familiar round of strikes and threats of strikes. It has taken Britain from a position of great financial strength and put us in the category of the speculative economy of Australia and the fragile development of Spain.

This is the situation which John Major, as the new Chancellor, has to put right, and he has at most two and a half years in which to do it. Like Spain, we should probably find convalescence more rapid, and confidence more easily won, inside the European Monetary Regime than out. The coming recession will cause debt repayment and liquidation; that should make it easier to bring the broad money supply back under control. It would certainly be helpful to set targets for M4, now that M3 has been abolished.

Broad money growth ought not to exceed 10 per cent next year, the level of Canada, Italy and Japan, or 6 per cent the year after, the average level of Belgium, France and Germany. The Bank of England ought to be set free of government with a remit to stabilize money and avoid inflation.

It would be ungenerous not to recognize what Mr Lawson did achieve. He was a major tax reformer, a strong controller of public expediture, a Chancellor who built an enviable budget surplus.

He probably had a better technical grasp of economic policy than any Chancellor since Hugh Gaitskell left the Treasury in 1951. He is a buoyant and determined political figure.

The best comment on his monetary policy may be an observation of Samuel Johnson's: 'We frequently fall into error and folly, not because the true principles of action are not known, but because, for a time, they are not remembered.'

30 October 1989

THE END OF DONALD AND RONALD'S DEBT PARTY

'I believe cash will be king over the next two to three years,' is the latest pronouncement of Mr Donald Trump, the New York real estate developer. He is now trying to refinance his assets, contemplating selling some of the most important of them, and is accused by *Forbes Magazine* of being a great deal less rich than he was previously thought to be. He may be a little late in his discovery that cash is king.

Donald Trump has been one of the most conspicuous of New York's speculative financiers, but what is happening to him may well also be happening to a number of other greyer figures who try as hard to stay out of the newspapers as he does to get into them. The evidence is that he is in some trouble, though it is not yet certain how acute the trouble is.

He has put a wide variety of his assets up for sale. To start with there is his yacht, *Trump Princess*, which was previously owned by Mr Adnan Khashoggi and contains a discotheque and theatre. The asking price is $115m. Mr Trump hastens to say that he is selling his yacht only because he wants to build a bigger one. The yacht brought no luck to Mr Khashoggi and it may not have brought luck to Mr Trump either.

Also for sale is the Trump air shuttle from New York to Washington, which he bought as recently as last June for $365m. He is also planning to refinance other assets, but he denies that he is facing a financial squeeze. 'I have the greatest assets in the world. They are all trophies, but they're all under-financed,' he told the *Financial Times*.

Mr Trump is angry with *Forbes Magazine* which has decided that he is not as rich as it had thought he was, by about $1bn. *Forbes*'s new estimate makes it doubtful whether Mr Trump is any longer seriously rich at all. He is said to have assets of $3.7bn, liabilities of $3.2bn and interest charges that come to $40m more than his income. This means the $500m that *Forbes* now thinks is Mr Trump's net worth amounts to no more than 13.5 per cent of his total assets.

These are the debt ratios of a first-time buyer. If a young couple in London owned a flat worth £100,000 with a mortgage of £86,500 and paid interest which came to £1,000 more than their income, we would not say they were rich but that they needed debt counselling. If *Forbes Magazine* is right, Mr Trump needs debt counselling.

What is the cause of the trouble? Of course, Mr Trump's debt ratios have gone badly wrong. If *Forbes Magazine* is correct, his liabilities are far too high relative to his assets, and he is paying far too much interest relative to his income. This is partly due to his reckless expansion in recent years, but even more to the rise in interest rates which has increased his costs and lowered the value of his assets.

'Interest rates are too high right now to justify a lot of deals if you have to borrow the money,' he has told *The New York Times*. He might have foreseen that happening.

Another cause of his difficulties is the decline in the cash flow from the casinos he owns in Atlantic City – Trump's Castle and Trump Plaza. Their combined cash flow was $92m in 1988, but fell to $37m in 1989, according to a filing with the Securities and Exchange Commission. Indeed, the cash flow problems seem to be becoming more acute. The SEC comments on Trump's Castle that sinking fund obligations 'in conjunction with the partnership's other debt service, capital expenditure and other working capital requirements, create cash needs that exceed anticipated cash flows from operations for 1990 and beyond'.

Mr Trump used $67.5m of what might be termed Trump bonds

to help finance his $1bn Taj Mahal casino in Atlantic City, which opened this month. It has been described by his publicists as 'the eighth wonder of the world'. The bonds have fallen by fifteen points in the past few weeks to seventy-five. The Taj Mahal itself is doing excellent business, but it has high overheads as well as interest costs.

Mr Trump stands on the edge of a financial precipice. A year ago he probably did have a net worth of $1.5bn; now he may have a net worth of $0.5bn; in a year's time, if interest rates fall and asset values recover, he could be back to $1.5bn, as the Taj Mahal profits flow in. Or interest rates might rise a little further, and asset values fall, and then farewell yacht, farewell shuttle, farewell Taj Mahal, farewell Castle and Plaza, farewell Trump. With his level of debts, Donald Trump is a bigger gambler than any customer in his casinos.

Of course there is nothing new in this. In every boom in history there have been financial speculators who have taken these risks, and in every crash in history there have been speculators who were destroyed by them. Yet Donald Trump is a figure of some symbolic significance because the boom has been worldwide and because the debt party is now coming to an end.

During the past five years most countries have gone through periods of excessive debt expansion. That was certainly true of Britain after 1985; indeed we may now benefit from having started to take anti-inflationary measures earlier than other countries. It was true of Australia, whose financial mismanagement in the 1980s was on a heroic scale. It was even true of Japan, which is now suffering from the aftermath of cheap credit and inflated real estate and stock market prices. But the real big debtor of the 1980s was the United States.

According to Grant's Interest Rate Monitor, the federal government borrowed $1.4bn overseas in 1980, the last pre-Reagan year. In 1989, the first post-Reagan year, the federal government borrowed $48bn overseas, twenty times as much. During the Reagan years, the total sale of federal debt overseas came to $225bn. Yet while the US government was borrowing heavily overseas, it was also borrowing heavily from its own people.

Professor Benjamin Friedman of Harvard estimates that in the

1980s the federal government was absorbing three-quarters of the domestic savings of the United States. That, in his view, deprived American industry of the funds that would otherwise have been available for re-equipment, as well as for turning the US from the largest creditor nation to the largest debtor nation on earth. He regards the day of reckoning as imminent and unavoidable.

Who saved the money that President Reagan and Mr Trump – Ronald and Donald – borrowed? Not Michael Milken, the junk bond king. The savings were made by the citizens of West Germany and Japan and were transferred through the international banking system to build Ronald's and Donald's debt pyramids, pyramids that could indeed be called 'the eighth wonder of the world'.

In the 1990s, the Germans and the Japanese are going to use their own money. West Germany had the largest surplus per head of any country in the world. All of that, and more, will be used to redevelop East Germany. Who is to say that the East German economy is not of greater social value than the Trump casinos of Atlantic City? The Japanese are determined to prevent their own inflation and Japanese bonds now yield 7 per cent. No longer will Japanese funds be forced overseas to earn a tolerable return.

In the first month of this year every country has experienced a rise in real interest rates. This reflects the demand for capital that now exists. The speculators are being crowded out. Mr Alan Bond has been crowded out already; Mr Trump is under pressure. But the great debt boom has been a financial phenomenon of nations and not just of individuals. If the Trump era is over, so is the Reagan era. The world has to adjust to a period when capital will be scarce, demand for it great, real interest rates high and asset values disinflated.

30 April 1990

PROSPERITY IS BORN IN A STABLE ECONOMY

'The country is not impoverished, but it has ceased to become richer. It is in a situation in which the least slip by the financial authorities could bring on very serious troubles. There no longer exists any margin for the unforeseen, either in the British budget or in the economy. The organism is intact, but it has become very vulnerable and could easily find itself in extreme economic, monetary or financial difficulties.' *Jacques Rueff, private report on 'The British Economy in 1930', to the French Minister of Finance, dated 15 April 1931.*

Different as the circumstances of 1930 and 1990 are, it would surprise no one if a French economist were to report to the French Finance Minister in similar terms today. Even some of Mr Rueff's specific criticisms still seem to apply: he reported high interest rates, a high exchange rate, a balance of payments deficit, a lack of competitiveness, a reluctance to face facts, a belief that financial skills will allow one to avoid the inevitable.

Britain's failure of economic policy in the Twenties was the result of an underlying intellectual failure. The economy was in theory run on classical free market lines – those were the days when bank chairmen would quote the nineteenth-century economist Ricardo, rather as, a century earlier, Chancellors could still quote Virgil to the House of Commons. In practice the Treasury and the Bank of England spent most of their time trying to buck the market, and the industrialists spent most of their time building up cartels. Throughout the Twenties the British were trying to rebuild a market economy without open markets.

This contemptible intellectual vacuum was followed by the long period when the ideas of John Maynard Keynes, variable and often inconsistent, dominated British economic policy. From 1940 to 1975 Keynesianism was the economic ideology of Britain, and it remains, along with abstruse mathematical theories, the most common ideology among our academic economists. By 1975 Keynesianism had proved to be cumulatively inflationary and had to be discarded because, like Leninism in the Eighties, the machinery had broken down.

From 1975 to 1985 the predominant influence on British economic policy-making was Professor Milton Friedman. The most important theoretical difference between Keynes and Friedman is that Keynes believed in demand management, principally through the budget, and Friedman believed in the stablization of prices and incomes through stable increases in the money supply. Keynes thought that the economy needed a recurrent stimulus; Friedman thought that this was inflationary, and that the best anyone could do was provide a stable monetary environment, a constant and low increase in the money supply.

This Friedmanite philosophy of money supply stablization worked reasonably well for ten years, even though it was not consistently applied. By 1985 Britain had a low rate of inflation, rising productivity, good export competitiveness and a modest surplus on the balance of trade. Unemployment was still high.

In his Mansion House speech in October 1985, Chancellor Nigel Lawson announced the abandonment of the monetary policy which had been adopted to give effect to Professor Friedman's ideas, and indeed he announced the total abandonment of broad money targets. This resulted in a classic case of a credit boom followed by a credit crash. This process had been given its fullest theoretical explanation in Professor Hayek's 1929 work, *Prices and Production*. That work explains why booms cause slumps.

Professor Hayek's theory, which we may call the Austrian Theory, states that actual interest rates fluctuate around 'real' interest rates. Real interest rates represent the return available on capital invested in plant or stocks. After a recession banks are liquid and lend freely and cheaply, below the level of real interest rates. That starts a cumulative process which is inflationary in character; it gives false signals which lead businessmen to invest too much in the wrong projects. 'When it stops,' as US economist Joseph Schumpeter puts it, 'and the money rate catches up with the real rate, we have an untenable situation in which the investment undertaken on the stimulus of an artifically low rate proves a source of losses: booms end in liquidation that spells depression.'

Britain went through the boom phase of this cumulative process in the years 1986–89; we are in the liquidation phase now. But while Nigel Lawson abandoned Friedmanism in the left luggage office of the Mansion House in 1985, we have not restored any general economic theory to explain the policies of the past two years, nor do we know on what theory the new Government will base its future policies. This is dangerous. In the absence of sound theories, unsound theories will prevail.

In 1977 Keynes's biographer, Professor Skidelsky, edited for Macmillan *End of the Keynesian Era*, a collection of essays which had appeared in *The Spectator*. One of the best of these essays, *Two Critics of Keynes: Friedman and Hayek* was written by a young economic consultant, Peter Lilley, who is now the Secretary of State for Trade and Industry.

He fully appreciated the strength of Friedman's critique of Keynes, but followed the Austrian view of the nature and consequences of credit booms. In particular he states that the Austrian analysis of the Great Depression blames the 'massive unsustainable credit expansion during the 1920s and believes that the resultant crisis was perpetuated by attempts to *resist* the liquidation of discoordinated capital projects'.

John Major inherited at the Treasury the consequence of the Lawson boom in Britain and the Reagan boom in America, both of which are now in their liquidation phase, as is the even more preposterous Australian boom. In Germany, where there was no such credit boom, there is no liquidation now, though even Germany is affected to some degree by the world monetary disorder of the Eighties.

As a result of his experience, the Prime Minister is certainly anti-inflationary, and he is a 'dry' on economic policy. One can indeed be inducted into the Austrian regiment – not by reading Hayek, but by the lessons of experience. The cumulative inflationary process really does happen; if you finance nonsense with cheap money, the nonsense really does have to be liquidated. Because he has inherited what has actually occurred, we can regard John Major as an honorary Austrian.

Peter Lilley has read the texts and has a coherent theoretical understanding of the process. I would like to see him draw on the work he did in the late Seventies and contribute to the theoretical foundations for the new Government's economic and industrial policy. Norman Lamont, the new Chancellor, also joined vigorously in the Conservative debate of the late Seventies. He was then, and I believe he remains, a Friedmanite and by no means a Keynesian.

What is needed – what is always needed – is stabilization. Business people can usually sort out their problems if they have a little time to do so. That is what business is about. When governments intervene, they usually make unstable situations even more volatile. They turn a storm into a hurricane. It would be nice to know that the Treasury ministers this Christmas are reading the economic works of Hayek and Friedman, and not those of Keynes and his followers. If they do, the eventual outlook will be one of calmer economic weather as the period of liquidation draws to a close.

24 December 1990

THE GREEN NOOSE THAT PUSHES UP HOUSE PRICES

The focus of John Major's Government is on Michael Heseltine. If he can solve the problems of the Department of the Environment, the Government is likely to win the general election and go on to prosper in the next Parliament. If he fails, then the Government may lose the election; even if it survives, it will certainly be in difficulty in the next Parliament. The Ribble Valley by-election shows that Michael Heseltine is the one man who could lose the Tories the election in an afternoon.

The poll tax is the most immediate of the Department of the Environment's problems, but it cannot be separated from the others. There are four great problems on Michael Heseltine's desk: poll tax, local government reorganization, housing and development and the inner cities. Whichever of the four he tries to deal with will turn out to involve the other three, and will affect the general economy as well. What is more, they are all politically explosive, and made a large contribution to the removal of Margaret Thatcher.

Perhaps one should start with the housing market, since it concerns the whole population, and is the key to the other three. Viewed simply in market terms, the present situation is bad enough, and the outlook is little less than catastrophic. Despite the recession, housing value for money in Britain is probably the worst in Western Europe. A family house costs twice as much, or more, in Britain as it does in most of the rest of the European Community. The average British housebuyer pays much more for worse accommodation. That is the case after almost three years of penal interest rates designed to lower house prices. These interest rates have ruined many businesses and raised unemployment.

Yet these poor values are likely to become still worse. Oxford Economic Forecasting has just produced its forecast of house prices for 1992 and 1993. It predicts that by mid-1992 house-price inflation will be about level with general inflation if base rates stay at 13 per cent, but would be about double general inflation if base rates were around 12 per cent, and would come close to three times general inflation if they were reduced to 11 per cent. In brief, any further reduction in interest rates from their present level is likely to restart a major house boom. The Chancellor has to choose between allowing house inflation to revive, or allowing unemployment to rise towards the three million mark.

These house prices are already socially unjust and economically inefficient. They mean that about 40 per cent of the population, more than twenty million people, is locked out of the housing market. They result in the homelessness one can see in the streets of London. High mortgage rates on high house prices involve a massive transfer of funds from the relatively young to the relatively old, and from the relatively poor to the relatively rich. The cost of a mortgage on a starter home in the South-east is likely to be more than ten times the cost of the poll tax.

The main cause of these inflated house prices is high site values. The system of planning controls which was introduced after the Second World War has produced a cartel of development land, theoretically administered without regard to market prices, but in fact bound to raise prices. There are two points to emphasize about this system. One is its complexity – it operates at four political and four bureaucratic levels, each having some impact on the outcome. It is a procedure I have been through several times, though never in a green belt.

There are three main types of plans: regional plans, county council structure plans and district council local plans. Each has its own process of formulation, consultation and appeal, and each interlocks with the others. A complete cycle of plans may never be achieved, but could not be achieved in less than ten years. The cost of these procedures is a factor in site costs, as is the cost of delay, but the main reason for high site costs is the shortage of approved sites. In the South-east Michael Heseltine has warned that the regional plan falls about 30 per cent short of need, and that is probably an underestimate. The whole planning system is designed to sterilize potential development land.

The other factor is the green-belt policy. Most green belts were defined twenty years ago or more. When they were originally allocated, urban land was left for development inside the belts. That land has now, in most cases, been used up. We therefore have many towns and cities that are actually shrinking in population, because the size of the average household is falling and no new houses can be built. For people who need to live in these towns and cities, the green belt has become a green noose.

This green-belt policy does have strong environmentalist support, though it can actually throw urban overspill beyond the green belt into deep countryside. That is why one sees so many cramped Eighties estates on the edges of country villages. The green noose is still being tightened, even taking in derelict land.

The main proposal for replacing the poll tax is to reintroduce a tax on housing. If house prices were at the European level, that would be reasonable enough. But they are already twice the European level, and our mortgage rates are about 50 per cent higher than Germany's. That means the cost to the new house puchaser is likely to be some three times the European level – not an encouraging basis for a new tax.

Local government finance cannot be separated from the structure of local government. Michael Heseltine intends to produce proposals for local government reform, cutting out one tier, either district or county councils. That will in itself abolish one tier of planning. He should concentrate on the productivity of local government manpower. One of the reasons why any system of local taxation is burdensome is that much local government is inefficient, a failure the poll tax was supposed to correct.

The fourth problem is the inner cities. Here again the question of house prices is vital. People are forced to live in slum conditions in the inner cities because they cannot afford better accommodation elsewhere. The inner cities are the sump for overcrowding. If the mortgage interest on the cost of a site in the South-east is £15,000 a year, then people earning less than £15,000 a year are not going to be able to afford many new houses. They have to take what they can get. Housing poverty is the inevitable consequence of excessive house prices; the high site costs make it impossible for housing associations or other benevolent housing providers to build for an affordable rent.

The starting point for new policy should therefore be the market for housing sites. The moment is favourable, because the recession has temporarily reduced their cost, and developers' land banks will cover a year or two of increased activity. The case study is not France, which has much more land than Britain, but the Netherlands, where planning controls have been operating in an even more dense environment, producing better quality housing at more affordable prices.

The green-noose policy is essentially anti-suburban. Most people in Britain would rather live in suburbs than in city centres or the deep countryside. If Michael Heseltine wants to avoid another house price boom, and the great suffering that will cause, he should allow the suburbs to grow, and should let suburban developers build at site prices that people not in the top 20 per cent of incomes can afford.

11 March 1991

INNOVATIVE, MOTIVATED
AND IN TROUBLE

Each recession has a different pattern and creates a crisis in different parts of the economy. In 1974, for instance, the recession most affected the stock market, which collapsed, the banking system – particularly the secondary banks – property and construction. The Bank of England launched the lifeboat to protect the banking system and a general financial collapse was prevented.

The present recession has hardly affected stock-market prices, and equity investors can realise their shares, if they need to, at very satisfactory prices. Nor has it been particularly severe in the manufacturing North, which was hardest hit by the recession of the early Eighties. This has been much more of a consumer recession, together with yet another slump in property and construction. Dun & Bradstreet report that a third of failed businesses are either in the retail trade or in construction. Tourism has been weak, and hotels and restaurants have done very badly.

The recession has damaged and, in some cases, destroyed large businesses, and others have had to lay off workers and close premises. Yet in the worst-affected sectors are large numbers of small businesses, many founded in the Eighties. By a small business I mean one that employs up to fifty people or has a turnover of up to £5m.

Both Dun & Bradstreet and the accountants Grant Thornton report a doubling of business failures between 1990 and 1991, and Grant Thornton expect to see 'the same level of receiverships until the end of the year and into next year'. That is bad news.

There is a general crisis of small business in the South and Midlands. 'One cannot tell who is solvent and who is not'; 'orders stopped coming in like a tap being turned off'; 'the bank is pressing him for £25,000 he is owed by an insolvent company'; 'running a manufacturing company in the East Midlands is impossible nowadays'. These are a sample of comments I have heard recently. I can never remember such widespread anxiety or so much personal distress. And, of course, the staff are as worried as the managers.

There are many small businesses that have not been much affected by the recession; some depend on overseas markets that may not have had recessions, others depend on markets where demand has been stable – undertakers are usually given as an example of a non-cyclical business. But the heaviest impact of this recession has been in sectors where small businesses are common, and in the South and Midlands it has been the worst recession for them since the Thirties.

By their nature small businesses are vulnerable. When they start they are always short of capital and usually over-dependent on the banks. They are seldom diversified in their markets. They do not have the reserves of larger and longer-established businesses. They do not have the same depth or range of management, though the management they do have is often very good and resilient. They can seldom spread their risks by operating in different markets. They tend to grow in niches in the home market; the small export businesses are important, but they operate in a different world.

The fall in consumer demand has been the real cause of the crisis. In many cases the decline was rapid and outside any previous experience. People stopped moving house, which affects not only housing, but many related businesses supplying the housing market. People deferred buying cars – even the last Budget discouraged business purchases. There are few new jobs on offer, and, therefore, no work for head-hunters and staff recruitment firms. Businesses have cut back on advertising, and the advertising agencies have suffered, as have newspapers and television. In all these areas well-estabished and well-run businesses found that there was a sudden stoppage of sales.

As the Government consistently overestimated future demand, one cannot blame the people running such businesses for failing to be better forecasters than the Treasury. Even if they had foreseen what was happening, they could not always have done anything effective to protect themselves. In general, it was not business inefficiency that accounted for the rise in business failures but reduction in demand, caused by the hard landing that followed the easy access to credit encouraged by Nigel Lawson's 1989 Budget.

These small businessmen are usually dependent on their bankers who, in many cases, have the power of life and death over them. Interest rates have been important. At the start of the recession, the base rate was still 15 per cent, which meant that small businesses were paying about 18 per cent. They could not earn 18 per cent on their capital, and as the recession progressed they might not be earning anything at all.

The commercial property market went into deep recession, which meant that the property security for bank loans was eroded. No less than 15 per cent of shops are now said to be for sale. Modern shop leases allow only for upward revision of rents; many leases have, therefore, gone from being assets to being liabilities.

This pattern of falling sales, sharply falling profits, high interest rates and falling balance-sheet values for business premises is so widespread as to be normal, and it puts pressure on the banks as well as on their customers.

Certainly the banks need to review their relationship with small businesses, as they have been doing. The shift from relationship to transactional banking has undoubtedly been taken too far, and bank managers tend to be changed too fast for the good of the customer relationship. But banks do not set base rate and they do not control demand in the economy. Many, though not all, small businessmen have found their banks helpful and supportive in the recession.

When he was Chancellor, John Major made two significant mistakes. He believed Treasury forecasts, and therefore underestimated the momentum of recession. He entered the ERM before bringing interest rates down to their appropriate recession level.

By the present stage of the business cycle, base rate should be below 10 per cent, and perhaps as low as 8 per cent. However, the objective of joining the ERM was right, because European monetary stability has been so much better than Britain's in the post-war period. Long-term stability is what business needs most.

Nevertheless, interest rates should continue to come down. The historic average for base rate is about a real rate of 5 per cent, though the fluctuations have been wide. In 1992 inflation should be running at about 3 per cent, which should allow base rate to come down to 8 per cent, and the actual overdraft rate for small businesses to 11 per cent.

With some recovery in demand, even if that is delayed, most small businesses that have not already been completely shattered should be able to survive in next year's conditions. That still leaves the structural problems of small-business finance. I hope that Citibank and NatWest's initiatives in offering fixed-rate mortgages at below 12 per cent will be extended to business loans. A fixed-rate, ten-year business loan would be a stable basis for small-business finance, and would allow much better financial planning. Both the Government and the banks should help these businesses.

They have great virtues of motivation, flexibility and innovation, and they still have growth potential. Banks lose money by lending on overvalued assets at the top of a boom; they seldom lose money by lending on undervalued assets at the bottom of a recession.

8 July 1991

HAUNTED BY THE GHOSTS
OF CHRISTMAS 1931

Perhaps it was not such a good idea to make British housing, jobs and the general election depend on the majority decisions of a non-elected, independent, German committee in Frankfurt. Before Britain joined the exchange-rate mechanism (ERM) last year, I argued that it could cost the Conservative Party the election. The Bundesbank's decision to raise the German discount rate to 8 per cent may prove those who have argued that way to be right. The Bundesbank is piling European deflation on deflation, and has fixed the highest German discount rate since 1931. That decision belongs to the old 'cure a headache with a bullet in the brain' school of economic policy.

This Christmas has something of the gloom and panic of the Christmas of 1931. Now, as then, we are about two years into a world-wide economic decline. Now, as then, we have world-wide stock exchange crashes behind us. Now, as then, the world's banking system is on the edge of insolvency. Now, as then, great speculators have crashed amid great scandals. Bob Maxwell had his true forebears in the late Twenties and early Thirties. Now, as then, there is a conflict between financial authorities still fighting the inflation of the previous decade, and those fighting the depression.

The big difference is that the downturn which started early in 1990 is much less extreme in the advanced industrial countries

46

than the one which began in the last quarter of 1929. A depression can be distinguished from a recession by three qualities; a depression is extreme, long-lasting and world-wide. What we are experiencing in Britain now is like a recession in severity, but more like a depression in extent and probably in duration.

The classic academic study of the depression of the early Thirties is Joseph Schumpeter's *Business Cycles*, published in 1939. He elaborated a theory of three business cycles operating simultaneously, and called after the economists who had first identified them. These cycles have a period of somewhat less than sixty years, somewhat less than ten years and somewhat less than forty months. We can, for the present, overlook the short cycle. The sixty-year cycle Schumpeter called the Kondratieff, after the Russian economist who was sent to a prison camp by Stalin and died there. The ten-year cycle he called the Juglar after the late nineteenth-century French economist.

Kondratieff depressions occur as a result of the coincidence between the low phase of the long and medium cycles. From peak to full recovery, they last about five years. The three Kondratieff depressions known to Schumpeter were those of 1825–30, 1873–78 and 1929–34. If we are now experiencing a Kondratieff depression, it could be expected to cover the years 1990 to 1994, and the after-shock may continue into the later 1990s.

There are earlier episodes which look like Kondratieff depressions going back to the 1630s, following the collapse of tulip-mania in the Netherlands; but, as Schumpeter admitted, the very existence of the long cycle can reasonably be doubted, and many economists do doubt it. You cannot prove a cycle on the basis of three or four recurrences.

The Juglar, however, looks to be alive and well. The recessions of the early Seventies and early Eighties are characteristic Juglar recessions, with the intensity and duration one might expect of them. The question is whether we are now experiencing a recession or a depression, a Juglar or a Kondratieff?

The main distinction is one of duration. An ordinary Juglar, as Schumpeter observed, is normally fairly short. The economy goes down for a year and recovers for a year. It is, therefore, a two-year economic event. A full-scale depression is a five-year event, with at least two and a half to three years of decline, followed by a recovery.

We are now about twenty-one months into this recession. It may have seemed relatively mild in the West, but in the Soviet Union it will look to have been very severe indeed, fully comparable to the early Thirties.

The trough of the Thirties depression was in June 1932, thirty-two months from the start. Timings are variable, but unless the present downturn lasts even longer than the great depression, we shall start to recover by the end of next year. Recovery could even start in mid-1992, but that does not mean we are through the worst. The last six months of a depression before the low point are usually the most alarming. A depression does its work by liquidating debt. The world's overload of debt may be starting to decline, but it is not yet liquidated to the necessary degree. The final liquidation usually occurs in a mood of temporary despair.

After a depression, the recovery, when it comes, can be rapid and strong. In the period between the third quarter of 1932 and the first quarter of 1934 – a period of only eighteen months – the London and Cambridge index of British industrial production recovered from 77.7 to 102.4, an extremely sharp movement. It looks as though 1993 could be a very good year, as 1933 was. But there is an economic and political chasm between us and 1993. The political impact of a depression wipes the blackboard clean of most of the statesmen and parties in power when the depression starts. The new leaders may be better or worse; 1933 gave us Franklin Roosevelt and Adolf Hitler. If we are in a depression, neither John Major nor George Bush can expect to be re-elected, nor can the Socialists in France or the Christian Democrats in Germany. The depression has already caused the fall of Margaret Thatcher, Mikhail Gorbachev and Bob Hawke and could well cause the fall of their successors, including Boris Yeltsin.

John Major's position is particularly difficult. The earliest likely date for the bottom of the depression coincides with the latest realistic date for the general election. May or June 1992 could well be the worst time for holding an election in sixty years, so far as the Kondratieff cycle is concerned.

In economic terms, the trough of the depression will come when debt liquidation has gone far enough to provide a base for a new advance at lower interest rates. In 1991, the US and Britain tried to form such a base and failed. Hence the double-dip recession. The US has reduced interest rates to the lowest level since 1964. That has opened a wide gap between American and European rates, and has already made the dollar an undervalued currency in terms of purchasing power. If the United States is first out of the depression, George Bush might survive.

At some point in 1992, panic will probably set in. Indeed, panic could now have a therapeutic value. Either the Germans will suddenly realize that the depression has already reached them and will reduce their interest rates, or there will have to be a major realignment of the ERM, or Britain, as in 1931, will have to abandon the attempt to maintain a fixed rate. The panic will signal not the end of the world depression but its low point.

The damage to the Maastricht programme is obvious. If we cannot trust the Bundesbank to co-operate in making the ERM work, we cannot trust a European central bank to operate a single currency. The damage to the European economy is obvious. Higher interest rates in a recession or a depression make the crisis worse. The damage to the Conservative Party is obvious. A recovery before the election was unlikely; it will now not even be possible to gift-wrap the depression for presentation to the electorate. There are only two pieces of good news. Those businesses that survive 1992 can expect to make a lot of money in 1993. The next Kondratieff depression is not due until 2050.

23 December 1991

WHICHEVER WAY THE VOTE GOES, RECESSION WINS

A t the general election the central issue will be economic policy: everyone is agreed on that. The central issue of economic policy will be how Britain can get out of the recession, which is probably the worst since the war. The recession has been sharpened by very high real interest rates. Britain has such high interest rates because sterling is in crisis in the Exchange Rate Mechanism. So the ERM will be at the heart of the general election.

What will happen? All three parties support British membership of the ERM, absolutely deny any willingness to leave it or to realign inside it, and are therefore committed to these destructive high interest rates. Vote Conservative and you vote for the ERM, high interest rates and recession. Vote Labour and you vote for the ERM, high interest rates and recession. Vote Liberal and you vote for the ERM, high interest rates and recession. It is an odious choice and recession comes out as the winner.

The character of this choice may not save the Conservatives, who have given us the late Eighties boom followed by the current recession, but it may help them. The vast majority of voters will have no alternative but to vote for a monetary system which is putting them out of their jobs, out of their houses and out of their businesses. Indeed John Smith, who is so widely praised, prides himself on his soundness because he is willing to destroy at least as many jobs, as many households and as many businesses as the Government. That is now Labour orthodoxy.

The voter may reflect that voting Liberal will mean higher taxes and voting Labour will mean much higher taxes. If one has to suffer from a prolonged recession, one might as well do so at Tory tax rates, so long as the other parties offer identical policies to the Tories on the central issue of economic management.

The other parties, both of them, have critized the Tories for not having been more Europeanist at Maastricht. Being more European would have meant being even more deflationary. Bad as the Conservative record is, the Opposition parties have usually criticized it in terms which would have made it still worse, urging interest rate cuts in the boom and commitment to a single European currency in the recession.

What should we do about the ERM? When I last wrote about this, in December, James Dickens challenged me in the letters column of *The Independent* to say whether, like Professor Tim Congdon and Sir Alan Walters, I wanted Britain to come out. It is a proper question, though I find it more difficult than they do. Tim Congdon and Alan Walters believe in floating rates as such; I do not.

Historic periods of fixed rates, such as the centuries of the gold standard or the decades of Bretton Woods [the system set up by the international conference in 1944 which created the IMF], compare favourably in real terms with periods of floating rates. They have tended to be periods of lower inflation, lower unemployment and about equal growth compared to the periods of floating rates. Fixed rates exercise some discipline over politicians. In a democracy, the requirement of securing re-election means that governments abuse flexibility.

In both fixed and floating rate systems, economic adjustment has to take place. Adjustment through the exchange rate is less painful and much faster, but also tends to be less real. Fixed rates reduce the businessman's incentive to gamble on high debt and high inflation. In principle, for these reasons I am sympathetic to fixed rates. In terms of the major economists, I am with David Ricardo rather than with Milton Friedman. The ideal is to maximize stability in economic management.

The difficulty is that fixed exchange rates only develop their benefits over quite a long time, and make adjustments over a long time. It is easy, therefore, to go from fixed rates to floating rates; in 1931 and again in 1972 that change produced a feeling of release and of necessary adjustments being possible. It is very much harder to move from floating to fixed rates. It took years to do so after the Napoleonic War, and was followed by a long recession. It took years to do so after 1918; the attempt produced a recession and broke down within a few years. The Maastricht proposal for a single European currency is supposed to take years and will probably never happen.

Despite Nigel Lawson's experiment in tracking the Deutschmark, which actually fuelled inflation, John Major's autumn 1990 decision to enter the ERM was not adequately prepared. Entry was made at the wrong price – as Britain's trade deficit in a deep recession proves. It was made at the wrong time. Britain had already entered a dangerous recession, and Germany was facing the inflationary impact of reunification. It was a political blunder, calculated to lose the Conservatives the election. It locked in instabilities rather than correcting them.

We can therefore be pretty sure that the decision to join the ERM, both when we did it and how we did it, was wrong. For those who in any case believe that floating rates are the only effective adjustment mechanism – and one can find support for this in some of the strongest passages of John Maynard Keynes's *General Theory* – the answer is obvious. Get out, and get out today. Even supporters of fixed rates may regard this as a failed experiment.

Such questions tend to be decided by events and not by opinions. Will the market allow Britain to remain inside the ERM, at the present rate, without imposing penalties and pressures which are more than we can stand? That is, to some extent, a question of will. Are we so determined to stay in the ERM that we are prepared for years of high interest rates, an indefinite further recession and deeper recession, more bankruptcies and higher unemployment? Presumably not.

To some extent the question is mathematical. How big are the disparities for Britain in the ERM? Can they be adjusted in a reasonable time? The three big disparities are the level of real interest rates relative to the recession, the position of the British economy relative to the German, and the rate of the pound relative to the dollar. Our interest rates are a third too high. We are at least 10 per cent less competitive in foreign trade than Germany. The pound at above $1.80 is at least 15 per cent overvalued in terms of the dollar, and in terms of the yen.

When one looks at these disparities, they do seem too large to be sustained, even with political will. The adjustment called for would be too painful and take too long, perhaps five to ten years of economic stagnation. If we had entered the ERM with these key relationships in a stable condition, it would have been right to stay with it. But we did not. We tried to perpetuate disparities, not to correct them.

The world has now been divided into two groups, the high interest rate European group, headed by Germany, and the low interest rate group of the United States and Japan. Conditions in Britain require us to belong to the second group; that is necessary to deal with the problems of the British economy. If we had not joined the ERM, that is where we would be.

We are, however, tied to high German interest rates which are quite wrong for us. We should therefore tell our European partners that we will leave the ERM if European interest rates are not substantially reduced. That is the only policy which will bring recovery to Britain and prevent a major recession in the rest of Europe.

13 January 1992

PART TWO

MEGAPOLITICS AND POWER

We need to look back to the Brezhnev era to see the beginning of the breakdown in the world system that was established after the war. The Brezhnev stagnation showed that the Soviet Union in the 1970s was already incapable of adapting to changes in the world economy. The motives behind the promotion of Gorbachev, and his introduction of perestroika, were not idealistic. The Soviet leadership had come to recognize that the maintenance of its own power, and of the Soviet Union itself, depended on the acceptance of change.

In the period 1989 to 1991, when Eastern Europe became free and the communists lost power in the Soviet Union, it was natural to see the process as being simply one of liberalization. Free societies are economically more efficient; people who are kept in chains naturally seek freedom. In 1992 however we can see that there has been more to it than that. The pressures which destroyed the old Soviet system seem to be worldwide.

In 1992 there is a genuine world crisis. The five main economic power groups of the world are the United States, the European Community, Japan, the Eastern group of ex-Soviet countries and ex-Soviet satellites, and China. Each of these groups faces acute economic and political problems and looks to the others for help in emerging from them successfully. This is the world crisis which James Davidson and I have been forecasting and discussing in the newsletter *Strategic Investment*, in our two books, *Blood in the Streets* and *The Great Reckoning*, and I have been writing about in *The Independent*.

The crisis in the United States is as much social as it is political. The American political system is under great pressure and has alienated a disturbingly high proportion of the electorate, but it is the oldest written constitution to survive in the world, it has overcome a civil war, a slump, two world wars and defeat in Vietnam. Plainly it has powers of survival. The real crisis of the American system is the breakdown of social order in the major cities, with whole areas given over to murder, drugs, poverty and disease.

This is a progressive disorder. When I visited New York first, in 1951, it was a safe city. One could take an evening stroll in Harlem or the Bronx without a twinge of anxiety. Except for a few people in the entertainment business, drugs were unknown. Race relations in the North were improving. Each decade since that time has seen a deterioration in the social life of the American big cities.

The United States also suffers from a progressive economic decline. Their recession has been more severe than in most European countries or Japan. The US budget deficit is out of control and the national debt has swollen alarmingly during the 1980s. In the post-war era American industry was the most inventive, the most productive, the most competitive in the world. Now the Japanese can export automobiles to Detroit. This has produced a loss of American industrial confidence and an actual loss of the high-paying blue collar jobs which were part of the bedrock of the old American society.

In Europe, Britain is the only major country with a stable and confident government in place. Germany is suffering from the absorption of East Germany which has proved much more difficult and expensive than was expected. *Länder* elections show the growth of a new and potentially dangerous right wing. Herr Kohl's Christian Democrats cannot be sure that they will win the next election, yet there is very little leadership on the left. In France the Mitterand presidency seems to be in an almost terminal stage of failure. Italy has no effective government and no coalition on which to base one. Recession is spreading through Europe and the Exchange Rate Mechanism, led by Germany, imposes high real interest rates which are quite inappropriate.

In Japan, as in the United States and Europe, there has been a major fall in asset values. So far in America and Europe that has concentrated on property. In Japan, following the boom of the late 1980s, it has also occurred in the stock market. The Japanese economy seems to be moving towards recession, and the Japanese banks are operating on a shrunken asset base and with large unrecoverable loans to write off. Many Japanese observers believe that 1990 marked the end of Japan's extraordinary period of economic expansion, and that other, lower-cost, Asian economies are now Japan's most formidable competitors.

The newly independent states which used to belong to the Soviet system are all in different degrees of economic and political crisis. They have in their favour exceptionally low labour costs, and valuable skills in their technological labour force. But they have abandoned the socialist command economy without yet being able to substitute for it an open market economy. China is probably the most successful of the major world economies, for technology transfer and investment are producing a Chinese miracle not unlike the Japanese miracle of the late 1950s and early 1960s. But China's political stability depends on a small group of communist leaders who are now in their late 80s.

In the major groupings of the world one can see the same political weakness, the same social problems, the same economic distress. Most countries exhibit all three of these symptoms; Britain at present enjoys an enviable political stability and China enviable economic growth.

One has therefore to look for common underlying causes, for what we have called the megapolitical reasons for this worldwide decline. In the economic sphere the 1990s are in the grip of the debt deflation phase of the long-term credit cycle. Because governments, through welfare programmes and defence spending, have maintained a much higher proportion of total expenditure than in the 1930s, the world is experiencing a controlled depression rather than a slump. But when governments cease to be able to maintain this expenditure, as happened in Russia, the slump follows. Russia is at present suffering a slump far more severe than America suffered in the 1930s, and will remember it for at least as long.

Western societies are trying to adapt to a steady rise in the levels of skill and application needed to obtain employment. The old skilled physical jobs used to last a lifetime. Now most physical skills require repeated retraining, and the mental skills needed to enter fully into the modern economy are not being created in the schools of the West. The inadequacy of schools, the increasing demand for skills and racial intolerance are cutting off the poorest groups from the rest of the community and creating in most big cities an underclass which becomes infected with crime and drugs, as well as with actual diseases.

The response of society at large is to subsidize these poor groups in the hope that the welfare subsidy will keep them from interfering with mass middle-class society. The dividing line between the haves and the have-nots has changed, so that there are now more haves than have-nots, probably by about three to one in the rich nations. But whereas society provided a place for the old poor, society excludes the new underclass.

This alienation extends from classes inside nations to nations in the world. About a billion people, 20 per cent of the world population, live in conditions of extreme deprivation. Comparisons of nominal income can obviously be misleading, but the gap between the richest and the poorest nations is extraordinary. In terms of gross domestic product per head, the range is from about $30,000 a year to below $100 a year, a range of 300 to one.

It is not the very poorest nations which produce most of the terrorists. In some cases terrorists come from the alienated middle-class young of rich nations. But alienation does produce urban crime, including frequent murder, and recruits for terrorism as a natural consequence. Both inside nations and between nations, modern economic systems tend to have this alienating effect.

The weapons available to the enemies of social order become more powerful as the order itself becomes more vulnerable. The most extreme example of this was the explosion of 200lb of Semtex by the IRA, amid the high-rise, glass-sided offices of the

City of London. Estimates of the damage caused, which will be met by the insurers, ranged to well above £1 billion. If 200lb of Semtex can cause £1 billion of cost, the equation is extremely favourable to the terrorists.

There are therefore three strong forces which are changing the world of the 1990s. The first is the economic force of debt-deflation, which will be very destructive in some countries, but milder in others, as it was in the 1930s. The second is the disintegration which is splitting the old communist empire into rival nationalisms but which can also be seen in the West, even in pressure to break up the United Kingdom. The third is the alienation of the poorest 20 per cent, both of individuals and nations. These are destructive forces, and political analysis has to take them fully into account.

THE US AS THE SICK
ECONOMY OF THE WORLD

I f I were illegitimate, or six years younger, I would be a citizen
of the United States, as my mother was. Even on my father's
side I have numerous American connections – there are some
250 Moggs in the United States, one of whom, Johnny Mogg,
died in Michigan in 1912, aged 125, the last surviving soldier who
had fought the British in the war of 1818.

I make these claims, rather in the style of St Paul emphasizing
his credentials as a Jew, because I want to write frankly about the
United States without incurring the suspicion of current anti-
Americanism. I am about as pro-American as one can be. I would
happily live in the United States, even if preferably in Georgetown, in Cambridge, Massachusetts, or under the good Mayor
Eastwood in Carmel, California.

I share many attitudes of American culture. I believe in the
competitive business society as a force for good in human affairs.
I have American heroes: my banker is Morgan, my statesman is
Lincoln, my philosopher is William James, my popular singer is
Jolson.

The proposition that has to be explored is the decline of the
effectiveness of the United States. There is an historical point of
view which sees almost the whole of the twentieth century as a
corruption of the idealism of the old America, a view expressed

by William James at the first stirrings of American imperialism, and argued now with conviction by Gore Vidal. Certainly, Teddie Roosevelt, the prophet of American imperialism, is an historic figure who seems the more repulsive the more one thinks about him.

One can well feel a regretful nostalgia for the virtues of late nineteenth-century America, for the residual Puritanism, the innocent isolation, the energy, the democracy, the Yankee combination of hustle and hucksterism with simplicity and intellectual curiosity. But can one believe that America could have remained a nineteenth-century country, of nineteenth-century values, in the maelstrom of the twentieth-century world? And should one not feel gratitude for American power, which prevented the twentieth-century world from being conquered by Nazi or Marxist totalitarianism?

It is a much more specific form of decline which has to be considered, the decline in the competitive performance of the American economy. There is a parellel in the decline of Britain.

We enjoyed a unique degree of advantage in the mid-nineteenth century, and became arrogant.

The United States enjoyed a similar peak in the mid-twentieth century; the cycle of America's own development came to its height when every other industrial economy had been weakened or destroyed by war. In terms of world trade, world competitiveness and the share of industrial production, the United States could only decline from the peak of the late 1940s.

The scale of the American advantage was so great that Americans too came to believe that they possessed unique virtues, that there was something about American culture which meant that the American economy would always stay ahead.

The British believed that in 1850, but had been proved conclusively wrong by 1950; that did not stop many Americans embracing the British delusion. We are sister cultures in our weaknesses as well as in our strengths.

The decline was gradual in the 1950s. The first person who gave me any insight into what was happening was Dr Steiner, George Steiner's father, then an elderly New York banker, in the early 1960s. He saw the rise in the free market price of gold against the dollar as an early warning of the erosion of American competitiveness. Gold is often a fascinating mirror of economic reality.

In the 1960s the decline was taken a major stage further by President Johnson's recklessly inflationary financing of the Vietnam war.

In the 1970s it was the bankers who did most harm, scrambling to recycle petro-dollars at a profit by lending them to nations who would never be able to repay them.

In the 1980s the Reagan administration behaved as though they had a master plan to devastate the American economy. They combined high defence expenditure with low taxation so as to produce an unparalleled budget deficit. They financed the deficit by borrowing abroad at interest rates which sucked money into the dollar. The dollar rose to levels which made American industry non-competitive both at home and abroad.

As a result an opportunity of an unparalleled kind was given to competitors, and most of all to Japan. In the early 1980s a generation of decline was packed into one four-year presidential term.

The result is that the United States, whose banking system has gaping holes in its own loan portfolio, has become the world's largest debtor nation. Last week the Commerce Department reported a $140bn current account deficit for 1986, up by $23bn in 1985, despite the devaluation of the dollar. The Budget deficit in February was $28.4bn, $3.8bn up on a year before.

The US current account gap has now reached 40 per cent of US exports of goods and services. Any rapid correction of so large a deficit, whether by devaluation, or by protectionism, would obviously destabilize world trade, and would trigger massive debt defaults. So large a gap makes the United States the sick economy of the world, as well as the biggest. It seems impossible to correct, but unthinkable to leave the crisis as it is.

The trade and budget deficits threaten world trade, world defence, the possibilities of world depression or of world inflation. They also threaten the political future of the United States. Meanwhile the stock markets of all nations, including Wall Street, continue to rise, in the characteristic current phrase, 'as though there were no tomorrow'. Unless the two great deficits are brought under control, tomorrow will be grim.

24 March 1987

THE END OF AMERICA'S CENTURY OF FINANCIAL PREDOMINANCE

The stock market crash has caused pain and fear throughout the world to all investors, and not merely to the rich or to large entrepreneurs. People have been affected in different ways, and have reacted in different ways, but the spread of anxiety is in itself an influence on the world economy.

There are, it is true, many people who have reacted very calmly. As so often, the smallest investors have been the calmest. The holders of unit trusts have not been cashing in their units on a falling market. Many small investors have been buying what they regard as bargains, such as the BP issue.

Yet they have lost money. This may make them want to save more. If a month ago you had saved £50,000 towards your retirement and your nest egg is now worth £30,000, you might hope the market would recover, but you would also want to increase your saving rate.

In the United States, where the saving rate is only 3 per cent, which is far too low, that will be no bad thing. Americans need to save more themselves, which is why their budget deficit is such an important issue, and they need to depend less on the savings of the Japanese. But a sudden rise in savings means less spending, and that has a deflationary effect. Fear also has a deflationary effect; an anxious businessman will reduce his risks, and he may be anxious because he has lost some of the value of his personal investment portfolio.

Of course, the crash has had its heaviest impact not on investors, but on speculators. The investor has seen a year's rise on the stock market wiped out. He is not as rich as he was in August, but he is still roughly as well off as he was this time last year. The speculator has debts as well as assets. His debts have remained the same, his assets have fallen sharply.

There must be many Australian stock market speculators who have been wiped out. It is quite normal for stock exchange speculators to operate on a fifty–fifty basis: half the money is their own and half is borrowed. Most of the Australian speculative stocks have fallen by more than 50 per cent; some of them by much more. It is the debt ratio to stocks that matters; arithmetic is as happy to wipe out $1bn as $1,000. Debt inside a company is less dangerous, so long as the company's cash flow holds up.

In 1974, it was the people who warehoused stock who found that they could not even realize those assets which they still had. In a crash, markets not only fall, they become much narrower. The greatest of the warehousemen of that time, Jim Slater, lost his business because of it. The even bigger Australian warehouseman, Robert Holmes à Court, is in a similar squeeze, which he is trying to fight his way through.

When investors lose money they do two things: they save more in order to try to replace what they have lost. They move from stocks to bonds – or into cash deposits – in order to avoid losing it again. That is one reason the bond market is so strong. They become averse to risk. When speculators lose money they are no longer able to speculate. Some of the folly of the markets is removed, but some of the buoyancy goes with it.

Of course, the consequences are not the same in all countries. Australia has supported a generation of speculative entrepreneurs on an optimistic stock market and generous banks. The crash, which has been accompanied by a weak currency and economy, has been a catastrophe. The foreign investor in Australian stocks has already lost well over half his money.

The Tokyo stock market, which is carefully managed, has fallen less than half of London and less than a third of Sydney.

The yen has been strong against the dollar. Japanese investors have been taught a sharp lesson against investing in the weaker stock markets, weaker economies and weaker currencies they can find overseas. That lesson is sure to have an impact. Japanese willingness to finance American debt must have been reduced.

In the United States, the lesson is the opposite. Americans have tended to do better on their overseas investments, because the rise in foreign currencies has offset stock market losses. The American investor in Japan has lost a little, but perhaps only a quarter of what he has lost on Wall Street. In a world crash, the movement of currencies either multiplies or divides the movement of stock markets.

Some commentators, and most politicians, are talking as though this worldwide shock will have little effect on what they term the real economy. I do not believe that. So far, the characteristic pattern of panic moving towards a temporary stabilisation has been followed.

I can see no reason why the normal sequence of rally and recession should not come after that. The rally will be assisted by lower interest rates, but the crash has changed people's perceptions of the world, and that points to a recession in 1988–89. What no one can tell is how deep the recession will be, but it is not likely to be mild.

After all, the problem which caused the crash has not been solved. In the American 1980 primaries, George Bush fairly described President Reagan's policies as 'voodoo economics'. That has not stopped Mr Bush supporting them for seven years as vice-president. The policies were really even simpler than that. They were credit-card economies. President Reagan bought a boom by spending without taxing, and the United States bought a boom by spending without saving. 'That will do nicely' has been the motto of the Reagan era.

The result is that the United States has in a few years become a debtor nation, grossly overdependent on Japanese finance, with a trade deficit running well over $150bn. That is comparable to the damage that happened to the British economy in the First World War. In 1914, Britain's century of financial leadership came to an end; President Reagan has bought to an end the American century of financial predominance.

Even a partial recovery can only be accomplished by a massive realignment of American resources towards exports and a reduction of American imports. Such a realignment cannot be achieved without a recession in world trade. Devaluation of the dollar without stringent domestic policies is not a cure – it is a symptom of the disease.

So long as President Reagan remains in the White House there will be no coherent attempt to restore the US economy, which his ignorant and optimistic policies have undermined. Washington still wants to avoid the pain of recession; the policy-makers do not begin to understand what they have done. Minor concessions on the budget are now too little and too late. The crash itself will have some effect in causing a recession; what the crash tells us is that a recession had become necessary, as well as unavoidable.

10 November 1987

THE EVOLUTION OF A NATION A LITTLE LIKE BRITAIN

At Kyoto last week I was taken to see the rock garden at the Temple of Ryoan. Everyone in Japan has heard of it; it is one of the wonders of the country. The rock garden consists of gravel, of fifteen rocks with some low-lying plants around them, but no trees or flowers. On three sides there are old walls, with mottled plaster panels; on the fourth side people sit to meditate. I took off my shoes to enter the enclosure which is ninety feet long and thirty feet wide.

The garden was designed in 1525 by Soami; he was a painter as well as a gardener. Its purpose, apart from its beauty, is to provide a setting for contemplation but, as with much Zen work, its aim is to open the mind, not merely to soothe it. It is designed to help the mind to enlightenment, both by the quietness of the garden and the subtle unexpectedness of the arrangement of the stones.

They told me they had taken the Princess of Wales to see the garden. She said she did not understand it. That is a good Zen answer; it meant the garden was working in her mind. The rock garden of Ryoan is certainly a good symbol for the culture of Japan. It has the beauty and love of art which are so important to the Japanese. It is also designed to be read in different ways. It is spiritually exciting, but enigmatic.

Of all the world's nations, one can make the strongest case

that the Japanese are insular and determined to maintain their own identity. One can make the strongest case that Japan is open to foreign culture. Some part of each attribute comes from the island history, so often parallel to that of Britain. Some part comes from the nature of Buddhism, the historic religion of Japan. Of course, most Japanese are post-Buddhist in the way most Britons are post-Christian.

The historic parallels are fascinating. Britain and Japan both owe their history to being large islands off a major continent. China has always exercised a gravitational pull over Japan's culture, as the Roman Empire and later Europe have over the culture of Britain. In both cases the sea has been wide enough, but only just wide enough, usually to defend against invasion.

In each case national unity was formed around a major religion which came from the neighbouring continent. Even the dates are virtually identical. Buddhism came from Korea to Japan in a period of a great statesman, Shotoko Taishi, who made it a kind of national religion. He lived from AD 523 to 621. Saint Augustine, sent by Pope Gregory the Great, landed in Kent in 597. The difference was that Buddhism absorbed the old Shinto religion and preserved it. Christianity absorbed the old Germanic gods and destroyed them.

An essential similarity of Buddhism and Christianity is that they are both advanced religions, capable of being practised at any level from the simplest peasant faith to the most profound intellectual abstraction. Both therefore were able to provide not just a structure for a nation but a civilization. An essential difference between them is that Christianity is exclusive – 'he who is not with me is against me' – while Buddhism is comprehensive. Christianity is an active religion and Buddhism a passive one. Buddha himself is thought of as comprehending the universe. Buddhists are taught that truth comprehends falsehood; good comprehends evil; indeed all are in the end equally illusions.

It is this spirit which has enabled Japanese culture to comprehend the West, while retaining its own nature. The first stage of comprehension, from the 1850s to about 1930, was a simple acceptance of Western trade and technology, but combined with an intense study of Western ideology. The Adam Smith Institute will be pleased to know that in Japan Adam Smith is still referred to as 'the pilot of policy', though Japan probably has more Keynesians as well as more Smithians than any other country.

The second phase, which ended in 1945, was a disastrous attempt to imitate Western imperialism, allied – partly because of a genuine fear of Stalin's Russia – to Germany in the Second World War. The third, post-war, phase has been Japan's astonishing industrial and financial success.

Yet the Japanese do not see these achievements as the sole reality of their national character or as more than a transient step in their national destiny. The central Buddhist belief is that enlightenment is permanent, and the phenomenal world is an illusion.

Some people in Japan feel that the Japanese destiny is moving on into a new phase, involving a reconstruction of parts of the Western culture. Since about 1980 the student age group has been registering an increasing disillusionment with the economic gains made by the post-war generation. Recent opinion polls show that a majority of university students want to direct their lives to spiritual rather than material objectives. Only about 10 per cent put either high income or status as priorities.

Japan is already an ageing nation, and one of small families. It is possible that Japan's economic growth will be self-limiting, if a new generation has different priorities. The older people themselves are nostalgic for the times when Japan was a country of gardens, rather than factories.

At the same time Japanese women are moving, gently but with determination, towards a new assertion of women's rights. Some older Japanese do not take kindly to this. Last week, over dinner in a Tokyo restaurant, I was discussing with a Japanese producer sex reversal in Shakespeare and Kabuki theatre. I said I had found the Kabuki actors convincing in women's roles. 'Yes,' he said, 'nowadays there is more femininity in our old actors than in our young women.'

In fact I found the young women students I met particularly heartening for the future of Japan. They are searching for a new way while retaining a traditional character. More than half of

Japanese women of working age are already working outside the home, and they are beginning to claim equal opportunities and status.

As I was shown around the Temples of Nara – which date from a period when our kings lived in huts – the archaeologist who was my guide threw a small coin and prayed before each shrine. He told me: 'Of course I do not believe in God, or anything like that. I make the observances for customary reasons.' At the next shrine he prayed again.

Two thirds of the Japanese live under the influence of a Buddhism in which they half believe. It is a religion which teaches that 'people call one phase of the moon a full moon, they call another phase a crescent moon; in reality, the moon is always perfectly round, neither waxing nor waning.' Japan is always changing, and is certainly changing now, but Japan remains Japan. I feel rather the same about Britain.

17 May 1988

A RENEWED SURGE IN SCOTTISH SEPARATISM

In the mid-Seventies, when the last revival of the Scottish Nationalist Party was at its height, I took the senior editorial team of *The Times* on a Scottish tour, to meet Scottish politicians, businessmen and trade unionists. We came back convinced that almost all Scots had a strong sense of nationhood, and that nationalism was an issue that would not simply disappear. Charles Douglas-Home, himself a Scot with a strong sense of British nationality, was the one of us who was most sceptical about the political implications.

After the failure of the Callaghan referendum on devolution and the election of the Thatcher government in 1979, Scottish nationalism did for a decade seem to disappear. Now with the Govan by-election victory, the SNP has returned as at least a serious political pressure group. How ought the English to react?

Most of the polls in the 1970s and the 1980s show that a majority of Scots want devolution, but do not want separation. It may be that the SNP will eventually succeed in converting the majority of Scots to complete independence, but that stage has not yet been reached. On the other hand, a majority of Scots are opposed to the present unitary institution, to London rule, and have been opposed to it for a long time.

The devolution proposals of the 1970s, which suggested a Scottish Assembly without taxing powers, were an unsatisfactory compromise, which could not have worked for long. They were supported in the referendum by a majority of Scots who voted, but not by a sufficient majority to meet the statutory test. In Wales the referendum led to a defeat of the Welsh proposals.

There are now five possible choices. The first, which is the Government's policy, is to defend the status quo to the limit. The second is to give Scotland and Wales devolved assemblies without changing the constitution of the rest of the United Kingdom – this was the option preferred by the Callaghan government.

The third is to turn the UK into a federation, of which Scotland, Wales and probably the English religions would form equal parts, a policy which has had Liberal support. The fourth is to create an independent Scotland inside the European community. That is SNP policy. The fifth is a separate Scotland, outside the UK and outside the EC. That used to be SNP policy.

The Government's policy depends on the consent of Scotland. If the Scots will not accept the status quo, they cannot in the end be made to do so.

If the SNP were to win a majority of Scottish seats in two successive general elections, Scotland would have voted conclusively for independence, and the only sane policy, at that point, would be to agree to it. If the Scots clearly and consistently prefer separate nationhood, that is not an outcome the English have the will, the power or the interest to deny them. But that situation has not yet arisen.

The Callaghan policy suffered from being illogical. It would have meant that Scotland would govern herself in respects in which England would not be self-governing. Under present arrangements there is already a weighting in favour of Scotland and Wales relative to the English regions, because of the Whitehall power of the Scottish and Welsh offices. That is keenly resented in the poorer regions of England. Any policy which gives Scotland and Wales home rule without home rule for England must break down because it will make worse this unfair distribution of resources.

The logical choice, if Scotland were to have home rule inside the UK, is the federal model, with Scotland, Wales and England, or the English regions, enjoying powers similar to those of the

Länder in Germany, the Swiss cantons, or the American states. In that case the major domestic decisions, covering taxation, industrial policy, social policy, education and police, become local matters, with an upper tier of taxation, defence, and foreign policy reserved for the Westminster Parliament.

This is logical and in some ways attractive, but England, since the Normans, has had no experience of it. Federation has only to be described for everyone to see how difficult the change would be to achieve – even if Mrs Thatcher herself were not absolutely opposed to it.

The SNP solution, a separate Scotland inside the EC, might even be preferred by the English to such a wholesale reconstruction of their own constitution. There are, however, at least equal difficulties in this proposal. Scotland has only historically known prolonged domestic peace as part of the UK. The tensions inside Scotland, between the Highlands and Lowlands, between Glasgow and Edinburgh, have more easily been reconciled from London, than they were before London became the metropolis for Scottish affairs.

There are other problems. As with Wales and Northern Ireland, Scottish benefits are greater than Scottish taxes – the English taxpayer has always subsidised the union, usually to a large extent. An independent Scotland would be poorer, perhaps more like the Republic of Ireland than like Norway.

Even the oil would cause disputes. A significant part of it is in Orcadian rather than Scottish waters; another part would be in English waters, and the boundary lines are open to argument. Would Scotland automatically take the Orkneys and Shetlands – or would those islands, like the Falklands, be entitled to local option? Orcadians are not Scots and probably distrust Edinburgh even more than they do London.

There is also the problem of defence. The EC is not a defence community. It would at least be desirable to continue to integrate the defence arrangements for England, Scotland and Wales – though a separate Scottish membership of Nato is conceivable, as is a Scottish decision not to join Nato.

For the present the first option – no change – will be taken; because Mrs Thatcher has the power and the will to take it. The reaction to that could lead to the SNP succeeding Labour as the main opposition party in Scotland. Of course, that would make Conservative victories in the general elections of 1991 and 1995 even more probable than they now are, and might result in the final break-up of the Labour Party. It could also result in the conversion of the majority demand in Scotland from devolution to independence.

The difficulty for the Labour Party is that it cannot deliver the defeat of Mrs Thatcher, whom the Scots dislike. It cannot deliver devolution – and because it has not thought it through it is not united on its devolution policy. It cannot stop the poll tax. As the Labour Party cannot deliver, the SNP has a real chance. Govan suggests that the danger to the Union is a real one.

15 November 1988

WHY THE POPE IS THE
ONE WHO SHOULD TALK
TO THE AYATOLLAHS

There has been a remorseless quality about the historic flow of Islam. In 1480, Mahomet II, the appropriately named conquerer of Constantinople, laid siege to the island of Rhodes. The island was successfully defended by the Knights of the Order of St John of Jerusalem, whose Vice-Chancellor, a Frenchman named Guillaume Caorsin, wrote an account of the siege.

As is often the case in resisting the forward march of Islam, the Jews were involved. The south-east corner of the island garrison, a weak spot in the fortifications, was the Jewish quarter. The Jews suffered heavily in the siege, and were joined by all the able-bodied citizens in the successful defence of that part of the wall.

Caorsin's account is part of the early history of British journalism. A translation by John Kay was published in London in 1483; that is the first printed news report in English. It reflects the degree of anxiety about the challenge of Islam, even in a country as remote as England.

Rhodes was saved then, but fell to the Ottoman Turks in 1522, and the Islamic military challenge to Europe was not finally defeated until the Polish general, John Sobieski, beat the Turkish army besieging Vienna in September 1683. With Islam, history has to be measured in centuries. Now Islam is again on the move, even if only to recover what it regards as its own. It is certainly a movement of faith, and could be a movement of boundaries.

In matters of religion, it is religious energy, the strength of the faith, that matters most. During the periods in which Christianity converted a large part of the world, it was a crusading faith. That was true of the Apostles, of the early Church, of the great saints who converted Germany, of the Jesuits in China or South America, but also of the great Protestant leaders such as Luther or Wesley. As Luther wrote, 'The Gospel cannot be introduced without tumult, scandal and rebellion . . .the word of God is a sword, a war, a destruction, a scandal, a ruin, a poison.' Luther was a great man, but not a moderate one.

Whether or not Khomeini would have used Luther's words, this was also the attitude of the Ayatollah; it was the way in which he made and maintained the Islamic revolution in Iran. A year after his death, millions of Iranians walked fifteen miles to his tomb, in burning heat, to show their devotion to his memory and to their faith. Some, no doubt, died on that dreadful journey, but they died in the expectation of Paradise.

This revival of Islam has many opponents. Khomeini himself believed that the greatest enemy was the secular modernism which he personified in 'the great devil', the United States. That is the essentially anti-religious influence which had inspired the regime of the Shah, and threatened – as in Britain it undoubtedly does threaten – to subvert the faith of the Islamic people. Pope John Paul II views the materialism of the West in much the same way; who can deny that the New York of Donald Trump is a modern Vanity Fair where the towering temples are dedicated to the great god Mammon?

As an idea, this atheistic materialism has always been present in the world; in terms of historic Jewish and Christian teaching, it is a form of idolatry, a breach of the first commandment, 'Thou shalt have no other gods before me.' It was the leading idolatry of ancient Rome as much as it is of modern New York. But its main centres of power are somewhat remote from Islam; they are to be found in Western Europe, the United States and Japan. There are, of course, outposts in the Middle East, but they can be regarded as secondary.

The three counter-powers which are near at hand are the Soviet Union, the nationalist dictatorships of the Middle East and the Zionist state of Israel (there is, of course, also India). The Soviet Union has about a quarter of its population in states which are predominately Islamic. Those states were occupied in the Tsarist era of primitive imperialism when Islam was at its weakest. They were retained in the period of Marxist revolution. Marxism in the Soviet Union is now dead; Marx was not only a false prophet, but, like all secular prophets, a short-lived one.

It seems certain the Islamic states will soon become independent of the Soviet Union. I hope the Russians have the sense to move their nuclear weapons out of these states before they leave. If Islam is exploding, it would be as well it had as few nuclear weapons as possible to explode with.

The second group of opposed powers are in the socialist dictatorships of the Middle East. When President Nasser was alive, authoritarian nationalist socialism seemed to offer a real alternative to Islam. Regimes of Nasserite character are still in power in Syria and Iraq, and Iraq's war with Iran shows how real the hostility between the two systems is. On the other hand, Colonel Gadaffi should be regarded as an Islamic dictator, and the likelihood is that Islam will eventually absorb all these dictatorships. Islam has a prophet, and they do not.

Obviously Israel is in the greatest danger, a danger made much greater by the benighted character of the new Israeli government. There was a period, from the death of Nasser to the fall of the Shah, when a determined Israeli government might have made a general peace with a largely moderate group of neighbours. That opportunity was missed. If Islamic fanaticism continues to increase, and is fuelled by major triumphs in reclaiming the Islamic independence of the Soviet states, then the threat to Israel will become even more acute. At present Israel has the advantage of nuclear weapons, but nuclear technology is now almost fifty years old. When the major Islamic states are all nuclear, Israel will have no deterrent advantage.

Islam is, therefore, likely to become steadily more powerful in political terms during the 1990s. By the end of the century the gradual depletion of the world's oil resources will again have raised the real price of oil. Soviet states will have joined the Islamic group. One or more Islamic states will have developed a significant nuclear capacity. No doubt, Islam will be held back, as throughout history, by internecine conflict – the Iran–Iraq war was the largest conflict in the world of the 1980s. But the trend of power and the threat to the interests of neighbouring nations is inescapable.

This is not just a question of political power. Nations without a faith are always exposed to nations which have faith. Of the world's leaders, it is not Mikhail Gorbachev, or George Bush, or even Margaret Thatcher, who is capable of responding to the new challenge of Islam. If any leader can make a valid response, it will be Pope John Paul II. Faith can only be met by faith.

11 June 1990

WEALTH, POWER AND
PREDICTIONS OF DECLINE

For some years I had known a little about William Playfair. I knew he had invented the visual presentation of statistical material; he is the grandfather of computer graphics. I knew that his brother, John, was a leading member of the eighteenth-century Scottish Enlightenment, a mathematician and an important early geologist. I had read somewhere that it was John who had first suggested the idea of what William called 'linear arithmetic'.

I knew William had edited and commented on Adam Smith. I knew that he had been in Paris during the French Revolution. I knew he had written numerous books and pamphlets, some of them illustrated with his brilliantly designed statistical charts. *The Dictionary of National Biography* states that he published forty works, and, rather sniffily, categorizes him as 'a publicist'.

What I did not know was that he had written *An Enquiry into the Permanent Causes of the Decline and Fall of Powerful and Wealthy Nations*, a substantial book, published in London in 1805, the year of the battle of Trafalgar. In the last two or three weeks I have been studying it, and have found it one of the great unknown books, unknown at least to me.

What first drew me to read Playfair's *Enquiry* was that I had long been interested in the early history of the decline of British power, and the views expressed by contemporaries about it. It is usually thought that the decline began in the second half of the nineteenth century, and that the high point of Britain's economic advantage was 1851, the year of the Great Exhibition. One of the earliest warnings of Britain's potential economic weakness, the first forecast of decline, was thought to have been given in Charles Babbage's *Economy of Machinery and Manufactures*, 1832. Babbage was the pioneer of the computer, and probably the first economist to have a thorough technical understanding of machine industry.

Now I found that Playfair had dealt with the question of national decline systematically, nearly thirty years before Babbage, at a period when the British economic lead was still rapidly increasing. Moreover, he dealt specifically with the prospect of British decline; his book had the thoughtful subtitle, 'Designed to show how the prosperity of the British Empire may be prolonged'.

Playfair's method is economic, statistical, historical and sociological, drawing on Adam Smith as an economist, on his own development of statistical practice, on Edward Gibbon, David Hume, William Robertson and Adam Ferguson for history, and Ferguson again as a sociologist. I do not know whether Karl Marx read Playfair, and I would guess that Playfair had never read Giovanni Vico, who invented historical sociology, but Playfair uses a combination of methods which seems entirely modern.

His conclusion is realistic, but must have seemed pessimistic at the time. 'The general conclusion is that wealth and power have never been long permanent in any place. That they have never been renewed when once destroyed, though they have had rises and falls, and that they travel over the face of the earth, something like a caravan of merchants. On their arrival everything is found green and fresh; while they remain, all is bustle and abundance, and, when gone, all is left trampled down, barren and bare.'

The frontispiece to the book is a chart of 'universal commercial history', showing the rise and fall of the ancient empires and, in the modern world, the rise and decline of Venice, Spain and The

Netherlands, and the rise, but not the decline, of Britain, Russia and the United States, Playfair already saw the potential strength of the US and Russia as very large developing economies.

The causes of decline Playfair gives also sound surprisingly modern. He held the eighteenth-century common view that wealth makes nations as well as individuals lazy, that the poor will always outstrip the rich, because their incentives are stronger. But he observed that this rule had been weakened by technology. In war, gunpowder had meant that rich nations could afford to defend themselves against the hordes of poverty. In industry, increasing capital was required, and poor nations did not have enough capital.

Nevertheless, Playfair thought that the children of self-made men never worked as hard as their fathers, and that this was true of nations as well as individuals. He saw over-mature economies as having certain common characteristics: high taxation, high prices, a very unequal distribution of property, strong special interest groups, monopolies, failures of motivation, a high tendency to import. He thought that these burdens tended to result in a flight of capital to nations who could employ it more profitably, and in a natural and irreversible decline.

If the present Government had read Playfair, they would certainly not have introduced the poll tax. 'Sometimes the manner of laying on the tax has given the offence, sometimes its nature, and sometimes its amount. The revolution in England, in Charles I's time, began about the method of levying a tax. The revolution of the American colonies began in the same way; and it is generally at the manner that nations enjoying a certain degree of freedom make objection. The excise [Walpole] had very nearly proved fatal to the government of this country, as the stamp duties did to that of France, and as the general amount and enormity of taxes did to the Western [Roman] Empire.'

Playfair was also well aware of the problem of local government finance. He thought local government was usually in the hands of inadequate and self-interested people. His views of lawyers were even harsher. 'In addition to the real dead expense, the loss of time, the attention and the misfortune and misery occasioned by the law are terrible evils.'

I suppose that the heart of Playfair's economic theory lies in the chapter headed 'Of the tendency of Capital and Industry to leave a wealthy country, and of the depreciation of money in agricultural and commercial countries'. He believed that the attraction of lending money to foreigners rather than employing it in domestic industry, enriched foreign competitors and impoverished the home nation. 'The capital, which, when employed at home, formerly maintained perhaps a hundred people in affluence and industry, only supported one single family living in indolence and splendid penury.' He was thinking particularly of Venice, but also of the Dutch of his time.

Yet Playfair's view was not purely monetarist. He emphasized the importance of education in which he thought that 'the education of the great body of the people' should be 'the chief object'. He believed that schools should be judged objectively by results in public examinations – 'parents would then have a measure by which they could estimate the merit of a school'. He believed in practical education: 'The useful should be preferred to the useless.' He believed very strongly in the importance of the education of women.

What Playfair failed to foresee is important. He could not have been expected to foretell the great twentieth-century wars, which did so much to destroy Britain's world position. He did not foresee Marxism, and its impact on our century. Yet he did foresee the importance of the diffusion of technology, of education, of capital flows, of different welfare structures, of comparative taxation, of changes in diet, of changes in population. He knew that riches and power will always tend to decline, and can never be made permanent. He had little use for what he regarded as the non-productive overheads of society, lawyers, special interests, the idle rich. He believed in the useful rather than the useless. That would not have been a bad motto for Britain.

18 June 1990

THE GATES OPEN TO AN ENLIGHTENED IRELAND

It was, unexpectedly, Ireland that last week produced the best news in a dark and gloomy world. The appointment of Dr Cahal Daly as Archbishop of Armagh and Primate of All Ireland marks a revolutionary change in the role of the Roman Catholic Church in Irish affairs. The election of Mary Robinson as President of Ireland marks an equally revolutionary change in the politics of that country. Where, until last week, every avenue for reconciliation seemed closed, now at least two gates stand open.

The saintly bishop and the reforming woman lawyer, one the child of the Church and the other, although a Roman Catholic, the child of the Enlightenment, have one vital characteristic in common. They stand outside the tribalism of Ireland.

The unfortunate Brian Lenihan, who is genuinely popular with the Irish people even though they have not elected him, is a wholly tribal figure, as thoroughly tribalized in his culture as the late Cardinal Tomás O'Fiaich or, in the other tribe, Ian Paisley.

The problem Ireland faces is reconciling the two tribes – the Catholic tribe, which represents the majority in the island as a whole but the minority in the North, and the Protestant tribe, of which the reverse is true. Both, however, are Irish tribes.

The Protestants arrived in Ireland, mainly from Scotland, following the setting up of plantations in the sixteenth and seventeenth centuries. Some had arrived before the Pilgrim Fathers landed in Plymouth, Massachusetts. Their ancestry makes them as much Irish as George Bush's makes him American.

Most of those who live inside the cultures of these two tribes seem unable to move outside their historic fears and loyalties. That has been equally true of most of the political leaders of both sides, whether they are moderate or extreme.

Politicians who lose the imprint of the tribal culture are usually rejected by their tribes, thereby condemning the tribes to repeat in each generation the horrific and bloody disputes of the past. This is not the case with Fine Gael, but Fine Gael remains the minority party in the Republic.

We still see the Protestant tribe repeatedly commemorating the victory of King William III at the Battle of the Boyne. Indeed, they still wear his colours. When one considers the legacy imposed on Ireland by King William – the penal laws of the Dublin parliaments of 1692 and 1694; the anti-Catholics oaths; the settling of more Protestants; the confiscation of Catholic property; the prohibitions on Catholics owning arms, holding public posts, being educated abroad or even owning a horse worth more than £5 – it would appear the Protestants are celebrating the destruction of the other tribe's status. It is an annual ritual of hostility.

Yet when one considers the use of terror by the Catholics, the terror of the seventeenth-century Tories – who were bands of murderous Irish Catholics – the terror of the nineteenth-century Fenians, the terror of the IRA, there has been only too much reinforcement of tribal hostility from the Catholic side also.

It has long been apparent, though not always well understood by the English, that there can be no political settlement until there is a reconciliation of these tribes. So long as they hate each other and wish to humilitate each other, no political solution is possible. If they could be made to love each other and to want to help each other, the possibility of a political settlement succeeding would be that much greater. In other words, the Irish issue is a spiritual one.

In theological terms, what is needed is a metanoia, a process of conversion, a fundamental change of heart, mind and soul. It is for this reason that the appointment of Bishop Daly is the more important of the two. In theological terms, such a metanoia comes as the result of grace, and such grace comes as the answer to prayer. There are many people in Ireland who already join in prayer.

What Ireland needs is that the two tribes should pray both for themselves and for each other. Nor can anyone be excluded from this. Even the terrorists on either side need to be prayed for; indeed, their conversion to a Christian and loving view of their neighbours would be a most valuable grace, both to them and to the entire Irish community. Catholics should take out their rosaries to pray for the spiritual welfare of the terrorists on either side.

In this work of mutual love and prayer, Bishop Daly has long taken a leading role. He has shared fully the suffering of his own community, having attended by now some fifty funerals of victims of terrorism. But he has also been active in seeking the co-operation of the Protestant clergy in Northern Ireland. In no part of the world is the ecumenical movement more important. It is scandalous that there should be hatred, rather than love, between one Christian community and another.

At the same time, Bishop Daly has been completely frank about the sin that is involved. It is always sinful to hate, rather than love, one's neighbour, whatever historic disputes one may have had with him.

Christian teaching does not tell one only to love one's neighbour if he is perfect; if it did, there would be very little love in the world. Bishop Daly has also reiterated that murder is always murder and that the sin of murder is not excused by political motivation.

If Bishop Daly offers the clearest religious guidance, Mrs Robinson is also a symbol of hope. One of the reasons many reasonable Protestants fear Dublin is that the city has been a tribalized centre of government, particularly when the tribal party of Fianna Fail is in power. The role of Cardinal O'Fiaich as a tribal Primate reinforced that fear. Mrs Robinson is a woman, an intellectual and a reformer, a president of the Enlightenment rather than a president of the tribe.

Middle-class Protestants in Belfast might not feel particularly English, but at least the British connection has been a link to a government based, however imperfectly, on the ideas of the Enlightenment, on the liberal values that have permeated British political life.

You hold out your hand to a British parliament, and you link hands ultimately with Maynard Keynes, John Stuart Mill and John Locke. You link hands with a Dublin Fianna Fail government and you are in touch with Pius IX, the syllabus of errors and a thousand political and religious ghosts. Now the enlightened Protestants of Belfast can deal with an enlightened President of Ireland.

There is, therefore, both a spiritual and an intellectual reason for hope in Ireland. And what should the British do? We should, in my view, join in the prayer for the reconciliation of Ireland, North and South, Protestant and Catholic, moderate and extreme. We should make it clear that the present direct rule is only a bridge towards a reconciled future for Ireland. We ask nothing for ourselves from the Union.

Indeed, we do not ourselves belong to either tribe, nor they to us. English Protestants have few cultural links to the Protestants of Northern Ireland. We who are English Catholics owe a great debt to Irish spirituality and Irish priests, but we are not Irish.

The two tribes belong culturally to each other rather than to us, for they have been forged in a common Irish history that we do not share.

Both Irish tribes should know that it is their reconciliation we aim for; and if reconciliation comes, we hope to enjoy a new relationship of friendship with both tribes in whatever constitutional form suits them best.

Britain does not want to retain the role of the neighbour who intervenes in a family dispute.

12 November 1990

RACE IN AN ANGRY AMERICA

Last week the trustees of City College, New York, decided not to suspend Dr Leonard Jeffries, the Professor of Black Studies in the college. He will remain for eight months while his performance is assessed. This was a compromise between dismissing him and confirming him for three years, and was reached by a majority of ten to four.

Professor Jeffries is a black anti-Semite. According to *The New York Times*, he has in recent years accused Jews of 'a conspiracy planned and plotted and programmed out of Hollywood' to denigrate blacks. He has referred to a colleague as 'the head Jew' at City College, and has accused the Jews of special responsibility for the slave trade.

He has been rebuked three times before, but City College has been afraid to discipline him further because of the threat of black demonstrations. It is absolutely unthinkable that a white professor could have survived in New York if he uttered such slanders against Jews or blacks.

In Louisiana, it is different. David Duke is a white racist who is running for governor. Although he was a Democrat until 1988, and has been disowned by the national leadership of the Republican Party, he is running as the Republican candidate. His opponent on 16 November will be Edwin Edwards, who has been governor three times before. Mr Edwards is an old-fashioned machine Democrat, but he may well win, and all good citizens hope that he will.

Until 1980 David Duke was a member of the Ku-Klux-Klan, ending his career in that organisation as a Grand Wizard. In 1980, he left the Klan, but there is evidence that he remained a Nazi sympathizer throughout most of the Eighties, celebrating Hitler's birthday and denying the truth of the Holocaust. He is even alleged to have expressed his admiration for Dr Josef Mengele as a plant geneticist, saying: 'You don't believe all that stuff he was said to have done, do you?'

Nowadays Mr Duke says that he has ceased to hold intolerant racist views, but he has not lost the support of those who do.

Since 1980 David Duke has been the fund-raiser, organizer and controller of the National Association for the Advancement of White People, a racist body he created and runs from his comfortable house in Metairie, a prosperous suburb of New Orleans. This body was able to raise $1.3m to spend on his successful primary campaign. It is said to have a mailing list of 100,000 in Louisiana, and has smaller numbers of supporters in other states.

Of course, New Orleans has had bigoted or populist politicians before. The most famous was Huey Long, whose national appeal, on the slogan of 'Every Man a King', seriously alarmed President Franklin Roosevelt in the early Thirties. If the Duke phenomenon were to happen anywhere in the United States, it would be in Louisiana, whose politics have been shaped by the profound poverty of the Mississippi delta, both among blacks and whites. Other Americans are horrified that a former Grand Wizard with a record of Nazi sympathy could have this appeal in 1991. It is as though time were marching backwards.

In terms of American race relations, perhaps it is. Of course, the situation is complex, as one saw in the Judge Thomas hearings, when the sex issue became involved, as it so often has, with race, and the conflict was between two middle-class black people.

One of the big changes has been the growth in the black middle class, and its growing importance both in black and US society. That needs to be offset against deterioration in other ways.

The life of the black urban poor, the so-called underclass, is even worse than it was. There is more violence, with the streets of large areas of most big US cities, including New York, Los Angeles, Washington, Philadelphia, Miami, Chicago and Detroit, being unsafe for blacks or whites.

There is far more drug addiction, particularly with crack, and there is the spread of Aids. In 1970, life for a poor urban black in the US was very difficult, though not lacking in hope. In 1991, it is catastrophic. For many, to be born into the underclass is an early sentence of death, by drugs, by Aids or by murder.

Inevitably, this has resulted in a black reaction. Black spokesmen have become increasingly aggressive and hostile to other ethnic groups. The ideas of Malcolm X are achieving wider support, and the leadership of the Revd Al Sharpton in New York puts Jesse Jackson into the role of a moderate, outflanked by more extreme leaders.

The lyrics of rap music attack white society in an extremely aggressive way, and express the feelings of young black people, including young blacks from the middle class.

Relations between blacks and Jews are particularly bad. Apart from Professor Jeffries, there is widespread anti-Semitism among blacks and widespread anti-schwarzer prejudice among inner-city Jews.

In the recent riots in Brooklyn, which occurred after the death of a young black in a traffic accident for which a Hasidic driver was responsible, an Australian Jewish scholar, in no way connected with the accident, was lynched by a black mob; some of the blacks shouted: 'Hitler was right. Kill the Jews.'

So we have New York blacks who sympathize with Hitler because he was anti-Semitic and Louisiana whites who sympathize with him because he was anti-black.

The themes of racial conflict are even more complex than that. There are tensions between black and Hispanic groups and outright war between black and Hispanic gangs over drugs and territory, particularly in Los Angeles. Blacks have boycotted Korean shops in New York.

There are even tensions betwen Caribbean and native US blacks in New York. If you pick up a cab with a black driver in

New York, the odds are that he will be an immigrant from the Caribbean who will regard native US blacks as too idle to drive cabs. By and large Caribbean blacks are likely to be friendly towards white people, while native inner-city American blacks are more likely to feel hostile.

In the 1992 presidential election the race issue wil be impossible to avoid. The overt issues will be crime and welfare, but the coded theme will be race.

There are now more than one million Americans in prison, a rate about four times that of Britain, which itself has one of the highest rates in Europe. Blacks have a far higher rate of imprisonment than other ethnic groups in the US, and it is said that there are now more blacks in prison than in college.

At the start of the last presidential campaign, George Bush was far behind in the opinion polls. His surge came when he used the case of Willie Horton, a black who committed rape while on leave from a Massachusetts prison. The charge that Governor Michael Dukakis was soft on crime was itself a coded message that he was soft on race. That charge helped George Bush win the election.

Already the recession, which is showing no sign of recovery, has made race relations worse than they were in 1990. Professor Jeffries and David Duke are extreme figures, but they represent real racist constituencies.

Black anger is bitter, and it is not going to be sweetened by the racist subtext that will be almost inevitable in the 1992 presidential campaign. This is the United States' biggest political issue, the cause of the greatest suffering and the worst threat to social order.

4 November 1991

THE EURO-DODO THAT
WAS TOO STUPID AND FAT
TO FLY

The interesting question about the new European order is not whether it can be created but whether it will survive. The laws of social survival have been studied for the past three centuries, but most originally in Gibbon's *Decline and Fall of the Roman Empire*, 1776; Adam Smith's *Wealth of Nations*, 1776; and Darwin's *Origin of Species*, 1859. The rules are the same for an individual, a nation, a species or any smaller institution – a family, a business, a university or a newspaper. To survive it is necessary to adapt to challenges, swiftly and decisively.

Western Europe faces three historic challenges. Between them they will determine the future of European life in the next decade, and in the next century. The most immediate is the crisis of Eastern Europe and the new commonwealth in the former Soviet Union.

The civil war between Croatia and Serbia is a warning of what could happen in many ex-communist countries where nationalist hatreds are explosive. The ex-Soviet republics also face famine this winter. It is said that they are short of a thousand shiploads of grain, and have only two major grain ports open. In St Petersburg, the bread queues are already four hours long, starting at five o'clock in the morning, and it is still only mid-December.

We cannot live safely in Western Europe if Eastern Europe is collapsing into anarchy, famine and war. We must not play Dives to the Russian Lazarus. President Bush has called an international conference for next month, which may produce some good results, probably when the famine is over. Europe has allocated some aid to the ex-Soviet republics. But little time was spent at Maastricht on the needs of Eastern Europe; it was an essentially inward-looking conference.

Indeed, the Eastern European countries were given little encouragement to believe that they will be able to join the rich man's club without enduring a waiting list longer than the Garrick's. The Maastricht document might raise their hopes by stating that 'any European state may apply to become a member of the Union'. They would soon be lowered again by the provision that applications will be decided by the European Council, acting unanimously, after consulting the Commission, and after receiving the assent of the European Parliament. The European club has adopted the principle that one blackball excludes, that all members shall have a blackball, and that the Parliament shall have a blackball as well. That is our good neighbour policy.

The second challenge is economic. The world is experiencing the worst recession of a decade, probably the worst since 1974, conceivably the worst since 1932. The world banking system is barely solvent, the summer recovery in the United States has failed, the recession in the United Kingdom continues, even in Germany there is a downturn. We are in some danger of a world depression in 1992. How did Maastricht deal with that problem?

The European monetary regime already imposes extremely high real interest rates on the member countries, rates which have made the recession far worse than it needed to be. Britain ought, on economic grounds, to have a base rate of between 7 and 8 per cent; our base rate is still more than 10 per cent.

The proposals for a single currency require in their first stage a deflationary adjustment by all the European partners between now and 1 January 1994: this is obligatory even in Britain, because the UK protocol only exempts us from obligation to the third stage. In particular, the Mediterranean countries – Italy, Spain, Portugal and Greece – face an impossible task. Maastricht is a

95

deflationary currency agreement at a time of severe world recession. That will either prove unworkable or catastrophic. It is the stupidest economic decision for the past fifty years.

The third challenge is Japanese competition in world trade. The United States, the European Community and Japan are the three great competitors in world export markets. In the past thirty years Japan has been by far the most successful. Maastricht ought, therefore, to have concentrated on improving Europe's competitiveness. Otherwise Japan will accelerate away from us in the Nineties.

The historic rules are clear enough. A competitive economy must have high productivity, advanced technology, good education, high investment, high savings, little bureaucratic regulation, low government expenditure, low taxation, low interest rates, low costs and relatively stable prices. That was Britain's formula when we led the world, was the American formula when they led the world, and is largely, though not entirely, the Japanese formula, now that they lead the world. We should be trying to build a low-cost, free-trade, lightly regulated, low-tax, high-productivity Europe.

I have counted forty Maastricht policy decisions which fall outside the area of the common currency. The large majority will tend to increase bureaucratic regulation and raise costs. Of these decisions, thirty will reduce the competitiveness of the EC, five will possibly increase it, and five may be neutral, though with some tendency to increase the bureaucratic overhead. As a way of competing with Japan, such a policy shift is suicidal.

Professor Tim Congdon, a leading economist, has made some forecasts of European public expenditure in the later Nineties. These show that the European Community countries, which have ageing populations, will have public expenditure drifting up to 55 per cent of national income, and above. Britain, thanks mainly to the work of Margaret Thatcher in the Eighties, can remain, in percentage terms, in the low forties. Anything above 45 per cent tends to be inflationary, puts excessive government burdens on the economy, and tends to crowd out productive investment. If Britain elects a Labour government, we shall join the non-competitive majority only too rapidly.

The Social Charter, to which Britain is not committed, and the Regional Development Policy, to which we are, will add to the Community burden on European industry. The regional policy will join the Common Agricultural Policy as a system of subsidizing the inefficient.

Maastricht was a qualified success for John Major. He did better than could have been expected in reducing the damage to Britain. He certainly did better than the Labour Party would have done; it would have joined every anti-competitive policy. But Maastricht looks like a disaster for Europe.

This is not anti-European sentiment. Good Europeans want what the founding fathers of the European Community wanted: a highly competitive, free-trade Europe, with low costs, minimum bureaucracy and a maximum capacity to meet the challenges of the outside world. The founders rejected Euro-socialism on the post-war British or Scandinavian model. Maastricht reflects the opposite ambitions and priorities of French socialists such as Jacques Delors and François Mitterand. Socialism in the twentieth century has ruined most European countries individually, and may be about to ruin them collectively.

Maastricht has failed to meet each of the three great challenges to Europe. It has done nothing to bring peace, food or hope to Eastern Europe or the Russian commonwealth. It will make the recession worse rather than better. It will turn Europe into a high-cost bureaucratic and rigid economy. It will hand dominance of the world economy in the Nineties to Japan. Why did the dodo perish? It was because the bird was too fat, too stupid and could not fly.

18 December 1991

CHINA'S ECONOMIC DAWN

ast Wednesday I was in China, visiting the recently opened floor of the Shenzhen Stock Exchange. On Thursday night I was taken to dinner on the Hong Kong island of Lamma. Outside the restaurant there was a stall of tourist goods, including Chinese hats, fans and parasols. I bought a hand-painted parasol for my wife; the painting was the familiar Chinese group of birds, rocks, flowers and plum blossom, done in the traditional style. The parasol itself was shaped like a flower, intricately made with thirty-six delicate spokes and about seventy-three moving parts. It cost HK$20, or about £1.50.

That parasol has been worrying me since. I bought it because it was pretty, not because it was a bargain, but it seemed too much of a bargain. My Adam Smith training made me work out how many manufacturing stages must have been required (there were at least sixteen), and how many stages of distribution (at least three).

So long as it is only parasols, that will not make much difference to the rest of the world. But already it is far more than that. Later this year the China Bicycle Company will be joining the six companies already listed on the Shenzhen Stock Exchange, the second stock exchange to be opened in China. The company already produces 30 per cent of the world's bicycles and exports 95 per cent of its production. I can remember when the world's bicycles were made in Birmingham.

Robert Lloyd George, the great-grandson of the prime minister, has just opened his new investment management company in Hong Kong. He has written an excellent book, *The East West Pendulum*, (published by Woodhead Faulkner) in which he argues that the Pacific Asian countries are the new driving force in the world economy. He compares the wage rates of China with those of the developed countries. 'A textile worker in Sichuan was reported to earn six dollars a week, compared to the equivalent textile worker in North Carolina where the average was $250 a week. The average wage in Japan was twenty-seven times that of a Chinese worker.'

So long as China remained a largely isolated peasant country with a strict communist regime, the wage level of its 1.2 billion people could have little effect on world competition. That era is now coming to an end. China has already set up nineteen enterprise zones, of which Shenzhen in 1980 was the first. They make China part of the industrial development of the Pacific rim, along with South Korea, Taiwan, Hong Kong itself, or in earlier years, Japan. The rise in their gross domestic product per head measures the progress these countries have made. Japan has reached $25,000, Hong Kong $14,000, Taiwan $10,000 and Korea $6,500. China has still only reached $350.

The influence of Hong Kong on south China, of Taiwan on the central China coast, of Korea on northern China and of Japan on China as a whole has accelerated the process of industrialization. That will continue unless there is some political catastrophe to delay it. For a long time there will still be hundreds of millions of Chinese peasants who will not be directly affected by this development. They give China an almost inexhaustible supply of low-cost labour, an advantage that will continue until at least the middle of the next century.

The scale of the potential development is staggering. If all China reached the economic level of Taiwan, the GDP would increase by $10,000bn, which is more than the present GDP of the United States or the European Community. At present growth rates, China will reach that level well before the middle of the next century.

In 1997, Hong Kong will become part of China. The cumbrous border, guarded by bureaucrats and with long queues on both sides, will disappear. Hong Kong is already the great trading port of China. As China develops, the absolute share of its trade moving through Hong Kong may decline as other centres, such as Shanghai, regain part of their position. But Hong Kong will continue to grow rapidly in absolute terms, and will be the funnel through which a very large and rapidly expanding trade will flow. Hong Kong, therefore, may be on the verge of even more spectacular development than that which took place in the Eighties. Again, there is a political risk, but the economic forces are extremely strong.

In the past twenty years the developing countries of Asia have been growing at a rate of about 6–7 per cent a year, compared with the American or European rate of about 3 per cent. Since 1980 China has performed as well as the Asian growth group, and the development areas on the coast have grown even faster. Between 1981 and 1990 the Chinese growth of GDP varied between a high of 13.5 per cent and a low of 3.9 per cent. In three years it rose above 10 per cent. The long-term sustainable rate, with inflation kept in single figures, could be as high as 8 per cent, and is certainly not less than 6 per cent.

From Hong Kong one can see the different world economies as so many clocks, set at different times. For the moment the Russian clock is stuck at midnight. The clock of China is still in the early morning, perhaps three o'clock. Hong Kong itself, with Taiwan, Malaysia and Singapore, is perhaps at six o'clock, halfway to the zenith. Japan is at 11.30, still a little before noon, but with a long afternoon of relative decline not so far away. In Tokyo, they tell you that China is bound to pass them at some time in the next century. They are right.

The United States and most of Europe are already well into the afternoon, and in Britain we seem stuck in the early evening, waiting for the others to catch up with us. Inevitably, the response of mature economies to low-cost competition is to raise the demand for protection. Europe and America can regard their markets as their greatest assets. We are on the defensive against the competition of more rapidly growing economies with far lower costs than our own, able to invest in the new technologies already in use in the rest of the world.

The European Community seems therefore to be moving inevitably towards a defensive state. In the United States there is fear and anger at the threat from Japan. These reactions are politically inevitable, but they are not likely to be effective. Relative to Asia's potential, the EC is like a sandcastle that children have built on the beach before the tide comes in; so is the US.

If we had the imagination, as a nation or as part of Europe, we might do much more to speed a development that will happen with us or without us. The faster China becomes rich the more imports it will require. But nations seldom have much foresight. The developed world is more likely to try to defend itself ineffectively against the inexorable advance of Asian competition.

When the twentieth century started 80 per cent of the British people were poor and about 20 per cent were prosperous. As we approach the twenty-first century, 80 per cent of the world's population is poor and in Europe we are among the prosperous 20 per cent. In the next fifty years, China, but not China alone, will be joining the wealthy nations. The future alone will tell how the world will solve the problems of resources or of pollution. But economic history is still on the march. In 1900, London was the economic capital of the world; in 1950, it was New York; in 2000, it will be Tokyo. By 2050, it will very probably be Hong Kong, or some other Chinese city. The competitive power which could sell the parasol for £1.50 will have won, and it will not only be the world market for bicycles that the Chinese economy will dominate.

3 February 1992

PLENTY OF SEX, BUT NOT ENOUGH PEOPLE

W hen you are looking out across the bay in Hong Kong, it is better not to think of Europe. Indeed the Chinese do not spend much time thinking about us. They do not wake in the morning and ask themselves what imperial decree Jacques Delors will that day issue in Brussels. They do not ask themselves even the most obvious quetions, such as how much oil will be left for the Scottish Nationalist Party or the name of Gianni De Michelis's barber.

They do, however, have the feeling – emphasized by the character of British withdrawal from Hong Kong – that Europe is shrinking and is on the defensive. They may suspect that the great days of the United States are past, but they know that the US is the only military superpower left in the world. They look to Japan as the example of an economic superpower, of an Asian country which has become the most powerful industrial competitor in the world. Japan is their role model.

Of course, they know Europe still has a concentration of wealth and skill. They do not see it as wealth which is going to grow in the future, but as an inheritance from the past. They think of Europe, as in England we might think of the Duke of Devonshire. Chatsworth is a wonderful palace, but you would not go there to buy a super-computer. Japan is for business; Europe for holidays.

The European Community is not seen as the next superpower,

but more as a friendly society of the rich. Indeed the image, which has been reinforced by Britain's scandalous immigration policy towards Hong Kong, is similar to that of those retirement villages for millionaires in Florida, with private guards to keep out intruders. The function of the EC is not to compete, but to keep out competition, to keep out foreign food through the Common Agricultural Policy, to keep out foreign manufacturers – the French even want to limit Japanese cars made in Britain – and to keep out foreign persons through ever stricter immigration controls.

This village of the rich is not seen as important. It has less than half the Pacific Asian growth rate in economic affairs; it is not a military power which matters much outside its own area. Even as a potential market it is expected to decline. Some Europeans are regarded as being good at making rather old-fashioned things. The French are good at making cognac, which the Chinese drink by the tumbler as though it were cider; the Germans are good at making big cars, which are smuggled into south China from Hong Kong. But all this is only a mixture of consumer brand names and middle technology. European science is recognized, but in many areas European technology is regarded as behind Japan and the US.

This dismissive view of the EC is no bad corrective to the rhetoric of Europe, or to the idealism which expects the creation of a European super-state to follow Maastricht. Apart from anything else, the demographics are against that. Which country has the fewest teenagers in the world? Not Mozambique, with its average income of $80 a head; in 1989 44 per cent of the population of Mozambique were under fifteen. It is the old West Germany, which in that year had only 14.3 per cent of its population under fifteen. Admittedly, population decline is associated with wealth. Japan's population is expected to decline from 2010 and the United Kingdom's from 2020. But Germany's decline has started already and will be steeper.

In 1991 the World Bank published a report on *The Challenge of World Development* that reviewed the comparative population statistics of the world. Richard Belous has just produced a paper on *Demographic Currents* for the British–North American Committee. World population in the decade of the Nineties is growing at 1.6 per cent, which means it increases by rather more than eighty million a year, or three a second. The EC population is virtually stable.

The EC is not all that big. At present we are about 6 per cent of the world population. The demographic estimate is that we shall have fallen to about 4 per cent by the year 2025. That is a rapid rate of relative decline. The total population of the EC in 1989 was about 326 million; by 2025 we are expected to be about 335 million. If one takes eleven of the largest Islamic countries, they have a present population of 741 million; by 2025 that is expected to be 1,539 million. Islam will double; we shall stay still. Before 2025 Europe will age; beyond 2025 Europe will shrink. Throughout this period, Europe will have to spend a decreasing amount on education and a greatly increasing amount on pensions.

There is only one European country that even has a fertility rate at or above the replacement level, which is usually put at 2.1 children per woman in her lifetime. That country is Roman Catholic Ireland, with a rate of 2.2; that is just sufficient to maintain the small Irish population. The average fertility rate for the EC is 1.65, or about a fifth below the replacement rate. The world is threatened with a population explosion in the twenty-first century; Europe is threatened with a population fall.

It is strange that this decline in Europe's fertility should coincide with the contemporary cult of sex, a cult such as Europe has not experienced since, perhaps, the Stone Age. Never in the history of sexual intercourse has so much been performed by so many to impregnate so few.

From a world point of view, the present stabilization and prospective decline of the Western European population must be welcome. Five billion people are a lot for the planet to support; ten billion would probably threaten the survival of the earth's ecosystem. But for Europe this population decline is not such good news. In the last centuries of Rome there was a mysterious decline of the Mediterranean population, accompanied by a surge in the population of the Asian and German tribes. These tribes filled the vacuum that the Mediterranean population fall had created.

The Maastricht structure is intended to create a strong federal Europe centred on a strong industrial Germany and organised on those French bureaucratic principles which go back to Colbert. This is a wheel of fantasy. It has no rim, no spokes, no hub and no locomotion. In the next century the West Europeans will be a small, declining population, exactly opposite to the major area of economic growth, surrounded on the globe by nations and religions which will be growing, probably too fast but certainly much faster than Europe. Europe's scientific lead, which propelled us into world dominance in the nineteenth century, will have been matched. Already Japan knows more about the most advanced computers.

Maastricht reflects one political reality, the reality of fear. In such a situation, people want protection. They want to be protected in their jobs because they know – as the small European farmers know – that they are not competitive. They want protection from immigration. Fear of immigrants makes ugly politics, and that can only increase if the population ratio between Europe and the rest of the world slips steadily downwards. The inevitable loss of our technological advantage, the now unalterable fact that European babies which were not born in the Eighties will not be there to produce their own babies in the next century, have changed Europe's position in the world. A narrow defensive federation is certainly not the best answer to this crisis of Europe, but it is unfortunately the answer that fear suggetss.

24 February 1992

PART THREE

RELIGION AND SPIRITUALITY

My religious life had a radical change of direction in my early thirties, shortly after my marriage to Gillian Morris, which gave me a personal happiness greater than I had previously known. Before then I was a liturgical member of the Roman Catholic Church, but had no inwardness in my faith. If I had not been a Catholic I would have found it easy to be an agnostic and in some moods I was one. I experienced the mystery of religion in a negative sense. What we cannot know for sure we cannot properly believe.

In my early thirties this changed. From that time my religious belief became inward, and my belief grew until now, in my sixties, it is undoubting. I am certain that we are all eternal spirits, with an eternal purpose. I have no doubt that love and prayer are the central purposes of our lives. I have no doubt that God exists, nor in the major affirmations of the Christian faith. These beliefs do not spring from an outward apprehension of dogma or ritual, but from a sense of the spiritual which occupies my inner space, however much my mind may also be filled with the selfishness, detail and business of the world.

I believe that the divine permeates all human nature, despite our sins. We are all like eggshells filled with spiritual realities we cannot begin to understand, filled indeed with the whole glory of Heaven. The blessed Trinity does not live outside us, in a place somewhere else, but inside us. When we pray to the Blessed Virgin Mary, we pray to a presence inside ourselves as well as outside ourselves. When we love people, we love by the spiritual in us the spiritual in them. If we accept this, the affairs of the world tend to work for us, not against us. The harassments of the world become no more than the raindrops pattering on the window.

In particular, death is not to be feared. We have not been told the full mystery of death and rebirth, of what we shall be doing next, or of what we did before. Sometimes we have momentary glimpses, but the curtain is not pulled aside. Perhaps the process of spiritual development requires many lives as the reincarnation-ists believe. When I met the Dalai Lama I found that easy to suppose, that successive lives could bring one closer to God, and that the saints of all religions enter life with more understanding of love than the rest of us. Perhaps confirmed atheists owe their superficiality to a lack of spiritual experience, and are not to be criticized for being young souls.

The spiritual does not age or die. So far as I can tell my soul is the same age as I can first remember when I was myself two or three years old. The people we love we know in the spirit. They too do not age or change. These things are already outside time. Spirits are as they were before birth and as they will be after death, which makes the change in death a small one, referring only to the physical and temporary, to the outside not to the inside. The person we lose on death is the shell of the real person, not the substance.

The acceptance of this changes one's whole attitude to life. We have lived before; we live now; we shall live in the future. 'Christ in us has died; Christ in us is risen; Christ in us will come again.' We need not wait until we have died for the love of the spiritual, for repentance for sins, for the new relationship to God.

The material world is also very patchy, and the spirit constantly darts through the holes in the wickerwork of the material. Sometimes it takes a ludicrous form, like Daniel Dunglas Home levitating in the drawing rooms of Victorian Belgravia. Sometimes it reveals itself in the direct spiritual understanding of the great mystics. Like William James, I treasure all these chinks, the minor as well as the major, because they remind the world of the immaterial.

Of course this sort of inner belief makes me realize what an absurdly inadequate person I am. I am not bowed down with shame and guilt only because I share this condition with everyone else. We are all selfish, limited, inadequate, unloving, cold boxes of clay. I see myself as suffering chiefly from an addiction to material gain, the sin of avarice, but I might just as well suffer from drunkenness, lechery or any of the other addictions which flesh is heir to. I sometimes fear that I have part of the nature of a cold clever man, like Lord Chesterfield or some senior members of the diplomatic corps. But God forgives those who do not love enough, even if He does it more reluctantly than He forgives those who have loved too much.

Such beliefs predispose one to family life. My children are spirits at least as ancient as myself. I have learned more from them than from anyone else. There is no teaching so much to the point as the teaching one receives from an infant, who comes into the world crammed with the wisdom of ten thousand experiences and the love of ten thousand ages. At sixty I am full of understandings which I have derived from my children, often from the natural insights of the earliest years. I remember Emma, when she was four, saying to me that she could understand what happened after one was dead, but that she could not understand where she had been before she was born. The remark was significant enough to my own development for me to be able to remember the spot on the front lawn where we were standing when she made it. Impact is often measured by image.

Plato believed that human beings brought knowledge into the world as memory. Each child has a different set of Platonic memories, or memory banks, from which a parent can draw. These memory banks contain strange things. I was born with a memory of old books, so strong that I became a collector by the time I was eleven, and have spent my life in and out of the rare book business. I think that might relate to an eighteenth-century ancestor, Andrew Henderson, who kept a bookstall in

Westminster Hall, though I am sure I am not a reincarnation of him. At any rate, I was, of all preposterous things, an innate bibliophile, as though I had a book-lover's gene.

All true religion seems to have the same core of direct spiritual experience, the knowledge of the light. This is the message of Plato and the neo-Platonists, of St John's Gospel, of the great Christian mystics and of Islam and of the Eastern religions. As Aldous Huxley showed in *The Perennial Philosophy*, the same light is seen by mystics who have lived in religions with very different formal doctrines.

Like most people I have had a glimpse of these insights; but only on the nursery slopes. Such an acquaintance starts one on the reading which leads to certainty of their truth. There is very much to learn, but fortunately there will be eternal time in which to learn it. The destiny of the human spirit is, I believe, to join God through Christ, but Jacob's ladder which leads to that unity has many rungs, each with its own necessity.

HOW THE SPIRITUAL LIFE BLOSSOMS UNDER ADVERSITY

Each year for the last five years I have spent a week in January in Rome. I attend the International Committee of the Pontifical Council for Culture, whose function is to advise the Vatican on the ways in which cultural changes may affect the work of the Church.

Culture is interpreted broadly – we can equally discuss Marxism, Buddhism, educational policy or television as cultural influences.

The Council has three Cardinals at its head, Cardinal Poupard, who is President of our Executive Committee, Cardinal Garonne and Cardinal Sales of Brazil. Our Secretary is a distinguished Jesuit sociologist, Father Carrier; he is a French Canadian who has spent the last twenty-five years in Rome.

The Committee itself is one of the most interesting with which I have ever worked. I am afraid I have learned much more from them than they from me. Our three women members are a Japanese professor of political science, the Ibo head of Nigeria's Catholic Women's Organization, and an Indian nun who is the ex-President of a college in Bombay.

We have ex-President Senghor of Senegal, who is not only an African statesman but a member of the French Academy. We also have Father Hesburgh, the President of Notre Dame, who has taken that college from being famous mainly for its football to being one of the leading universities of the United States, with a law school comparable to Yale.

We have representatives from Poland, Germany, the Arab world, Unesco, Brazil, Peru and a number of other countries. At our annual meeting each member reports on the changes in the cultural circumstances of his or her part of the world.

Each year we have also had an audience with Pope John Paul II; he was responsible for setting up the Council for Culture and follows the work closely. When one sees him repeatedly one becomes amazed by the joys as well as the strength of his faith.

The world view from Rome is very different from my more familiar view from London. To take an instance, vocations to the priesthood and to the religious orders are a particular problem in Western Europe. Two countries which stand out for the number of vocations are Poland and Chile. From Rome one sees very clearly both the extent of world suffering and the strength it can give.

Apart from the impact of the Pope himself, I have become very conscious of what might be termed the Polish paradox. Poland is an oppressed country, forced by Russian power to suffer an alien government. The Catholic Church has, particularly since the eighteenth century, been the symbol of nationhood – rather as in Ireland.

The result is a country of great material and personal distress, but of a confident and resilient religious life. In post-war Europe Poland has been an economic failure; West Germany is perhaps the greatest economic success. Yet Poland flourishes spiritually; West Germany is spiritually impoverished.

It is a sign of Poland's confidence that despite poverty and persecution, and despite many state abortions, the Polish birth rate is the highest in Europe – West Germany's is about the lowest. One European baby in five is Polish. Religion can be reinforced by persecution and it can certainly be undermined by prosperity.

When we started, five years ago, it was the pressure of Marxism and the seductive materialism of the West which seemed to be the main threats to the development of Christianity.

Perhaps now Marxism seems less threatening, an ideology in its later stages, still offering an appeal to the oppressed in Latin America but itself an obvious – and cynical – oppressor in Europe.

The new force – both a force of religion and a threat to other religions – is the aggressive fundamentalism of the new Islamic movement. Khomeini-ism, an aggressive resurgent Islam, is a political and religious force in the Middle East, in Africa and undoubtedly in the Soviet Union as well.

In Africa the period of very high oil prices has financed a forward movement of Islam which presses on tribes which are predominantly Christian and those which still hold animist beliefs.

It is strange that the most rapidly expanding religious groups of the late twentieth century in many cases belong to the most fundamentalist sects.

In the United States this can partly be attributed to the influence of television, which has proved an ideal medium for the propagation of fundamentalist Protestantism.

Yet Khomeini-ism in the Middle East, the animist cults in Africa and Latin America, the new Buddhist sects in Asia, or militant Sikhism in India, all seem to belong to the same branch of religion – religion at its simplest, its most emotional and its most convulsive. Even inside the Catholic Church there are some extreme charismatic cults of which the same could be said.

The Protestant fundamentalists pose a particular threat to the established Protestant churches in America, whose numbers have been dropping almost as fast as the moral majority preachers have been winning converts.

Yet in the United States the Catholic Church has also been increasing in numbers – there are now fifty-five million American Catholics, and with the new Hispanic immigration, the Catholic Church of the United States remains closely linked to the immigrants and to the poor.

In Europe the anti-religious force of scientific materialism remains powerful; it has emptied the pews of many churches, even if one can see a reaction to the spiritual emptiness of modern European life.

But this does seem to be primarily a West European phenomenon. Bernard Williams may find the religiosity of California a shock after the agnosticism of Cambridge.

In the rest of the world, in India, Africa, Latin America, in many parts of Asia, it is the opposite movement which is so striking. There religion, in some of its purest and some of its most passionate forms, is strengthening its hold on the spirit of mankind.

The West European five per cent are not the leaders of the new movement of mankind; we seem to be a rather lonely culture which has temporarily lost touch with its spiritual vitality.

Those whose European experience has led them to believe that God is dead seem to be making a most provincial as well as a preposterous mistake.

27 January 1987

WHY THE SYNOD IS INCAPABLE OF ASCERTAINING CHRISTIAN TRUTHS

I have every sympathy with the bishops of the Church of England. The Synod has developed into a quasi-parliamentary referee on matters of faith and morals.

It seems to me that Plato was right to argue that matters of faith and morals cannot be determined satisfactorily by majority votes. Nor can they be settled by a debate which is concerned not with the definition of truth but with the achievement of agreement.

I entirely support the principle that the government of my country should be regulated by a majority, and can see no better way in which government can be given authority. I would regard it as an outrage to regulate my conscience by the same system.

After all, a majority in Parliament has legislated for permissive abortion, which I regard as murder. David Steel's Abortion Act, each year since it was passed, has cost as many British lives as the Battle of the Somme. The fact that a majority of Members of Parliament, each enjoying a majority in his own constituency, voted in favour of that Act, does not mean that I have to regard it as morally right to kill unborn babies.

Yet I recognize that the practical question whether abortionists should be prosecuted is a proper one for Parliament. A majority has no rights over my conscience, but it does have a political right to make laws, even including laws which permit doctors to kill babies.

The distinction is much harder to maintain when it comes to church affairs. Until modern times, the main Christian churches have not pretended to be democracies – the bishops have had authority as the heirs to the Apostles, who were given their authority by Jesus. The Roman Catholic Church claims a special authority for the Pope as the successor to St Peter, the rock on which the Church was built. The bishops and the Pope sought, and have claimed to have been given, the guidance of the Holy Ghost.

On this pattern, episcopal churches have derived their authority to teach on matters of faith and morals ultimately from divine revelation. Various Protestant churches and chapels offer an alternative model in which the congregation has been the ultimate authority. This was a natural development of non-episcopal Protestant churches after the Reformation. The history of such bodies shows that they are very vulnerable to internal conflicts and subdivision. No one who, for instance, knows the early history of New England will doubt the difficulty of operating such a system of church government. Read Cotton Mather and beware.

The Synod is itself a compromise between the congregational and episcopal. That is a very English contradiction; we are more imbued with parliamentary ideas than any other nation. Unfortunately, the Synod has also been accompanied by a marked bureaucratization of church government.

Many or most English people regard it as in some way un-English that Roman Catholics accept the authority of the papacy, an external and non-democratic power. They may see that the compromises, fudges and conciliations of assembly debate are unlikely to reach any valid truth, but they still feel that it is wrong to put one's faith in a church run on the principle of an ultimate individual authority.

The English Catholic, of course, does not see things that way. He sees the universal Church not as the inventor but as custodian of truth, and the Pope not as the master but as the servant of the Church. He sees the Christian role as service to the truth which

comes from God, not from man. He does indeed see the importance of Church councils, but because they are assemblies of
bishops, not as quasi-parliaments. He sees popes, bishops and
laity – the whole Church – as respondents to an immutable truth
which does not belong to them or their context in history, and
not as the leaseholders of an estate which they are entitled to
develop according to their own lights. In this, the Catholic is
closer to the evangelical position than to the modernist. To the
evangelical, also, truth is an absolute, even if it is to be found in
the Bible alone, rather than in the Bible as taught by the Church.

To the Catholic, and that certainly includes Anglo-Catholics
such as the Bishop of London, the subjective and relative
response to questions of faith and morals is a dangerous error.
Evangelicals and Catholics do not agree on what propositions are
true, but they do agree on what it means to say that a proposition
is true.

The Synod neither is nor can be an appropriate body for
determining the truth in this sense. Both its method and its
language are based upon compromise, and compromise depends
upon watering down truth and mixing it with fragments of
falsehood. But there is a further difficulty. The Synod is a quasi-
parliament; it is not a parliament. The reason why the British
Parliament has been such a great historic institution is that there
has for 300 years been government in Parliament. Mrs Thatcher
has a majority; she has whips, she can enact laws, and if she
ceases to be able to govern, out she goes.

Not so the Archbishop of Canterbury. He is no more than a
very influential voice in the Synod. He has no majority, and
never has had. His authority is purely persuasive, and he is
himself pressed to voice the compromises the Synod requires. A
bishop who votes against him suffers no loss of authority. Dr
Leonard is still Bishop of London, but Michael Heseltine is no
longer Secretary of State for Defence.

A partly democratic assembly, answerable to nobody and
supporting no system of government, is in theory an unworkable
way of running or supervising any institution, ecclesiastical or
lay. The practice seems to bear out the theoretical insufficiency.

The Synod of the Church of England is genuinely conscientious, thoughtful, prayerful and engaged. But it is also genuinely incapable of reaching those decisive judgements on which government can be based, and it does not even look like a suitable way of ascertaining, let alone affirming, the mysterious truths of the Christian religion.

This leaves the bishops of the Church of England unable to govern the Church of England, and it makes the Church of England appear a much less effective body than the totality of its work suggests that it is. However high-minded its intentions, no one will respect an ultimate authority which cannot make up its mind on any contentious issue. As St Paul observed to the Corinthians: 'If the trumpet give an uncertain sound, who shall prepare himself to the battle?'

17 November 1987

GHOSTS, POPULAR MIRACLES AND A RATIONAL ROUTE TO PROVIDENCE

I n Wiltshire they have stone circles and flying saucers; in Somerset we have ghosts. They do of course have ghosts in Wiltshire too, and Longleat is much haunted – a great-uncle of mine saw the grey lady as he was coming downstairs for dinner and caused consternation by asking his hostess who she might be.

Yet in Somerset we have so many ghosts that most houses of a respectable age are reputed to be or to have been haunted. I have myself never seen a ghost, and lived comfortably for fourteen years in a house where an eighteenth-century lady wearing a lace cap has recently appeared in what used to be our bedroom. She appeared and disappeared, going out like a light, in front of two respectable witnesses.

We also have family ghosts. Dorothy Mogg of Farrington Gurney married a Mr Churchey of Wincanton early in the eighteenth century. They lived in a small but pretty house called The Dogs, now too much overlooked by Wincanton's milk factory. William of Orange is reputed to have spent the night there on his march to London. Until exorcised, Dorothy Churchey used to walk about the upstairs bedroom, a small figure but apparently a disturbing one. I rather resented the exorcism of a relation.

A few years ago I visited a house near Stratford-upon-Avon,

where Shakespeare is said to have visited his fellow poet Drayton. When I was at school I used to stay there with my cousins, who both died in the 1940s. The wife was an invalid, of sweet and kindly personality, who loved her garden and sat long days in a summer-house. I had her described to me by the modern owner when I visited; she had seen an old lady who left a feeling of peace and happiness, seated in the summer-house. This owner had no clear knowledge of the previous owners of the house.

What is one to make of all these ghosts, happy and unhappy? What is one to make of the ghosts of dogs – another cousin regularly saw the ghost of C. Aubrey Smith's terrier – or of the ghost horses who draw ghost carriages to remote rectories?

The fact that can be asserted is that ghosts are seen, and have been recorded in many cultures, in many parts of the world and in many historic periods. Whatever ghosts may be, the existence of these perceptions is not to be doubted. It is rational to deny the existence of ghosts, if by that is meant the denial that ghosts are departed spirits; it is not rational to deny that people see ghosts, because plainly large numbers of people do see them.

There are numerous explanations offered. It is not an explanation to say that they are hallucinations; that is merely another word for the perceptions which have to be explained. Many of the people who have seen ghosts are sane, and their faculties show no other abnormal signs. One explanation commonly offered is that ghosts are some sort of video of past events, perhaps imprinted on a particular place by some strong emotion. That would require some at present unknown means of transmission through time, but it does not require that the ghosts should be departed spirits – they would merely be living people who are seen, as though recorded on film, by other people living at a later period. The possibility of this seems less remote in post-Einstein than in Newtonian physics.

Such an explanation seems plausible for many sightings. C. Aubrey Smith's dog stretches out in front of the fire in the early 1920s; he dies; he is seen stretching out in front of the fire years after his death. That is odd, but could be accommodated inside the natural scientific view of the world without impossible difficulty.

There is however a much smaller group of ghosts who are recorded as interacting with the living. They utter warnings, they convey information, they even converse. The same cousin who saw C. Aubrey Smith's dog had a long conversation about beetles in the New Forest with an entomologist from the British Museum who had died ten years before. He recognized the old man's photograph only later on when he went to the museum.

Such cases, like the fictitious one Shakespeare tells of Hamlet's father, are not merely natural occurrences falling outside their natural time order, but interactions between different periods of time. Yet the cases of this interaction, though many fewer than the recorded cases of non-interactive ghosts, are sufficient to need explanation.

They may of course belong simply in the mind of the beholder; the ghost may be a sort of waking dream. Indeed people do often dream vividly of dead people they have known, or even people they have known of. What is surprising about ghosts, as reported, is that they so often seem to be representations of real people not known to the person who sees them. My great-uncle had no knowledge of the grey lady at Longleat, and something, one would think, must have triggered his perception of her.

Natural scientists often become extremely angry when ghosts are spoken of. In a sense they are right to do so. Since Hume there have been two alternative explanations of the world contending for mastery. One is a materialist world view which explains the whole development of nature as an automatic system, a chain of cause and effect not interrupted by any non-material intervention. Even human consciousness is merely a product of this natural process.

The other is the religious world view, which regards natural science as an explanation of no more than part of the development of the universe, and accepts a dualism between the material and the spiritual. Ghosts fit uneasily enough into the religious world view – what do they think they are doing? – but the interactive ghosts, at least, have to be explained away for scientific materialism to subsist. Nature abhors a vacuum; science abhors a miracle.

I like ghosts partly because they are miracles of the people.

Authority, whether scientific or theological, has seldom felt comfortable with them. They are awkward things, certainly not repeatable and therefore not testable, seldom showing any interest in the questions we would all like to ask of them. They fit with no one's logic.

Yet I also like ghosts because I believe that what they sometimes suggest is true – that life is influenced and often dominated by non-material forces which impinge on time but exist outside time. That is true for evil as well as for good. I do not believe that the evil which dominated the world in the second quarter of this century had merely natural causes, whether Hitler's Freudian childhood, Stalin's paranoia, or Germany's inflation in 1923. I believe that real evil was there, and that it infected the world, like a pandemic. I also believe in the real influence of holiness. Ghosts hint at the existence of non-material causation, and another word for non-material causation is Providence.

23 December 1987

EAVESDROPPING ON A CONVERSATION LIKELY TO BE RENEWED IN HEAVEN

first saw John Gielgud as Macbeth at the Haymarket in 1943. Last week, I saw him play Sydney Cockerell in Hugh Whitemore's *The Best of Friends* at the Apollo. It is unusual to have seen an actor's performances over a period of forty-five years. In fact, Sir John Gielgud has been on stage for sixty-seven years, not a record but nevertheless a long time.

I was brought up to believe that Gielgud was the greatest English actor of the twentieth century and, by the classical standard, he is. This was my mother's view. She was an American Shakespearian actress who came to England in the summer of 1920 to join the Old Vic Company. She met my father, married and left the stage.

She had been taught by the old English actors and actresses who, in the early years of this century, still had such an influence on the American stage. She had heard their stories of Henry Irving and Ellen Terry, of David Garrick and Sarah Siddons, and had imbibed their theatrical values. She herself in 1916 had played on Broadway with an even greater theatrical figure than Gielgud: Sarah Bernhardt.

This traditional acting school is now usually portrayed as over-theatrical, and Henry Irving himself was obviously one of those great actors who have in them more than an element of the great ham. But it had also always been a naturalist tradition, going back to Garrick and beyond. Its central instrument was voice and the sound of language; its greatest admiration was reserved for the ability not only to speak, but to act Shakespeare's verse.

The method was partly an accumulation of traditional memory of the way in which great actors had performed. I remember our reading *Macbeth* in the nursery, and my mother telling us what she had been told about Sarah Siddons's emphasis in the lines:

> 'If we should fail, – '
> 'We fail!
> But screw your courage to the sticking-place,
> And we'll not fail.'

She told us that Sarah Siddons had pronounced '*We fail!*' fatalistically and not scornfully, accepting failure as a possible outcome, not deriding it as an impossible one, with a firm but falling emphasis on the second word.

There is no doubt that John Gielgud has been the master of speaking Shakespeare's poetry. His Hamlet, which I also saw, was the greatest theatrical performance I can remember. Hamlet himself is an intellectual, and Gielgud's special gift as an actor has been his ability to portray the intellect, just as his contemporary, Lord Olivier, has had the special ability to act physical energy, the physical will. Olivier failed to achieve Gielgud's mental projection in *Hamlet*, just as Gielgud could not have matched Olivier's physical projection in *Henry V*.

It is therefore right that John Gielgud's latest performance should be playing the part of an intellectual. The night I was there the atmosphere in the house was itself most unusual. It was a very English audience – not very smartly dressed people of middle age with kindly faces – and there was a feeling of peace and gratitude which was most moving. I thought there was a slight danger that something might be overlooked in this friendly adulation for John Gielgud's performance.

The play itself, which appears simple enough, is a great play because it deals validly with universal issues. There is, indeed, little or no plot. *The Best of Friends* is an account, without a decisive story, of the friendship between Sir Sydney Cockerell, the museum curator, George Bernard Shaw (played by Ray McAnally) and Dame Laurentia McLachlan, the Abbess of Stanbrook, played by Rosemary Harris. It is about the unfashionable subject of friendship, a friendship the details of which survived because it was largely followed by correspondence.

The message stresses the value of friendship not just for comfort but for intellectual and spiritual well-being. There is a religious message, mixed with the personal one. The three friends are the scholar, the writer and the nun. We see that it is the nun who is the happiest of the three, and she is the central figure.

When contrasted, the three qualities of scholarship, artistic creation and worship fall into a hierarchy, with worship at the top, artistic creation in the middle, and scholarship at the bottom. All three characters see that and accept it.

But the relationships are also those between two men and a woman. The characters understand the relative permanence of the feminine principle and the relative fretfulness of the masculine. It is a pro-woman play, if not in a way that all feminists would accept.

The play is concerned with people growing older; again unfashionably, it takes an optimistic view of age. The play suggests – which our grandfathers believed – that as people grow older, they are likely to grow wiser, both because of the benefits of experience, and because the strivings of youth have dropped away. Both Cockerell and Shaw improved as they aged. What we are told about their earlier years makes them sound immature at least until fifty.

The same is not true of Dame Laurentia, because she had voluntarily adopted in youth principles which the men move gradually toward in old age. The truths they are coming to see she has known all along. Beside this growth in wisdom and affection, the troubles of old age, physical disabilities, bereavement, death itself, seem unimportant. Ripeness is all.

The play also has in it the suggestion that friendship in this life is one of the things most likely to be transferred to the next. There is a stage of dying in which people can become confused about which world they are in. I have been asked by a friend on his deathbed whether he was yet dead, and he seemed rather surprised to be told that he was not. *The Best of Friends* has something of this atmosphere.

As the curtain falls, only one of the friends is left alive, but we feel that the conversation which we have been overhearing has hardly been interrupted by the accident that the other two have died first. The conversation is to be renewed in heaven, a heaven to which, as Shaw foresaw, the two men will be led by the woman, the intellectuals will be led by the nun.

From a religious point of view, old age is a kind of adolescence to death, not the least important part of life, but perhaps the most valuable as it is closest to the next world. All love supports the capacity for love; love of friends supports the capacity to love God. Therefore, the quiet friendships of the old, which are bound to be interrupted, are among the strong influences for good in life. But how much one delights in a play – a rare benefit – in which the values are friendship and prayer, innocence and peace.

15 March 1988

FLYING MAHOGANY, A LEVITATING BELLRINGER AND THE DEAD RAPPING

like to revisit the great Victorian mysteries, because they pose such intriguing questions. What did Dr James Gully see that evening in July 1860 at a house in Hyde Park Terrace? Was it a paranormal event, a collective hallucination or a fraudulent conjuring trick? Should Dr Gully's evidence be discounted because he was something of a quack, or because he was later involved in one of the great Victorian scandals?

If we do discount his evidence, do we have any reason to doubt that of James Wason, the Liverpool solicitor in extensive practice, who described the same scene in terms very similar to those of Dr Gully? Should we disregard the evidence of the 'eminent literary man' who wrote an article for the *Cornhill* because he remained anonymous?

What Dr Gully saw, or thought he saw, or said that he saw, was 'a man, between ten and eleven stone in weight, floating about the room for many minutes'. What Mr Wason saw was a man who 'as he floated along, kept ringing the small hand bell to indicate his locality in the room, which was probably forty by thirty feet'. Although the room itself was not lit, there was sufficient light from a gaslamp in the street for both Dr Gully and Mr Wason to see the man as he floated past the windows or the door.

Mr Wason in addition handed up a pencil with which to write

on the ceiling. 'Stretching upwards I was enabled to reach his hand, about seven feet distant from the floor, and I placed therein a pencil, and laying hold and keeping hold of his hand, I moved along with him five or six paces as he floated above me in the air.' Dr Gully felt the man's foot touch his head as he floated above him.

The *Cornhill* published the anonymous author who saw the 'figure pass from one side of the window to the other, feet foremost lying horizontally in the air. He spoke to us as he passed and told us that he would turn the reverse way and recross the window; which he did . . . He hovered round the circle for several minutes, and passed, this time perpendicularly over our heads.'

The author also touched the floating figure: 'The foot was withdrawn quickly, with a palpable shudder. It was evidently not resting on the chair, but floating, and it sprang from the touch as a bird would.' Three witnesses saw, heard and touched.

The figure was Daniel Dunglas Home, and Hyde Park Terrace was not the only recorded instance of his levitation. Because of the witnesses, this seance marks a high-point of Victorian physical mediumship, and raises most acutely the question: was it a hoax?

Daniel Home, a young Scottish American, claimed to come from a family endowed with second sight. His mother, who died when he was seventeen, was said herself to be a seer, able to predict family deaths, including her own. Of all the mediums who demonstrated physical events in the mid-nineteenth century, Home is the most impressive. His powers, whether psychic or not, were extensive and well attested. Although he was accused of fraud, he was never in fact caught out. He appeared in the United States, London, St Petersburg, Paris and Italy. He even met the Pope, though at a time when his powers were not operating.

The story is a very strange one, whichever way one looks at it. What happened was that tables, often very heavy ones, rocked around Victorian rooms, as did chairs and well-stuffed settees. The dead communicated, often by rapping. Apart from the occasional identification of mislaid documents, they did not have

anything very interesting to say. Hands appeared, and sometimes wrote the names of dead people. They patted people's
knees under the table. Flowers appeared and were scattered
about.

Suppose this to be true, suppose Home's levitation to be true,
what does it all mean? Daniel Home thought that it was intended
to prove the spiritual nature of existence. He was himself a
devout Christian, and became a convert from his early congrega-
tionalism to Roman Catholicism. He records the effect that some
of the first experiences had on him. 'Whilst we were thus engaged
in prayer, at every mention of the holy names of God and Jesus,
there came gentle taps, whilst at every expression of a wish for
God's loving mercy to be shown to us and our fellow creatures,
there were loud rappings. I was so struck, that there and then,
upon my knees, I placed myself entirely at God's disposal.'

The sequence of his early life is clear enough. There were some
apparently psychic events in childhood, then some poltergeist
phenomena in adolescence; he was exposed to New England
Swedenborgian ideas, like those which influenced Henry James
the elder, father of William James, the philosopher, and of Henry,
the novelist; he was also exposed to the mediumism which had
been started by the Fox sisters in Rochester. Home experienced a
lucid dream, very like modern reports of near-death experiences.
He went out of his body, reviewed his past life, saw dead
relations, experienced a vivid light, met a wise counsellor, was
told to return. Yet this spiritual conversion led to levitating tables
in front of crowned heads. It is hard not to laugh at all this flying
mahogany, but of course a miracle – if it was that – is not less a
miracle for being comic.

Levitation itself is widely recorded in the lives of the saints,
when it is usually treated by the saints themselves as an embarrassing manifestation of grace. St Teresà of Avila in prayer had to
be held down by her nuns, and there are other instances of saints
who levitated in front of better witnesses than Dr Gully. St
Francis of Assisi's secretary, Leo, records that the saint, in
meditation, would be raised into the air so that his feet were level
with Leo's head.

The unnamed author of the *Cornhill* article quotes a reply of Dr

Treviranus to Coleridge: 'I have seen what I would not have believed on your testimony, and what I cannot, therefore, expect you to believe on mine.' That perhaps puts the dilemma of the evidence as well as it can be put.

Then of course there is the problem of Dr Gully. The *Dictionary of National Biography* states the later scandal objectively: 'In 1876 Gully's name was frequently mentioned at the sensational inquiry into the death of a barrister named Charles Bravo who, it was suspected, had been poisoned by his wife. Disclosures as to Gully's intimacy with Mrs Bravo gravely damaged his reputation. On the conclusion of the inquiry his name was removed from all the medical societies and journals of the day.'

A witness to one of the great unresolved Victorian mysteries, an actor in another, Gully's connection makes one uneasy. Whatever else Daniel Home's levitation may have achieved, it did not do Dr Gully much spiritual good. Perhaps a Liverpool reader can tell us what became of Mr Wason.

28 June 1988

LEFEBVRISM MEANS IRRATIONAL PRIDE AND A FEAR OF FREEDOM

Anyone who can look at the four successive popes since the opening of the second Vatican Council – John XXIII, Paul VI, John Paul I, John Paul II – and declare that 'the throne of Peter has been occupied by anti-Christs' must be suffering from some deformity of mind. The language used by Archbishop Lefebvre is not the language of truth, nor is it the language of Christian charity.

That he should have led his followers into schism with the Catholic Church is both illogical (how can any Catholic defy the papacy in the name of Saint Pius X?) and breaks the loyalty of a Catholic bishop. The contradiction between his hypercatholicism and his own rejection of the Church's authority makes him unfit to be trusted with the care of souls.

The Lefebvre cult is based on a complete rejection of the second Vatican Council; it is not, however, a reassertion of the first Vatican Council which in 1870 defined the doctrine of the papal infallibility. The Lefebvrists are anti-papal; his consecration of four bishops without papal authority has an essentially Protestant character. It is the central doctrine of Protestantism to reject the authority of the Church in favour of private judgement.

Archbishop Lefebvre's private judgement is that four popes have been anti-Christs, and he therefore rejects them. He rejects popes; he rejects councils; he rejects the teaching authority of the

Church; he puts his own judgement ahead of all other consider-
ations. That is legitimate for avowed Protestants, but ridiculous
in an extreme anti-Protestant.

So far as the archbishop is concerned, one can therefore only
feel anger at his presumption and hope that he will come to
repent. The act of schism itself should be condemned, but the
appeal which has led thousands to follow Lefebvre needs to be
understood.

There is little doubt that Pope Paul VI's handling of the changes
of the Roman Catholic liturgy in the 1960s was inadequate. The
so-called Tridentine mass, the historic mass to which the council
of Trent in the sixteenth century gave a codified and uniform
character, was abruptly discarded.

It was replaced by a dialogue mass, which is normally said in
the vernacular; the English translation is not eloquent. When said
reverently, it is a lucid and sanctified form of worship; it has,
however, also been used by Charismatics as the basis of a folk
mass as noisy but seldom as cheering as a Salvation Army band.

The other main difference is that the Tridentine mass focuses
its worship outside itself; the priest has his back to the congregation so that both priest and congregation can face the host in
unity. The Pauline mass has its focus of worship inside itself,
between the priest and the congregation, emphasizing the community of worship.

There are arguments for both views. At its worst the Tridentine
mass could be a rite in which the congregation left the mass to
the priest. At its worst, the Pauline mass becomes a barely
reverent conversation in which the host has its significance
diminished.

For a contemplative temperament, the sense of projecting
worship towards God and the beauty of the traditional mass
probably provided a better opportunity for reaching the calm
prayer which is at the heart of the psychology of religion. For
others, and particularly for the young, the Pauline dialogue
vernacular is more accessible.

What is certain is that it would be better if the old mass had
been kept as a much-loved option, as the Church of England did
with its historic form of service. The Pauline mass, spoken in

many languages and accompanied by a variety of sacred and profane music, is inherently pluralist. In a pluralist liturgy, it was harsh to deny the one option that adhered to the tradition of the Church. Today, the Tridentine mass is rare and requires special permission.

Of course Lefebvrism is much more than a matter of liturgy. The second Vatican Council was called after a century of relative failures on the part of the Church. They were not failures of the central core of faith, but failures to give a heroic Christian leadership to the world.

The isolation of the Pope in the Vatican after the loss of the papal territories, the intellectual inadequacies in the face of modern science, the failure to prevent or mitigate two world wars, both of which started in the European heartland of Catholicism, the ineffective but obsessive attitude towards communism, the failure either to prevent or even adequately to condemn the Nazi massacre of the Jews, the clerical introspection of Rome, all called for a new effort to reopen the Catholic Church to the Holy Spirit.

Inevitably such a reopening was perilous; the Holy Spirit has always been a disturbing companion. Yet those of us who lived through the change from the old Catholic Church to the new can hardly question that the new is the more open, the more loving and the more alive.

Archbishop Lefebvre challenges all this; he wants to go back to some of the merits but also to the worst faults of the Church of his childhood. He particularly condemns the new role of the laity, modernism, liberalism, attitudes to communism, ecumenism and Zionism. He does not accept that the Church should be in dialogue with the modern world, that the Church should understand the virtues of the liberal respect for individual freedom – indeed his political sympathies appear tainted with some sympathy for Fascists. He wants to return to the obsession about communism just at the point when communism is changing; he rejects ecumenism and openness to other Churches and religions, and he rejects Judaism. His supporters include anti-Semites.

There are two common threads to Lefebvrism: in his dealings with the Pope the main thread has been pride, that irrational pride which sometimes invades old people; in his doctrines, the thread is fear – fear of change; fear of freedom; fear of communism; fear of even talking to other religions or to Christians of other Churches; fear of Jews. Pride and fear are two of the evils which Jesus himself most often and most explicitly condemned. Where one can make clear distinction between the doctrines of the Church and the doctrines of Lefebvre, it is the doctrines of the Church, and of the second Vatican Council, which are Christian and those of Lefebvre which are anti-Christian.

Catholics who follow Lefebvre do so because they are traditionalists. Yet the tradition of the Church is one of acceptance of the ultimate teaching authority, and of a serious commitment of loyalty to the papacy as an institution. A man who attacks the papacy in grotesque language and defies its authority is not to pretend that he stands in the Catholic tradition. Thank goodness it is John Paul II and not Archbishop Lefebvre who is the Pope.

5 July 1988

LOOKING BACK BETWEEN
THE RAINSHOWERS OF
SILVER TEAPOTS

On Wednesday last I attended the last Arts Council meeting, of about seventy, in which I have taken the chair. I hand over the chairmanship to Peter Palumbo at the end of this month. The council very kindly gave me a farewell visit to the National Theatre, followed by a supper, a very friendly speech by Roy Strong and the presentation of a leaving gift, a water colour by Gerald Mynott.

This is not by any means my first retirement, nor is it likely to be my last. I was given a gold watch when I left *The Financial Times* in 1960, and I still wear it on grand occasions. I was given a set of silver spoons when I retired as the Conservative candidate for Chester-le-Street after the 1959 election. I was given a silver salver, bought by Charles Douglas-Home, and an excellent lunch cooked by the managing director's wife, when I left *The Times* in 1981. I was given an engraved glass bowl when I left the BBC, although it was clear that some of my then colleagues would have given more than that to see me go.

I still have a number of different jobs which I enjoy, so I expect the sky to rain silver teapots for years to come. Nevertheless, retirements which take place after one reaches sixty seem to have a finality which is lacking in retirements which occur when one is still in one's early thirties.

I have never regretted a retirement. I do not wish to work for

The Financial Times, contest Chester-le-Street under whatever name the constituency now has, edit *The Times*, govern the BBC or, after 31 March, preside over the Arts Council. I have been fully absorbed in the work of each of these functions while I was doing them. I miss the friendship of old colleagues, but I look back on passages of personal history almost as detached from my continuing activities as if the tasks had been performed by someone else.

My ideal time for each piece of work seems to be about the seven years which I did at the Arts Council. I worked for *The Financial Times* for eight years, at *The Sunday Times* for seven years, for *The Times* for fourteen – probably too long – and at the BBC for five. There has to be a learning period at the beginning of each job, and there ought then to be time to develop a strategy and see it through. But in journalism at least the freshness of ideas is essential. Papers which have been edited by the same person for too long lose imagination and go stale.

I find no difficulty in looking back and seeing the mistakes that I made. When I was writing the leading articles on *The Financial Times* I ought to have seen the likely inflationary consequences of Harold Macmillan's acceptance of Peter Thorneycroft's resignation – Harold Wincott, our senior columnist, got it right. On *The Sunday Times* I should not have been taken in by Harold Wilson's professed interest in new technology. By the stage I reached *The Times*, I should have known that a formal incomes policy cannot be made to work – so should Ted Heath.

In 1978 I should not have agreed to the decision to close *The Times* without a clear Wapping-type alternative being accepted first. The BBC was in difficulties when I got there, remained in trouble while I was there, and has now been put into better condition. As I have not yet left the Arts Council, it has not yet become obvious to me what I have got wrong, but no doubt that too will be made clear in due time.

What I do not regret is the rows I have had. The people who seem to me to achieve most, who do the most good to the world, are those who follow their own logic and face the disputes which follow from that. It is a quality which occasionally takes people to the top, though it may be safer to develop it after arriving at the top. It is a quality I regard myself as possessing only in some degree. There are those who have found me difficult, but my own judgement is that I have not been difficult enough.

When one retires at sixty, even from only one section of one's work, one is conscious of a certain shaping of life. It is like a mound with a flat top: there are twenty years of becoming, forty years of doing, then with luck twenty years of being. The appetite for doing seems to me to be at its peak for ten years before and after the age of forty. After sixty there is still plenty of doing left, but the rewards of achievement come to look more and more illusory; 'it's only a paper moon, a Barnum and Bailey world'. The pleasures of being, however, become more intense and the pleasures of family and friendship have a colour that is even brighter than in the glass of busy ambition. I feel happier at sixty than at any earlier time of my life.

Roy Thomson, who started to make a really large fortune when he retired to buy *The Scotsman* at the age of sixty – he retired worth $9m and died twenty-five years later worth $650m or so – might be taken as an example of doing continuing to the end. Yet even he thought that his need to make a few more hundred million dollars in his eighties was something of an eccentricity, even a joke. When he was in his eighties he was lunching with Paul Getty and said: 'Paul is richer than I am; but I'm six months younger than he is.' In their later years, people should do what pleases them, and if it pleases them to make millions or govern great nations, that is a forgivable weakness. Reagan, Adenauer, de Gaulle and Churchill show that old men can make good statesmen.

Certainly I find that the process of age changes one's attitude to religion. Islam seems to me a religion of young manhood: fervent, daring, intolerant and expansionist. Christianity is a religion of middle age: strong, truthful, serious and trustworthy. Buddhism is a religion of old age: humble, pacific, tender to life, quiet. There comes to be an element of Buddhism in the Christianity of most people as they become older.

The Buddhist view of a very long succession of different consciousnesses also acquires a new plausibility. At sixty, one finally starts to perceive how short life is. My friends in their seventies tell me that perception sharpens with every year. Not much can be done in any one life – forty, even fifty or sixty, years of great bustle make little mark on the world, and perhaps not all that much mark on the individual spirit. In the twentieth century it is the wicked who have left the deep scars on human history.

That said, I have much enjoyed my seven years at the Arts Council. It is a bridging job between government and the artists – mainly the performing artists. Next to the vocation of the religious, the vocation of art is probably the highest human activity. And the vocation of politics, though often absurd and in human terms usually tragic, is in its own way an admirable vocation as well. It has, as they say, been a privilege to be part of a yoke which ties those two ill-matched oxen together.

7 March 1989

HOW A NARROW-MINDED CHURCH CAN PRODUCE A GOOD CITIZEN

The Lord Chancellor is an admirable character, one of the best men in public life. I do not at all agree with his Green Papers on law reform, but he is obviously an exceptionally fair-minded, serious, diligent and caring servant of the public interest. Until last week he had spent his life as a member of a singularly intolerant Scottish Calvinist sect which finally excommunicated him for an act of charity, the attendance at a Roman Catholic funeral. There is a question to ask. How is such a good man produced, and his personality shaped, by so defective a Church?

One can put the question more broadly. The most highly disciplined religious sects in Britain include Orthodox Jews, strict Muslims, the Plymouth Brethren and other ultra-Protestant groups, Mormons and perhaps some others. All of these groups accept disciplines which to the rest seem irrational. Most people would not regard it as sinful to drive a car to a synagogue on the Sabbath, to read Salman Rushdie, to have a meal with someone not an exclusive brother, or to drink a cup of tea or coffee. For that matter, unlike Lord Mackay, most people would not think it sinful to give an interview to a Sunday newspaper, although I can think of one or two it might be imprudent to talk to.

Yet as one looks at the figures of crime, a very different picture appears. There are hardly any observant Orthodox Jews in prison, very few strict Muslims – though perhaps more than there were before last weekend's demo – few Plymouth Brethren and few Mormons. I doubt whether, to use the old cricketing cliché, Lord Mackay's Church often troubles the scorer when it comes to the crime statistics.

For believers, the message of their religion is simply true. But plainly they cannot all be absolutely true. Moses, Mohamed, Calvin and Joseph Smith did not preach a single religious doctrine; they differ on important questions. From the outside we can only note that dogmatic and highly disciplined religious groups have the common characteristic of producing orderly, honest and useful citizens, and that their ability to do so does not seem to be affected by a discipline or dogma which, from the Enlightenment's point of view, is irrational.

No doubt these groups can also damage the psychological health of some adherents. Narrowness and puritanism can distort the human personality, produce neuroses, and lead to much bitterness and unhappiness. Equally these sects can be intolerant, as the Free Presbyterian Church – or Ian Paisley's Presbyterian Church – are intolerant of Roman Catholicism. Calvinism is a system of spiritual apartheid.

At the extreme this intolerance, as in the case of the Ayatollah Khomeini, can become an unqualified evil. Nevertheless the rest of us, liberal Christians or non-Christians, children of the Enlightenment, must contrast the failures in our own societies with the capacity for self-discipline of theirs. In the United States there is the new threat of the epidemic of crack. Which religious groups are successfully able to resist it? Roman Catholics? No, crack abuse is extremely common among the Hispanics of the inner cities. Charismatic Protestants? No, for theirs is a major religion among the blacks of cities such as New York, Washington or Atlanta which are among the worst affected.

You will find very little use of crack among observant Jews or Mormons; if an American wants to minimize the risk of drug abuse for his children, Brigham Young University in Utah is probably the college of first choice. My own experience is of belonging to a Church which has in my lifetime moved from a high discipline to an acceptance of the Enlightenment. Half my life was lived before the Second Vatican Council and half since. As it happened, I was myself brought up in a liberal Roman Catholic atmosphere. My father was a disillusioned Anglican who had heard too many long sermons in his childhood.

My mother had been born into the Irish American Catholic Church. Shortly before the First World War, she attended the College of New Rochelle, outside New York City, a liberal arts college run by nuns. There she was influenced by a remarkable chaplain, Father Meister, a German Jesuit who had been silenced in the purge of modernists under Pope Pius X. He had been sent by his order to a teaching post in America where it was thought that he could do no harm. His views, though they would now seem rather conservative, were those which prevailed in Vatican II.

I was therefore brought up in a moderately liberal and modernist Roman Catholic belief which only became orthodox in the 1960s. My mother's combination of liberalism and Irish tradition made the old English ghetto Catholicism, with its strict adherence to points of detail such as are obvious in other highly disciplined groups, unsympathetic to her. Probably the only American pronunciation I've retained all my life is the use of the short 'a' in 'Mass' to rhyme with 'lass' rather than 'grass'. 'Mass' with a short 'a' represents a significant difference of religious attitudes.

I was also brought up to take what was essentially the modernist view of the primacy of the individual conscience, the impertinence of the index of prohibited books, the impossibility of a fundamentalist interpretation of the Bible, and the need to respect scientific findings.

I went to Anglican schools and had few Catholic friends until I went to Oxford, and those not particulary close. Indeed the first Roman Catholic whose religious outlook I found approximated to my own was Shirley Williams, whose religious formation also had a degree of American influence. Of course she always scored higher in charity than I did.

Obviously, therefore, I find the modern Catholic Church more congenial than the old one, and closer to the truth. The lifting of the imposed guilt which hung over the childhood of so many Roman Catholics, the abolition of the fear of hell fire for some

143

trivial offence, and of the preposterously oversensitive pseudo-deity that implied, has been a return to a more valid Christianity. But I am not sure that the new Catholic Church has the power of the old to form consciences.

The question is not one which will go away. At what step along the road to religious liberalism do we lose the vital ability of religion to form personal character and stability? Perhaps the first generation of liberalism has the best of both worlds – the character formed by a strong discipline, the intellect moving on to a broader enlightenment. In history the formation of the religious personality – the man for all seasons, the life lived for others – has been one of the objectives of religious discipline and practice. The ideal has always been rare, but a liberalism which does not even attempt it is bound to fail.

30 May 1989

AMSTERDAM, WHERE
NOTHING IS SACRED

did not go to Amsterdam to be shocked. I went as a tourist
with my family, to take a trip around the canals, to visit the
artificial rain forest at the Arnhem Zoo (as described in *Blue
Peter*), to walk through the old city and to visit museums and
churches. We did all these things, seeing the Vermeers and
Rembrandts at the Rijksmuseum and the Van Goghs at the Van
Gogh Museum.

We admired great Dutch art and architecture; we ate excellent
Dutch food, a solid cuisine to support long tourist walks. We had
in every way an enjoyable weekend, and felt grateful for the
mild-mannered efficiency of Dutch services. The people are
among the friendliest and most helpful in Europe.

It was the churches that shocked me. Amsterdam has two
great medieval churches, much painted by Dutch artists, the
Oude Kerk of St Nicholas, built on the right bank of the Amstel
River in the early thirteenth century, and the Nieuwe Kerk,
originally dedicated to Our Lady, built on the left bank about a
hundred years later. Both of these were Catholic foundations,
and remained so until Amsterdam joined the Calvinist Party in
the 'alteration' of 1578. As a result, the basic architecture of the
churches is Catholic; they are designed for the celebration of the
Mass. The interior decoration is Protestant.

The two great churches dominate the centre of Amsterdam in

rather the same way that St Paul's and Westminster Abbey dominate the centre of London. In ecclesiastical terms, they are still affiliated to the Dutch Reformed Church, and indeed a few services are still held at the Old Church. We were visiting on a Sunday morning. The Old Church was firmly closed, although there had been an 11 a.m. service. Judging by the notices outside, it appeared to be the only service performed in the course of the week, although there were advertisements for concerts and opening hours for tourists.

It was the New Church, the more prominent of the two, which was disturbing, although I must admit the graffiti at the back of the Old Church gave a depressing impression of neglect. The New Church has been turned into a museum. I had thought that the practice of turning great churches into museums was confined to communist or at least to avowedly non-Christian countries. The atmosphere of the New Church was almost equally Godless.

Indeed, I have seldom been in any place where there seemed to have been such a determined effort not to desecrate but to desacralize, to remove the idea of the sacred. I was reminded of the rhyme in *The Scarlet Pimpernel*: 'They seek him here, they seek him there, those Frenchies seek him everywhere. Is he in Heaven, is he in hell, That damn'd elusive Pimpernel?' God is the Scarlet Pimpernel of the New Church.

The process of desacralization has been going on for a long time. It started in 1578 when the image breakers, the iconoclasts, plundered the church and largely destroyed the interior. It continued in 1645 when the church was burnt out in a great fire, but at least that was the result of a plumber's negligence and not intention. It went a stage further in the late 1670s with the erection of Michiel de Ruyter's tomb, an act of blasphemous vulgarity made none the better by its high quality as a work of art. The tomb takes up the entire apse, where the high altar stood in the Catholic period of the church's history.

De Ruyter was a great Dutch admiral; he defeated the British, among other navies. It was entirely reasonable that he should be lavishly commemorated, as we commemorate Nelson in Trafalgar Square. But the statement made by his tomb is the same as would have been made if the high altar at Westminster Abbey had been ripped out to accommodate a funeral monument to Nelson. They put their great admiral in God's place.

On Sunday morning when we visited the New Church, there was a museum exhibition of Dutch glass, which filled much of the church, with another exhibition of nineteenth-century photographs of Venice, which filled the choir. The bookstall had a selection of books on art, such as one might see in the Tate Gallery, including a paperback on the work of Andy Warhol. Yet this is a church so important to the Netherlands that the monarch takes her constitutional oath here, and did so as recently as 1980.

The National Foundation of the New Church was brought into existence in 1979. The foundation's board 'consists of representatives from ecclesiastical and social spheres'. The statute of the foundation sounds largely secular: 'The foundation shall direct itself toward promoting Nieuwe Kerk in Amsterdam, in accordance with its origin and appropriation, as well as with the significance it has gained for the entirety of the Dutch nation; to help it function as a meeting place for the Christian community and the world it inhabits. Without excluding other aspects, this encounter will take place on social, economic and religious levels. City and republic shall both contribute to this and in accordance with their capacities.'

The guide book tells us what the result has been. 'During the spring and summer months, the church bustles with activities such as public assemblies, concerts, lectures, exhibits and discussions. The Knyper Hall has been set up as a foyer and a café, and the Eggert Hall can be hired for receptions, lectures, exhibits and concerts.'

That, of course, is a conceivable use for a redundant church, but it says something about the Reformed congregation that one of the great national churches of the Netherlands should be treated as redundant. At least that has not been proposed for Westminster Abbey.

The total secularization of a great church, a progression unremittingly continued over more than 400 years, has only been possible because of the secularization of Dutch culture. It is one of the most secularized societies of any I know, perhaps the one in which liberalism has been taken the furthest. The stripping out of God from the New Church is as complete as modern man can make it. There was not a scent of the divine in the whole place, but a sort of sad absence and withdrawal, a cave where the tide had gone out.

Outside, you only have to walk a few yards to see the sex shops displaying their fly-blown rubber phalluses in the ground-floor windows of beautiful seventeenth-century houses. At night, the windows beside the canals are often lit up with red strip lighting, where bored-looking prostitutes, many of them Asian, display themselves in unappetizing poses. It reminded me of Smithfield, another great meat market. The fruits of this ultra-liberal society have included a commercial degradation of woman more open than in Britain, or in any of Europe's Catholic countries.

A church is not sacred, so it is turned into a museum. A woman is not sacred, so she is sold in a shop window. Human life is not sacred, so the Dutch are moving towards euthanasia. This desacralization is natural to our modern liberal secular society, not only in Amsterdam, yet the Dutch have taken it at least one stage further than we have.

Cultures need a recognition of the sacred to retain their meaning and even their life. The Dutch culture has much that is good left in it – tolerance, friendliness, efficiency and a tradition of visual art. But there is a sense of death about a desacralized culture. The New Church in Amsterdam seemed to me not just a depressing, empty church, but also a symbol of the rejection of the Christian culture of Europe which is terrible in its implications.

22 July 1991

WHY SHOULD THERE NOT
BE LIFE AFTER DEATH?

Since 1859, when Darwin published *On the Origin of Species*, there has been a fatal duality in human thought. On the one hand there are the materialists who believe in natural science as the one road to truth, in evolution through selection of random genetic mutations, in the brain as a machine for consciousness, in the impossibility of human survival of brain death and the unreality of religious or psychic phenomena. On the other side are those who adopt a religious view of life, who see spiritual growth as the aim of human existence, who believe in some purpose in evolution, and expect the human spirit to survive death.

Ever since Darwin there have been those who have tried to reconcile these two positions; they have been criticized from both sides, but particularly by the scientists. There is nowadays as great a hostility among devoted science-bound thinkers to the spiritual statements as there was in the seventeenth century among religious people to the new science. It is now scientism that appears afraid of the inadmissible observation.

One contemporary leader in the brave attempt to bring this division to an end is Peter Fenwick, who is the chairman of the Council of the Scientific and Medical Network, and a consultant neuropsychiatrist at the Maudsley Hospital in south London. The network takes as its motto a statement from Niels Bohr: 'We must continually count on the appearances of new facts, the inclusion of which within the compass of our earlier experience may require a revision of our fundamental concepts.' It began in 1973 and has 700 members.

I recently had a meeting with Dr Fenwick and his colleague on another body, David Lorimer, because I share their interest in near-death experiences. Our conversation turned on the central issue of the nature of the brain. Is the brain simply a machine that produces the phenomena of mind, including consciousness, or is it something else, and if so, what? If it is a thought-producing machine, then presumably when the brain dies, mind dies and we die, finally and for ever.

We discussed the ideas of William James, who was the leading American psychologist and philosopher at the turn of the century, the author of the standard late-nineteenth-century textbook on psychology. He was the elder brother of Henry James, the novelist.

A few days ago I was able to buy from an American bookseller a first edition of William James's Ingersoll Lecture, *Human Immortality*, published in Boston by Houghton Mifflin in 1898. In it he deals with the brain death objection to the possibility of immortality. Of course, he knew much less about the structure of the brain than is known now, but he knew what the questions were.

William James described himself as a physiological psychologist. Dr Fenwick is a neuropsychiatrist, and would accept the same description. James asked his audience to subscribe, at least as a hypothesis, to what he calls 'the great psychophysiological formula: Thought is a function of the brain'. He went on to ask what type of function the brain performed. Does it produce thought, or transmit it?

Most, if not all, the major organs of the body are transmitters. The lung takes in air and transmits oxygen to the blood, the stomach transmits nutrients to the rest of the body. There is, therefore, nothing unusual about organs that absorb and transmit; the difficulty would rather be to find an organ which, in any perfect sense, produces. The body neither manufactures the air it breathes nor the food it eats. If we do not manufacture what we eat or what we breathe, why assume that we manufacture, rather than regulate, what we think?

This idea was not original to James; he quotes from Ferdinand Schiller, an Oxford philosopher who published *Riddles of the Sphinx* in 1891. Schiller wrote: 'Matter is an admirably calculated machinery for regulating, limiting and restraining the consciousness which it encases. Matter is not that which *produces* consciousness, but that which *limits* it. It is an explanation which no evidence in favour of materialism can possibly affect. For if a man loses consciousness as soon as his brain is injured, it is clearly as good an explanation to say the injury to the brain destroyed the mechanism by which the manifestation of the consciousness was rendered possible, as to say that it destroyed the seat of consciousness.'

The French philosopher Henri Bergson, a contemporary of James and Schiller, suggested there was a general force which, as it were, applied intelligence to evolution. If one adopts these ideas of an intelligent force outside ourselves, a number of difficult problems are resolved. The first is the apparently universal human instinct for religion. If there were such a universal consciousness, it would be likely to be recognized as sacred. The place of the Holy Spirit in Christianity is of this character, as is the idea of the logos in Plato or in St John's Gospel.

Another problem that would be resolved is the nature of certain types of mental illness. Schizophrenia often produces hallucinations of an external bombardment by spiritual forces, sometimes interpreted as radio rays. Schizophrenics can have visions of the divine. Whatever the correct diagnosis of his illness, Christopher Smart, the eighteenth-century poet, appears to have been suffering from a breakdown of mental limits on the inflow of divine consciousness. Dostoevsky describes similar passages in an epileptic condition. And terrible panics can also be seen by the mentally ill as invasions from outside.

The transmission theory also removes the difficulty of admitting, cautiously, the reality of some psychic phenomena. It is hard to exclude all the evidence for telepathy, precognition, inspired conversions, clairvoyance, out-of-body or near-death experiences, or even for levitation or ghosts. There is too much evidence, from people of good reputation, for an absolute a priori refusal to accept any of it to be rational.

The chief scientific difficulty of neo-Darwinism itself, that random genetic change could not account for the sequence of development of some complex structures, was criticized by Bergson eighty years ago, and is now being explored in the laboratory. If there were a universal source of consciousness, transmitted through the brain, as oxygen is through the lungs, its influence might explain what appears to be the purposive development of complex structures that require multiple mutations to be effective.

William James, in his doctrine of pragmatism, used results as a test of truth. The transmission theory of the brain has the advantage that it solves problems, rather than creating them. The problem of the human instinct for religion, the problem of the inrushes experienced in some mental illness, the problem of psychic phenomena and the problem of pure randomness in neo-Darwinism are real difficulties for the scientific world view.

The Schiller-James-Bergson theory proposes a natural force of intelligence, which is perhaps received and transmitted by the brain, and also influences evolution in the direction of survival. That would restore purpose to nature, but it would also make possible, as James argued, the concept of human survival after death. Such a theory is repugnant to many scientists, but it is not contradicted by scientific observation.

Indeed, it can contain scientific facts that are difficult to fit with the pure randomness required by orthodox neo-Darwinism. If this theory were to be accepted, it would reconcile the division of human thought that has done so much harm in the past century and a half.

29 July 1991

CASTRATORS OF THE
HUMAN INTELLECT

E
very columnist is influenced by his audience. When I write an article that produces a large number of letters, whether to myself or the newspaper, I know I have at least interested some of my readers, even if I have also irritated some of them. I have written about the desacralization of the Nieuwe Kerk in Amsterdam and William James's views on human immortality. To date *The Independent* has published fifteen letters on what might appear to be relatively obscure subjects. What they had in common was that they referred to the supernatural, and most of the letters came from people who regard the supernatural with disfavour.

In his lifetime William James was not considered a particularly controversial figure. He was the authoritative theoretician of the American school of psychology; he was a leading intellectual figure of the late nineteenth century at Harvard; his theory of pragmatism is one of the major American contributions to philosophical debate; his work on the psychology of religion was original and widely admired, even by sceptics. Yet when I recounted his theory of the human brain as a transmitter of consciousness, there proved to be fires of controversy to be lit in the columns of this newspaper. As he delivered the lecture I was quoting in 1898, that is something of a tribute to him. It shows his thought is alive after a hundred years.

Lynne Reid Banks's letter (1 August) shows, as do a number of others, how disturbing the idea of the supernatural is to people who reject it. What troubles her is that the relationship between the scientific and spiritual views of life should be discussed at all. 'One of the most baneful aspects of religious belief is the incalculable amount of time and mental effort that is expended by intelligent believers in their struggle to come up with theories aimed at reconciling the irrational with the rational.'

This puts my work rather high. At the worst I have wasted some of my own time and some of that of the readers of *The Independent*. In Ms Reid Banks's terms there are far greater figures than myself who have been guilty of similar time wasting; they would include Socrates, Aquinas, Spinoza, Locke, Berkeley and Kant among many others, and they would, of course, include William James himself. If their works are to be regarded as 'among the most baneful aspects of religious belief', then religion has a good deal to be proud of.

What she and many other scientific materialists believe is that there is a body of knowledge and a method of acquiring it that can be defined as rational, and that anything outside that is irrational and therefore a waste of time. That view is not a new one, though it is perhaps harder to maintain in the light of modern scientific knowledge than it would have been a hundred years ago. Yet the real difficulty facing this argument remains the same: how are we to recognize this rationality and why should we believe it to be complete?

William James discussed the problems in an article on 'The Sentiment of Rationality' in the philosophical journal *Mind* for July 1879. 'Philosophers desire to attain a conception of the frame of things which shall on the whole be more rational than the somewhat chaotic view which everyone by nature carries about with him under his hat. But suppose this rational conception attained, how is the philosopher to recognize it for what it is, and not let it slip through ignorance? The only answer is that he will recognize its rationality as he recognizes everything else, by certain subjective marks with which it affects him. What, then, are the marks? A strong feeling of ease, peace, rest, is one of them. The transition from a state of puzzle and perplexity to rational comprehension is full of lively relief and pleasure.'

These objectors to my article, or to William James himself, are content with a world view that they regard as rational, that probably gives them this feeling of 'lively relief and pleasure'. To many of the rest of us it seems seriously incomplete, and cannot be made to fit our experience. William James commented, rather sharply, that 'these most conscientious gentlemen think they have jumped off their own feet – emancipated their mental operations from the control of their subjective propensities at large and *in toto*. But they are deluded. They have simply chosen from among the entire set of propensities at their command those that were certain to construct out of the materials given, the leanest; lowest aridest result – namely the bare molecular world – and they have sacrificed all the rest.'

Why is it that an article on the desacralization of the Nieuwe Kerk in Amsterdam produced far more letters to *The Independent* than would, say, a thoughtful article about the likely result of the next election? It is because the sacred is more interesting to the human mind. The mind is not merely a rational grid, designed for purely intellectual tasks. It is designed for action, as well as for thought, and is shaped by its own predispositions and will. The natural mind is a buzzing hive of insights, intuitions, sympathies and affections that from time to time swarm round an idea which seems to take further the possible understanding of a mysterious world.

Human beings can perform the rational job, but in itself it belongs to a superficial level of their experience. Our inner minds are the arena of the half known and the sacred. We may opt for the reductionist understanding of the modern scientific view of the world. But it is at the expense of what is really most important to us. If we admit as knowledge only what we mistakenly believe that we can know for sure, we remain ignorant about everything that matters most.

It will be apparent how much I admire William James; I would regard him and Alexander Pope as the two great dead writers from whom I have learnt most, and I feel a strong gratitude to both.

James wrote, in 1880, another passage which probably best describes his own intellect, and it argues for the broadest possible approach to truth.

> But turn to the highest order of minds, and what a change! Instead of thoughts of concrete things patiently following one another in a beaten track of habitual suggestion, we have the most abrupt cross-cuts and transitions from one idea to another, the most rarefied abstractions and discriminations, the most unheard-of combinations of elements, the subtlest associations of analogy; in a word, we seem suddenly introduced into a seething cauldron of ideas, where everything is fizzling and bobbing about in a state of bewildering activity, where partnerships can be joined or loosened in an instant; treadmill routine is unknown, and the unexpected seems the only law.
>
> They will be sallies of wit and humour; they will be flashes of poetry and eloquence; they will be constructions of dramatic fiction or of mechanical device, logical or philosophic abstractions, business projects, or scientific hypotheses, with trains of experimental consequences based thereon; they will be musical sounds, or images of plastic beauty or picturesqueness, or visions of moral harmony. But, whatever their differences may be, they will all agree in this, – that their genesis is sudden and, as it were, spontaneous.

The scientific materialists try to force this human mind into the strait-jacket of their limited logic.

What they achieve is a castration of the exuberant power of the human intellect. They also deny the sacred, and try to put out the candles in the temple of the human spirit.

5 August 1991

KILLINGS OF CONVENIENCE, FROM CRADLE TO GRAVE

In an average year the National Health Service may possibly take more lives than it saves. I am not referring to the illnesses caused as side-effects by modern drugs, although I have noticed that the best physicians prescribe as few drugs as they can, but to the fact that most people die at about the time nature suggests, and that the abortion service on the NHS has killed babies by the hundreds of thousands for more than twenty years. Certainly, as babies lose more than seventy years of life expectancy, and those successfully operated on for cancer often gain only a few years, the total of human years added by the work of the NHS can be no more than a fraction of those lost.

The advocates of killing inconvenient people, having had such a triumph with the holocaust of abortion, are now setting their sights on people at the other end of life, taking in a few depressives from the middle years on the way. In the United States, in Britain and in Europe, euthanasia, its time perhaps delayed a generation by the sponsorship of the Nazis, is now the progressive cause of the hour. If it succeeds – and it has the same complacent momentum as the abortion case had in the mid-Sixties – the National Health Service will take us not from the cradle to the grave, but from abortion to euthanasia.

Both abortionists and euthanasiasts claim to be motivated by compassion, but it is a dangerous, lethal compassion, and the motives are not unmixed. The power of death is a terrible power for any human being to take; we are none of us wholly rational about death. Human nature has in it a killer instinct. The adviser who pushes a young woman to have a convenient abortion, the doctor who invents a death machine to help other people into the next world, the judge who orders muffins after donning the black cap, the red-tabbed general who sends men of his son's age on a suicide mission, cannot be far from that musky delight in death which brought the crowds to Tyburn or to the Roman circus. There is an unholy glee somewhere in human beings at the thought of other people dying; if you doubt that, turn on the television set any evening of the week.

The central issue is religious. Most of the atheists I know are in favour of both abortion and euthanasia, though they are opposed to capital punishment. I, too, am opposed to capital punishment, though I am not a pacifist. Yet I find it hard to accept that life may only be taken if it is innocent, the life of the embryo or the ancient, but that the life of the mass murderer is sacrosanct. I am not in favour of the state killing people, save in self-defence against aggression, but if the state really enjoys killing people, I would prefer that it should choose adults who have themselves murdered.

It is logical that atheists should regard life in a strictly utilitarian way. A child is going to be born on an overcrowded planet. Its mother has perhaps several other children, and finds them difficult to look after. Some of them may grow up to be criminals, perhaps the child itself will grow up to be a criminal. The mother wants, or half-wants, to be free of the responsibility.

Will it not contribute to the greatest happiness of the greatest number if this child is not born to share the overcrowded trough of life with the rest of us, perhaps to steal the radios out of our cars, or commit some other grave offence?

An old woman is suffering from cancer. She is occupying a bed in an NHS hospital. If she leaves the hospital, she will have to be looked after by her children, who are themselves already middle-aged. She does not want to be a nuisance. Her children are divided between a sense of duty, and the strain that caring for her will put on them. She is in pain, though it can be controlled by drugs.

A hint from the doctor, a word from the nurse, the reluctant consent of the children, and how can she decently refuse the last exit from life? It would certainly improve bed turnover in our hospitals, and would relieve society of some expense and trouble. And if she does not consent, then, as has been found in the Netherlands, consent can be assumed.

The utilitarian arguments are real enough. They were indeed the arguments that were used by the Nazis, who were not altogether intellectually isolated. Eugenics, as a theory, was founded by the English scientist Francis Galton, who was Charles Darwin's cousin. People such as George Bernard Shaw believed in it. There are misshapen and idiotic children who can never care for themselves or enjoy an ordinary life. The Nazis put them in bath houses where poison gas came out of the shower nozzles. They argued that it was a kindness to remove these innocents from a life that could never be anything but a burden to them. They went on to use the same methods, and others, in killing six million Jews, most of whom were perfectly healthy, apart from malnutrition.

Either God exists, or He does not. Either man is an immortal spirit, or he is not. We all have to make the choice between these propositions, and it is a choice which wholly changes our attitude to life. If we are immortal spirits living in the hand of God, then we are not free to treat human life as a purely utilitarian matter; we are certainly not free to kill other human beings, who are also immortal spirits, because they are embryos, mental defectives, lunatics, cancer sufferers, Alzheimer's sufferers, homosexuals, Buddhists, Jews, kulaks, old people, bourgeois, or because they belong to any other of the categories which have been taken to justify killing in the twentieth century.

Atheists, however, do not believe in God, which removes one restraint, and do not regard themselves or other people as immortal, which removes another. Some atheists are humanitarian; others hate God very much indeed. 'Every religious idea, every idea of God, even flirting with the idea of God, is unutterable vileness,' Lenin wrote to Maxim Gorky.

The logic of even a benign atheism is utilitarian; if human beings are simply machines, then it is reasonable to disassemble them when they no longer serve their purpose, or to abort them if they seem likely, on balance, to be of no service to society. The Chinese, who send troops into peasant villages to impose compulsory abortion, abortion by rape, only take this to a logical conclusion.

We like to believe that the response to the question of God and of immortality is simply a personal preference, that it does not matter. It is indeed a personal choice, but it matters supremely, not just to the spiritual development of the individual, but to the logic which rules society. If we start from a logic that denies the sacredness of human nature, we move rapidly to a conclusion that human life is disposable as a matter of social convenience.

Lenin, who thought that any idea of God was vile, accepted terror as an institutionalized, political instrument. In *The Brothers Karamazov*, Dostoevsky wrote these disturbing words: 'If you were to destroy in mankind the belief in immortality, not only love, but every force maintaining the life of the world would at once be dried up. Moreover, nothing then would be immortal, everything would be permissible, even cannibalism.' As belief in God has been eroded, we have indeed lived in the century of death.

18 November 1991

AN AGE BETRAYED BY ITS
WORSHIP OF MACHINES

The other day I behaved badly, or was thought to have behaved badly, at a wedding reception. The reception itself was quite delightful. It was held at Cliveden, the home of the Astors, built by Frederick, Prince of Wales, the father of George III; it is the house where 'Rule, Britannia' was first sung in public.

While waiting for the bride and groom, the guests were shown into the library down a corridor lined with busts. One of the busts was of Nelson, who had, in pure white marble, the face of an untrusthworthy colt, with a nervous instability about the nostrils. When we reached the library I tried to restrain myself from looking at the books that the Astors had left behind. In vain. Inside ten minutes I was sitting in a corner reading the second volume of Thomas Carlyle's *Essays*, 1842.

Another guest, who was discussing educational questions with my daughter the next day, mentioned 'the social skills expected of a seven-year-old'. Asked what they were, he replied: 'Not to go to a wedding reception and sit in a corner reading a book.'

I am sure he is right, but I am not the least sorry to have done as I did. I found an essay of Carlyle's that put so well what I have been trying from time to time to write here that I felt invigorated and reinforced. I have since obtained the volume from the

London Library and have been able to confirm the first powerful impression.

The essay I was reading was relatively early Carlyle. It was published in the *Edinburgh Review* in 1829, when he was only thirty-four. He called it 'Signs of the Times'; it is not mainly about newspapers, though there is an excellent passage on the triumphalism of contemporary journalism.

> The true Church of England, at this moment, lies in the Editors of its Newspapers. These preach to the people, daily, weekly; admonishing Kings themselves; advising peace or war, with an authority which only the first Reformers, and a long-past class of Popes, were possessed of; inflicting moral censure; imparting moral encouragement, consolation, edification; in all ways, diligently 'administering the Discipline of the Church'.

I have been in that trade myself, and recognize what Jung called 'psychic inflation' as a professional risk to the health of editorial persons, on television as well as in print. Our most primitive popes nowadays are programme controllers; the servants of the servants of the box.

Carlyle writes of his own period, now as long as 160 years ago, that 'were we required to characterize this age of ours by any single epithet, we should be tempted to call it, not an Heroical, Devotional, Philosophical or Moral Age, but, above all others, the Mechanical Age'. He contrasts this with what he terms 'Man's Dynamical nature', by which he means the sphere of 'Poetry, Religion and Morality'.

Carlyle saw great dangers from the dominance of the mechanical principle. 'The truth is, more have lost their belief in the Invisible, and believe, and hope, and work only in the Visible; or, to speak in other words; this is not a Religious age. Only the material, the immediately practical; not the divine and spiritual, is important to us. The infinite, absolute character of Virtue has passed into a finite, conditional one; it is no longer a worship of the Beautiful and Good; but a calculation of the Profitable.'

He does not argue for an absolute reversal of this trend. In his view the mechanical tendency was both 'fruit-bearing and poison-bearing'. He believed that both the religious and the mechanical principle must 'work into one another'. He writes that 'only in the right co-ordination of the two; and the vigorous forwarding of *both*, does our true line of action lie'.

But his fear is of the neglect of the inward and religious because of a sort of worship of the outward and mechanical. 'Undue cultivation of the outward must in the long run prove more hopelessly pernicious.'

Our age is the great-grandchild of his, but we still live in a period when the outward and mechanical is cultivated at the expense of the inward and spiritual. Indeed, so much so that some of the things Carlyle writes are made to sound visionary to the point of the ridiculous. Even the BBC, which does talk of the ideal of public service broadcasting, would not say that television ought primarily to be concerned with 'the Beautiful and Good'.

Again and again, in practical social decisions, we retreat into the mechanical as a pseudo-solution to our problems. Abortion is a mechanical answer to unwanted pregnancies; the instinctive religious view is that the unborn baby is a sacred life, deserving of infinite love and care, the same love and care we give to a newborn baby. The mechanical view is that the embryo is only a redundant artefact, mechanically conceived, mechanically removed.

In dealing with the Aids epidemic, the religious answer is to strengthen lifelong relationships of love and mutual support. The religious answer is also to care for Aids sufferers with love and compassion. No matter how they caught the disease, to the Christian they are the images of Christ, and are sacred in their sufferings. The mechanical answer is to emphasize condoms and to pretend that a solution can be found in a mechanical way. Some mechanists involve themselves in truly spiritual caring; others recommend euthanasia.

I am not at all opposed to people who are taking the risk of catching the disease being encouraged to use prophylactic measures. If people are having penetrative sex with temporary partners, of course they ought to protect themselves by reducing the physical risk of the virus passing between them.

But the pretence that condoms are a substantial answer to the epidemic is false. For two-thirds of the world, they are either unavailable or too expensive; some cultures regard them as repulsive; those who use them do not in practice use them all the time; they do not even given total protection when they are used. Condom use should be advised where it can save lives, but we should not delude ourselves that it is likely to prove more than a secondary defence against the virus. One can see, from the rates of infection in different countries, that religious culture can be an extremely important factor in reducing the spread of Aids.

In one way, I feel more optimistic in 1991 than Carlyle did, or could be, in 1829. He saw clearly the physical advantages that machinery was going to bring; he also saw the social damage and spiritual devastation that would follow; the poison in the fruit. We have in the twentieth century drunk that poison. After all, the machine-guns of the Somme made a factory of death; so did the death camps of the Second World War, and the atom bombs that were dropped on Japan.

The mechanical philosophy is still dominant in the modern world; it dominates our politics, our economies, our universities, our communications, even our entertainment. But Carlyle had to live in the morning of that philosophy, while we live in the afternoon. He foresaw some of its horrors; we look back on the worst of them. The leaders of the mechanical philosophy were great men in those days, with ideals of social benefits and with the future on their side. Now they are usually rather ridiculous, vain, self-congratulatory and superficial persons, with the past against them.

The twentieth century – just take the nuclear wasting of vast tracts of Russia – has been betrayed by the worship of machines. The way is open in the next generation for the inward and the outward to be brought back into balance.

9 December 1991

WE HAVE THE PLAGUES; NOW WE MUST LOOK FOR ANGELS

saac Newton, the greatest of all English scientists, was fascinated by chronology. He wrote *The Chronology of Ancient Kingdoms Amended*, which was first published in 1728. His short chronicle collates the events recorded in the Old Testament, Greece, Persia, Egypt and Babylon; he verified historic dates by calculations of astronomy.

His chronology helps to bring out the extraordinary synchronicity that occurred around the date 500 BC. He gives 521 BC as the year of the introduction by Darius of monotheism in Persia under Zoroastrian influence. The dates of the historic Buddha, who was a prince of the minor royal house of Gautama on the borders of Nepal, are approximately 560 to 480 BC. Confucius was a close Chinese contemporary of Buddha, living from 551 to 478 BC.

In Greek philosophy, Socrates comes only a little later. He was not born until 469 BC and died in 399 BC. Aeschylus, the father of Greek tragedy, does overlap with Confucius and Buddha; his dates are 525 to 456 BC. The period around 500 BC is therefore one in which geographically separate civilizations simultaneously experienced religious and cultural revolutions; these experiences were on so great a scale as to have influence to this day, two and a half thousand years later.

One cannot visit China, or the overseas Chinese communities, without seeing that Confucius has had far more influence on

Chinese society than Marx; Confucianism will remain when Marxism has been obliterated. The aesthetic of Aeschylus created tragedy; Shakespeare would not have written as he did if Aeschylus had never lived. A modern synthesis of Buddhism and Christianity is now the underlying religion of many young European and American intellectuals, and, of course, Buddhism itself is a major religion. In little more than a century, and with little or no direct connection with each other, enlightened masters created a new fabric for human consciousness which still shapes our lives.

There are many other examples of ideas occurring simultaneously in different places and to different people. Newton invented calculus independently of Leibniz but at the same time. Yet the example of 500 BC is both the greatest in importance and the strangest. It is as though the people of the world came to a certain stage of maturity at the same time but separately.

There are still many people who feel that the wisdom of the sixth century before Christ has more to offer our world, and the twenty-first century which is to come, than any contemporary wisdom. Confucian doctrines of family, order and moderation look reassuringly rational in modern New York, where Tom Wolfe's *The Bonfire of the Vanities*, or Tina Brown's *Vanity Fair* could be taken as tracts on the desolating absence of the Confucian virtues in modern America.

Similarly, the Buddhist teaching of detachment from strenuous material ambitions and even from the normal comforts of life makes good sense to people disillusioned by the materialism of the West; Buddhist respect for nature is inspiring to people who fear the destruction of the environment. In the modern world, a good Christian would attempt to lead a Buddhist, a Confucian and a Socratic life.

Perhaps the greatest of Aeschylus's tragedies is *Prometheus Bound*, which was excellently translated by Samuel Johnson's friend, Bishop Potter, in 1777. *Prometheus Bound* deals with a very modern problem, the penalties that follow the benefits of scientific discovery.

Prometheus claims to have opened the consciousness of mankind: 'I formed his mind; and through the cloud of barbarous ignorance diffused the beams of knowledge . . . They saw indeed, they heard; but what availed or sight, or sense of hearing, all things rolling like the unreal imagery of dreams, in wild confusion mixed? . . . At random all their works, till I instructed them to mark the stars . . . To man I gave these arts; with all my wisdom yet want I now one art, that useful art to free myself from these afflicting chains.'

Perhaps Aeschylus is giving an echo of the human frustration on emerging from the truly primitive state of mind to the organisation of knowledge, perhaps it was that frustration which drove mankind to seek the great teachers, of whom Christians believe that Jesus was uniquely inspired. Civilization advances irregularly, by sudden breakthrough movements. If the first of those revolutionary changes in knowledge led to the new consciousness of the period around 500 BC, is there any hope our age will develop a similar response to a similar revolution?

There have been those who thought so. W. B. Yeats believed that humanity moved in a gyre, ascending what might be called a spiral staircase of developing consciousness. Aldous Huxley, who came from a scientific family, turned back to *The Perennial Philosophy* which owed most to Buddhist beliefs. Bryan Appleyard, from another scientific family, has written an excellent new book on this theme, which I hope to discuss later.

There is also the fear of apocalypse. There are now several potential threats to the survival of human society in its present form, perhaps even to human survival on earth. There is the nuclear threat; there is the threat of disease, with both the HIV virus and malaria spreading widely; there is the threatened breakdown of the ozone layer; there is the threat of global warming; and the threat of gross overpopulation leading to some sort of population collapse. There is also the fear of what grim mutant might come out of genetic engineering, the possibility that some lethal artefact might escape from the laboratory. Those are six plagues which a reasonable man might consider could conceivably destroy our society at some time in the next hundred years. I am not a scientist, and can only accept expert opinion on the risks, but there clearly are risks in each case.

One used to be able to regard the book of Revelations, with its seven angels and seven plagues, as a work of morbid theological psychology rather than plausible prophecy. But modern society, without angels, faces at least six potentially fatal plagues.

The seventeenth-century expert on prophecies of the Apocalypse was Dr Joseph Mede, a fellow of Christ's College, Cambridge, which was also Milton's college. He assembled quotations from the Bible and ancient literature, and preached on the sound modern theme of *The Apostasy of the Latter Times*. He records an ancient Jewish prophecy, 'the tradition of the House of Elias', which states 'the world doth continue six thousand years, two thousand years before the law, two thousand under the law, and two thousand years the days of Christ'.

As we approach 2000 years after Christ, this ancient human fear of some final calamity is not as unthinkable as it would have seemed fifty years ago, and much less than it would have seemed a hundred years ago. Like Prometheus, we have opened the secrets of nature and are not able to control the powers we have released.

There seem to be two ways in which this crisis might be resolved. In 500 BC, there occurred an almost worldwide spiritual revolution which gave mankind a new religious consciousness, one which rejected materialism, respected nature and took a spiritual view of the nature of humanity.

Such a world spiritual revolution could happen again. Or we may simply go ahead with our immensely powerful material projects in a spiritual vacuum. In that case we could well prove Dr Mede, the House of Elias, and St John the Divine to have been uncomfortably prescient forecasters.

10 February 1992

SAINTHOOD BY THE
PRAGMATIC METHOD

The argument between science and religion has for at least the past 130 years – since the publication of Charles Darwin's *On the Origin of Species* – been a false one. The two disciplines operate under different rules. It is like confusing two different games, with the scientists playing cricket and the theologians playing chess. The atheist scientists are like a man who moves his queen to Q7 and appeals for leg before wicket.

Atheists are, however, entitled to ask whether there are rational grounds for believing that religious propositions are true. One test to apply is the pragmatic one. Do spiritual events make any difference? This is an entirely orthodox question for a Christian to ask. Indeed Jesus gave precisely this test to determine which are true and which are false prophets: 'By their fruits ye shall know them.' Pragmatism as a philosophy was developed by the American philosopher William James, around the year 1900, and has influenced many philosophers of the twentieth century, including agnostics.

'The ultimate test for us of what a truth means is indeed the conduct it dictates or inspires.' William James gave this definition in his 1904 article on 'The Pragmatic Method'. If purported spiritual experiences have no effect on conduct, then they are meaningless; they cannot be shown to be untrue, but they do not pass this test. That is one reason why saints are so important in the spread of religious belief. They profess their faith, but their conduct is the real evidence of its truth.

For many people the most Christ-like public figure of the modern world is not a Christian at all, but a Buddhist, the Dalai Lama. His sufferings, and his people's sufferings, at the hands of the Chinese communist regime have been terrible. Yet he offers the world an example of serenity of mind and love, even towards the persecutors of his nation, which is quite exceptional. Christ was capable of this conduct: 'Father, forgive them, for they know not what they do', he said of those who crucified him; but even good ordinary people are incapable of it.

In 1988, the Dalai Lama gave a series of teachings in Dharamsala in India with the title: *Path to Bliss: A Practical Guide to Stages of Meditation*. It was published in paperback by Snow Lion in the United States, and is distributed by Element Books in the United Kingdom. These teachings are based on the Tibetan system of meditation, *lamrin*, which dates back to the eleventh century.

His reference to the men who inspired the invasion and brutal persecution in Tibet shows the quality of the Dalai Lama's compassion. 'We find that the lives of some people who were connected to the fate of the Tibetans – such as Mao Tse-tung and Stalin – have not in the end been quite admirable. Such people have meted out a lot of destruction and have not been able to accomplish even the negative actions that they set out to do. They have had to live their whole lives under great anxiety and pressure. That is an obvious fact.'

This seems to me to meet two vital tests. The first, and greater, is that it is genuinely Christ-like, and the second is that it demonstrates the difference in conduct caused by the Dalai Lama's spiritual faith. The Christian injunction to love one's enemy, to do good to those who hurt one, is too much for most Christians. It is the rule of the Dalai Lama's life, deeply present in his spiritual being.

In Buddhism, such a state is rightly called 'the extraordinary or special, unusual attitude'. It clearly meets the pragmatic test. Undoubtedly the Dalai Lama has reached this state through Buddhist contemplative practice, but he emphasizes that 'all the masters of the major religions of this world should be respected and should be admired, be they Buddhist or non-Buddhist.'

Indeed, when one reads the main *lamrin* meditations, one is more conscious of their compatibility with Christian belief than of the differences. The first precept is 'reliance on a spiritual teacher'. For the Christian, the supreme religious teacher is Jesus himself, as revealed in the Gospels, though I think modern Christian practice underrates the importance of spiritual guides, and that many Christians would benefit from the personal spiritual supervision found in Tibetan Buddhism. We tend, too much, to go it alone.

The second contemplation is one of 'recognizing the human potential'. To a Christian this is a welcome affirmation of the importance and opportunity of human life. It fits with the Christian idea of the Incarnation of the Divine.

The third contemplation is on 'death and impermanence'. This is designed to detach people from the delusions of the present life. 'If one is not aware of the eventuality of death, one will be totally concerned with the affairs of this lifetime . . . Having too much worldly involvement ends in confusion.' This again is the teaching of Christianity as well as Buddhism.

Not all the meditations are Christian as well as Buddhist to this degree, but many of them are. The contemplative method known as *samadhi*, which is translated as the 'calm abiding of mind' is, as the Dalai Lama says, 'common to both Buddhists and non-Buddhists'. The doctrine of karma, the law of causality in which there is a kind of chain reaction of good and bad consequences, is not the same as the Christian doctrines of rewards and punishments, but is certainly similar to it.

The sense of the delusions of human life, which is so strong in Buddhism, is paralleled by Christ's teaching that we want the wrong things, and seek happiness in treasure that does not last. The pressures of the world produce a general condition of suffering, which we are reluctant to face. 'For instance, we Tibetans suffer on a national scale . . . In very powerful and developed countries such as the United States – although they are regarded as superpowers and are materially developed and superficially appear to be quite successful – at the level of the individual you find a lot of anxiety to the degree that many people have to live on sleeping pills and tranquillizers . . . There is always this suffering of want and lack of contentment.'

The differences between the metaphysical structures of Christianity and Buddhism remain important. Christians have a belief in an active and personal God which Buddhism does not have. Buddhists have a closeness of connection with nature through the belief in unlimited reincarnations which Christians do not have. But Christians can only benefit from exposure to Buddhist forms of contemplation, and Buddhists can only benefit from exposure to the teachings of Christ.

What is certain is that we can answer the question – whether religious faith makes a difference – by pointing to the Dalai Lama. Here is a monk who, by the path of contemplation, has formed a spirit that seems to be an evolutionary advance on the ordinary human consciousness. Who is the noblest politician of the Western tradition? Perhaps Abraham Lincoln. The noblest artist? Perhaps Rembrandt. The noblest writer? Perhaps Tolstoy. The noblest scientist? Perhaps Einstein. The noblest atheist? Perhaps David Hume. There is a transcendence in the Dalai Lama's consciousness that one cannot find in any of them. 'By their fruits ye shall know them.' That is the pragmatic test.

11 May 1992

AN ENGLISH SAINT AT THE HEART OF GERMANY'S SOUL

I n the period following the unification of Germany, the other European nations have been trying to reassess the German character in order to foresee future German behaviour. These reassessments naturally look to German history, to the rebuilding of the post-war period, to the Nazi terror and to the Prussia of Frederick the Great, Bismarck and Kaiser Wilhelm. Some historians point to the great traumas of the Thirty Years War in the seventeenth century and the Napoleonic invasion in the early nineteenth century. Cultural historians emphasize German romanticism and the wonderful tradition in music. Philosophers look to the work of Kant, Fichte and Hegel.

Less, or no, attention has been given to Germany's history as a Christian nation, though any nation's religious history has a profound effect on its culture and character. Of the three outstanding figures of German Christianity – St Boniface, Meister Eckhart and Martin Luther – the average Englishman has only ever heard of Luther.

Of course, German Christianity has been marred by war, persecution and anti-Semitism, although Nazi anti-Semitism was pagan and eugenic Darwinist rather than Christian in origin.

St Boniface (680–754) was the missionary who first converted the Germans to Christianity. He was, in fact, an Englishman, born at Crediton in Devon and educated at Exeter. His mission had three characteristics: a direct approach to the heathen tribes, strong central organization backed by the Pope and Charles Martel, and a strong sense of orthodoxy.

Meister Johanne Eckart (1260–1327) was the first of the German school of mystics. He taught at Paris. He was the provincial of the Dominican order in Saxony in 1303 and vicar-general of Bohemia in 1307. He was given the title Meister by Pope Boniface VIII, but some of his views came to be regarded as unorthodox and he was condemned and excommunicated by Pope John XXII in 1327, shortly after his death.

Meister Eckhart took his preaching to the laity, and spoke in German, rather than the Latin which was the normal language of teaching at the time. He has been described as 'the father of the German language'. His doctrines are those of advanced mystical contemplation. 'When God made man, the innermost heart of the Godhead was put into man.' 'What could be sweeter than to have a friend with whom, as with yourself, you can discuss all that is in your heart?' 'Only those who stand with Christ in depths of bitterness will ever taste eternal bliss. Nothing is more bitter than suffering, nothing as honey-sweet as to have suffered.'

Martin Luther (1483–1546) was the first Protestant reformer, the greatest religious genius of his time. Like Meister Eckhart, he preached a doctrine of faith. Like Eckhart, he made a great contribution to the German language and, therefore, to the German sense of nationhood. He went far beyond Eckhart in being willing to challenge the orthodoxy of Rome. Luther was also a nationalist – one of his tracts is entitled *The Nobility of the German Nation*.

German Christianity has, therefore, deep national and mystical roots and a close connection with the development of the German language. From the Middle Ages it has made a direct appeal to lay people; even Boniface preached a very direct conversion to the heathen tribes. From the time of Meister Eckhart, the orthodoxy of this popular individualist and mystical religion has been questioned in Rome. These characteristics continue to the present day; they can be found in the German theologians of the twentieth century, both Protestant and Catholic.

Luther's great hymn *Eine Feste Burg ist Unser Gott* ('A safe stronghold is our God') sums up the detachment from the world so strongly expressed in Eckhart's mysticism. 'And tho' they take our life, goods, honour, children, wife, yet is their profit small; These things shall vanish all, The City of God remaineth.' *'Das Reich Gottes Muss uns Bleiben.'* The translation is Thomas Carlyle's, but it lacks the authentic resonance of Luther's German.

Eckhart's ideal is the man whose soul is filled by God. 'There are five things which are sure signs in whoever has them that he will never lapse from God. First though this man experiences terrible things from God or man, he never complains: no word but praise and thanks is ever heard. Again, at most trying times he never says one word in his defence.

'Thirdly, this man derives from God what God will freely give, and nothing else; he leaves it all to God. Fourthly, nothing in heaven or earth can ruffle him. So settled is his calm that heaven and earth in topsy turvydom would leave him quite content in God. Fifth, nothing in heaven or earth can sadden him, so neither can it gladden him, except as trifles can.'

The ideal German Christian has therefore an interior faith which gives him a fullness of the spirit of God and a detachment from the affairs of the world. If he follows Eckhart, he will believe that his soul has been with God from the Creation in the eternal now, that life with God is its natural state, that concern for material things is against the soul's true nature, and can only make it unhappy. Yet this mysticism is closely allied to a feeling for Germany, the German language, the German religious tradition and the German people. It is a tradition of religious detachment, but it is still psychologically a German tradition of mysticism, popular and open to everyone.

If all Germans practised these contemplations, Germany would be a nation of saints. Obviously most Germans do not, and are as much caught up in the allures and harassments of the modern world as the rest of us. But this belief, related to the German language and to a specifically German tradition, has influenced the most ordinary commonsense Christian practice in Germany, whether Lutheran or Catholic.

The sanctity of the German tradition is unquestionable. St Boniface, Meister Eckhart and Martin Luther are among the most

God-filled men in the history of Christianity, as was Dietrich Bonhoeffer, martyred by the Nazis. In so far as German Christianity directly influences German conduct in the world that must be all to the good; it has undoubtedly sustained the best of Germans in the soul-disturbing repentance they have had to experience since the Second World War. In such a repentance, after such an evil, only God can give people strength, and post-war Germany has been strong in its moderation and neighbourliness.

Some people would argue that this detachment contains the risk that good men will withdraw from the active world, and leave the arena of life to men with questionable motives. That does not seem to be borne out by experience. Devout Christians were active in the resistance to Nazism, and have been active in post-war development.

Luther is the last religious leader one would give as an example of ineffective and cloistered virtue. Even Eckhart specifically teaches that 'in this life no person can reach the point at which he is excused from outward works . . . those who lead the contemplative life and do no active works are quite mistaken'. Boniface was one of the most active and organizational of missionaries.

The world should therefore recognise and welcome the strength of the German Christian tradition, with these mystical elements. The common culture of Europe is a Christian culture. Germany has been, and still is, one of the major contributors to it. The British can be proud that this noble tradition had its birth in Crediton, thirteen hundred years ago.

15 June 1992

PART FOUR

WORDS AND IMAGES

n my last term at Oxford, in the summer of 1951, I was President of the Union, the celebrated Oxford undergraduate debating society. I owe that to Dick Taverne, a friend from my days at Charterhouse and a fellow candidate for Union office. He passed me in the Balliol quad and suggested I should have a final try for the Presidency. He had decided to concentrate on reading for a first, which he duly obtained. I had half promised my College that I would do the same, but I consulted my tutor in modern history, Hugh Stretton, an amiable Australian. His advice was that the final examiners would either take to my papers, and give me a first, or take against them and give me a second. It has indeed always been my fate as a writer to irritate some groups as much as I please others. Further work, in Hugh's view, would make little difference. In any case he thought I would rather be President of the Union than have a first. So I stood for a third time and won.

From that more or less accidental change of mind it followed that in the next term I was profiled in the Oxford undergraduate magazine, *Isis*. The profile was written mainly by three Somerville undergraduates, Anne Chesney, Val Mitchison and Shirley Catlin, who later married my Balliol contemporary Bernard Williams. In those happy days an undergraduate could luxuriate platonically in the friendship of beautiful and intelligent young women. The profile, called 'An Isis Idol', reported correctly that I read *The Financial Times* over breakfast every morning.

By good fortune the press cutting agency employed by *The Financial Times* saw the Isis article and sent it to the paper. As they were then recruiting young graduates, but had hardly met one who regularly read the paper, the management of *The Financial Times* made enquiries about me of Roy Harrod, the biographer of Keynes. Lord Drogheda, then Lord Moore, the Managing Director, was responsible for the initial enquiry, though Gordon Newton was the Editor who eventually interviewed me. On the first day of my final exams, Roy Harrod sent me a note and asked me whether I would like a job on *The Financial Times*, on a trial basis. I went for eight weeks, and in the event stayed for eight years.

That was my real education. At Oxford I had been rather idle, though very political. The second I was awarded as well deserved, in the sense that I did not deserve to get a first. At *The Financial Times* I learned the craft of journalism, in so far as I ever did learn it. I also learned to work, or at least to produce a lot of copy, though I think I had there, as I did later on *The Times*, a certain reputation for high productivity in relatively short hours.

Gordon Newton was the ideal first editor for a young journalist. He was not easily satisfied. My first leading article, on the death of Sir Stafford Cripps, had to be written three times. This imposition of meticulous standards did not always please me, but I am extremely grateful for it now. He later told me that he sometimes had to go downstairs to have a quick brandy at the bar before he gave me back a leading article to amend or rewrite. Certain technicalities of journalism I never learned. I never had shorthand; I never learned to type. The compositors on the *F.T.* learned to cope with my not easily read handwriting. But this was something of a mask. The only profession I have is journalism, and I owe that to Gordon Newton and the *F.T.*

I also benefited from the company. One of the elders who was there when I arrived was Andrew Shonfield, the perfect example of the serious European journalist, a tutor to the rest of us. The young journalists included Ronald Butt, Nigel Lawson, Jock Bruce-Gardyne, Shirley Williams, Sam Brittan, Robert Colin and

Arthur Winspear, an economist who was later drawn to War-burgs. We were an academy of ambitious and intelligent young people – perhaps the largest group of really able people with whom I was to work. The average ability of the young journalists on the *F.T.* in the 1950s was higher, in my judgement, than that of the average Cabinet. We were able to take Nigel Lawson in our stride, which is more than any Cabinet was able to do.

We debated with each other all the issues of the British economy and the modern world, and particularly the issues of Europe and of the decline of British power. These were to be the unresolved themes of my professional life as a journalist and, not surprisingly, they are to be found arising repeatedly in this book. For five years, from 1955 to 1960, I was the chief leader writer, so I was at the heart of these debates, discussing with highly intelligent colleagues what line the newspaper ought to take. At the same time I was a Conservative candidate, fighting the solid Labour seat of Chester-le-Street in County Durham in 1956 at a by-election, and again in 1959. I was a very political journalist, but independent in my views, not then a great admirer of Harold Macmillan who became Prime Minister in 1957. I had always been an admirer of Winston Churchill and from quite an early stage close to Rab Butler.

I also involved myself in purely journalistic development of a sort which I enjoyed. I persuaded Gordon Newton to let me start a personal answers column called 'Finance and My Family' which still exists forty years later. I also persuaded him to let me restart the *Financial Times* gossip column. These have proved lasting contributions to the paper.

In 1960 I had lunch with William Clark, subsequently Editor of *The Banker* and then City Editor of *The Times*. He told me that he had been asked to become City Editor of *The Sunday Times*, which had recently been bought by Roy Thomson, the Canadian press proprietor. I pressed him to take the job, on the grounds that he would never make his name in the anonymous tradition of *The Times*. He decided not to take it. I was offered it, and took it, for exactly the reason I had advised him to do so.

So I arrived at *The Sunday Times* by a series of accidents. If I had not met Dick Taverne in the Balliol quad, if Shirley Williams had not mentioned that I read the *F.T.*, if the press cutting agency had not cut 'The Isis Idol', if Bill Clark had taken my advice instead of leaving me to take it myself, I would not have gone to *The Sunday Times*, and the course of my life would have been largely different. When I went there I invited Gillian Morris, whom I had met as a press secretary in Conservative Central Office, to come as the secretary to the City Office. She accepted the job, and later, to my great good fortune, she accepted me. That too – I suppose – might not have happened if I had not met Dick Taverne in the quad. Though when I now look at my children, and at my granddaughter, Maud, I do not think that their destiny was wholly based on so fragile an accident. Destiny has a way of making itself.

I came to *The Sunday Times* at a particularly interesting moment in that newspaper's history. It was the period in which, under Denis Hamilton's editorship, the modern and dominant *Sunday Times* was created. We proliferated sections and supplements; the paper grew in editorial, in advertising and in circulation. I moved in six years from City Editor, to Political and Economic Editor, to Deputy Editor. Denis assembled a strong team, including Harold Evans and Frank Giles, both of whom were later to be Editors of *The Sunday Times*, and Mark Boxer who founded the colour supplement.

Denis worked on a shrewd principle of balance. Frank Giles and I were supposed to be the scholar journalists, rather academic gentlemen journalists of the old school. Harold Evans was the brilliant working journalist – and he proved a great Editor in his turn. Mark Boxer was the sophisticated metropolitan figure, who gave the Colour Magazine a certain smartness and a contemporary feeling.

We were head over heels in helping to fashion the 1960s; *The Sunday Times* was the leading journalistic contributor to the 1960s zeitgeist, the paper where it was at. 'Thank you very much to *The Sunday Times*, thank you very, very, very, very much.' I was always an uncomfortable participant in these revels. I made a good effort at being a contempoary figure in later years, in the 1970s and 1980s, but I did not sympathize with the 1960s when they were happening and I do not like what the 1960s stood for now. To me it seemed a decade in which society took its values from photographers and hairdressers, that is to say from people who lived by externals and not by an internal logic. However it was an excellent decade for me professionally.

My main theme was the need for a revival of the British economy which I argued could only be achieved through higher productivity. This introduced me to Arnold Weinstock, who was reforming the productivity standards of the electrical industry, and to Leon Bagrit, who was the industrial prophet of the potential power of the computer, a man ahead of his time. It made me resentful – rightly – of the Conservative decision to make Alec Douglas-Home, who had no knowledge of these things, leader of their party. It led me – wrongly – to flirt with support for Harold Wilson until I found out what a fraud his pose of modernizing Britain really was. I was guillible in 1964, but had ceased to be gullible by 1966.

In 1963, when he became Secretary of State for Industry, Ted Heath took me to lunch at Brooks's Club to celebrate his appointment. I think he thought that I might have some new ideas about the industrial renovation of Britain. I certainly supported him on Europe, and regarded entry to the European market as one essential element in economic recovery. At the lunch I suggested that he should use his new office to dramatize the potential future of computer technology, in which Government backing might then have helped Britain to take a lead. He was, I think, disappointed in this idea, which was not quite what he wanted, and opted for the abolition of resale price maintenance, which was not quite what I wanted.

These were the ideas which I advanced in *The Sunday Times*, and they fitted well the modernizing and youthful image of the paper. As with *The Financial Times* in the 1950s, we were preoccupied with the apparently unavoidable decline of Britain. The energy we devoted to this issue may have been one of the factors which made *The Sunday Times* an attractive newspaper. Yet it did little or nothing to halt or slow Britain's actual decline. We did, of course, support Ted Heath for the leadership of the Conservative Party as the most anti-decline candidate. One could not believe that Reginald Maudling, whom I much liked, would generate the psychological energy to halt the decline of a nation.

In the summer of 1966, Denis Hamilton began a negotiation with the Astors for Roy Thomson to buy *The Times*. He told me in July that if they were successful in buying *The Times*, I would be appointed to succeed Sir William Haley as Editor. They did succeed; in January 1967, I was appointed Editor of *The Times*, and Harold Evans Editor of *The Sunday Times*. No doubt it was the right way round. I was always more at home with *The Times*, and he with *The Sunday Times*.

I was Editor of *The Times* from January 1967 until March 1981, a period of over fourteen years, which I came to think was probably too long. It covered the whole of the period in which the Thomson family owned *The Times*. It took me about three years to learn the job, and reach a proper balance between maintaining the tradition and reforming it. From 1970 to the death of Roy Thomson in 1976 I was, I think, doing the job as well as I was capable of doing it. From that point until the end of my editorship the newspaper was increasingly harassed by the printers' trade unions who nearly killed it. Their willingness to stop the newspaper and their refusal to accept modern computer methods led to a year's stoppage, to the sale to Rupert Murdoch and eventually to Wapping. Trade union crises were an unpleasant interruption to the proper work of editing.

In any case I think that from ten years onwards I was increasingly becoming stale. The real contribution an Editor must make is his enthusiasm, his imagination. If that candle is flickering the whole newspaper becomes dimmed. My excitement over each new turn of history was not as great in 1977 or 1978 as it had been in earlier years.

On the night of the tenth anniversary of my editorship I took some of my chief colleagues to dinner at the Garrick to celebrate. Although Roy Thomson had died, January 1977 was a good point in the history of the newspaper, a period of good journalists. As I was walking down the steps of the club with Peter Jay I thought that perhaps I should have announced my resignation at that dinner. My life might have been easier if I had; I would certainly have avoided a lot of trouble.

The reason I stayed on was that I felt doubtful whether Ken Thomson really wanted to maintain the burdensome responsibility of owning *The Times*. He was indeed much more of a Canadian than his father and much less attracted by British life. He spent tens of millions trying to provide the paper with a secure future, but when in 1981 he came to sell it was, I think, with relief. When the Thomsons left, I left also.

Until I started writing for *The Independent*, that closed my professional life as a journalist. In 1982 I became Deputy Chairman of the BBC, with the promise that I would succeed George Howard on his retirement two years later. I was not well suited to either post, and chose to become Chairman of the Arts Council rather than succeed to the BBC. I thought that the BBC needed reform, but was pretty certain that I would not be the right person to do it.

The difficulties of relationship with an institution can be important in one's life. I was never a good Balliol man, and I never became a good BBC man. In each case I resented what seemed to me an exaggerated, progressive complacency. In the BBC's case I also disliked what I regarded as a Byzantine bureaucracy. I fought some good battles on the Board of Governors, for the employment of women in senior posts, for broader opportunities for ethnic minorities, for the BBC to obey its own codes, to save Radio Two. But the relationship was not a good one. I liked many individuals, but I did not like the institution and the institution did not like me. I worked with George Howard's successor as Chairman, Stuart Young, very happily, but he was too ill to carry out the reform both of us knew was needed. I thoroughly support the work of Duke Hussey, but by then I was gone. Five years had been long enough. Yet the BBC is in many ways a great and admirable institution.

My final post connected with broadcasting has been the Broadcasting Standards Council. At some point, after I have retired, I expect to write a proper account of what I expect to prove a transitional body. However, I am sure that our code, our research and our specific answers to complaints have helped to maintain broadcasting standards, without the power or will to censor. I also believe that the public has a right to complain to an independent body.

The last piece in this section was written immediately after the death of Robert Maxwell. I have left it unchanged, as it represented my reactions at the time. Now I know that when I drank his champagne it may have been fraudulently paid for. Like Trollope's Melmotte he was indeed a grander crook than I had any idea of.

A FARCE WITH OLD
FRIENDS AND A CHORUS
OF MADMEN

What Mr Justice Powell has called the 'danse macabre' of the MI5 trial has been for me more like one of those cocktail parties at which one is surprised to meet so many old friends. I seem to have known most of the participants, some of them for several years. They include several people of whom I am particularly fond.

I first corresponded with Lord Rothschild in 1943, about a cancel leaf in Swift, and came to know him in the late 1960s when I persuaded him to write some excellent articles for *The Times*. He is a man who does not have the luck to be mediocre.

His genetic intellectual inheritance, far more than his wealth or his name, has set him apart; he thinks far more powerfully than ordinary people, and is not always at ease in trying to guess how they will think. His courage, his patriotism, his seriousness of purpose are not in doubt. Nor is the affection his friends feel for him.

Margaret Thatcher I first met in the spring of 1946, when we sat together on the committee of the Oxford University Conservation Association. She was a serious girl then, and a very likeable one, and she is a serious lady now.

I suppose we were all rather serious in the 1940s at Oxford, made so by the experience of the war that was just past and the cold war that was just developing. Margaret Thatcher has a personal sense of humour, but I am not sure she has much enjoyment of public farce, and what has been happening in Mr Powell's court is undoubtedly a black public farce of the most absurd kind.

Robert Armstrong I first met in about 1954 when he was a Private Secretary in Reggie Maudling's office at the Treasury, and I was working for *The Financial Times*. I have every fellow feeling for him. We would both have to confess to being members of the Establishment – indeed, he is probably the leading figure of the establishment. He is also a kind, sensible, intelligent, moderate and highly cultivated man. All paidup members of the Establishment know that we are born to be figures of fun, the perfect target for the custard pie. To go to give evidence in ockerish Australia is as certain to invite farcical retribution as for a Victorian missionary to try to impose trousers on a cannibal island.

I never met Roger Hollis, though I knew his brother Christopher, the Catholic MP, well, and I remember my father remarking that he had met Roger at some function in Wells. I very much doubt Mr Wright's view that Hollis was a spy. I do not believe he was an ideological type of man at all, much more an old-fashioned, patriotic, upper-middle-class Englishman. Nor did he strike those who knew him as particularly clever – Christopher was the clever brother. It does not seem to me that Wright ever understood Hollis, though I can see why he resented him.

Wright I never met, nor the Australian cast of Philips and Turnbull. I do not know why so many Australians have chips on their shoulders; Gallipoli seems to me to be a long time ago, and Botany Bay an even more remote piece of history. Yet the atmosphere of the court seems to be seething with class resentment, as though Philips and Turnbull were citizen *sans-culottes* relishing sending M. le Comte d'Armstrong to the guillotine. Of Wright we know three things; he writes because he is short of cash, he has been obsessed by Hollis for twenty-five years, he is not a man who keeps his word on matters of secrecy. These are not reasons to trust his judgement.

I rather like the *Daily Mail*'s idea that the whole drama is being produced from London by Miss Pat Hewitt, Neil Kinnock's

Australian press secretary. Press secretaries seem to be important in modern politics and Miss Hewitt is certainly a match for that mighty Yorkshireman, Mr Bernard Ingham. Miss Hewitt I have met, at lunch at the BBC. She struck me as clever, amusing, formidable and probably dangerous – all rather attractive qualities. That she should be master-minding an Anglo-Australian plot to rubbish the British establishment seems perfectly likely and perhaps even to her professional credit.

Mr Chapman – a tough-minded journalist – I do not know well, though I am now chairman of Sidgwick & Jackson, which publishes his books. I did, in the late 1960s, once take him to lunch at the Savoy to try to persuade him to leave the *Express* and join *The Times*. I failed. Unfortunately, I did not join Sidgwick & Jackson until some years after we had published *Their Trade is Treachery*. Otherwise, I should have a proper *locus standi* in the whole *brouhaha*. Michael Havers I first met after he defended Mick Jagger in 1967. He is a skilful trial lawyer and a clubbable man.

How have so many good people, all of them shrewd by profession, found themselves mixed up in so ludicrous an affair? The reason is, I think, quite fundamental. Farce depends upon disorientation – the respectable family man is found in his shirt in a brothel, which he is visiting for entirely honourable reasons.

Secret service work depends upon disorientation – it is the one bit of the state that is not only allowed to lie and cheat, but exists to lie and cheat.

The trouble with lying and cheating is that you cannot control them by systems of truth and honour. Once you abandon truth, you enter a perverse world in which nothing is what it seems and anything may be anything else – the world of Alice in Wonderland.

To this world people of intelligence and integrity are particularly unsuited. They exist by clarity of logic, by relating truths to their own magnetic north. This is a world without a compass, a world designed for the spirits of the night like Kim Philby, a world where the ultimate reality is disorder. Such a world is essentially mad, for sanity depends upon relating oneself to a valid standard of truth.

The secret world is not one for sane people, and it does not produce sane decisions of state. Britain is fortunately suffering only an embarrassing farce in an Australian court-house. But look at President Reagan and the Iran arms scandal. See what damage the whole imperium of the United States is now suffering from the president's entrapment in the hallucinated fantasies of demented spooks.

2 December 1986

WHY THE HEALTH SERVICE SHOULD FOLLOW THE ARTS COUNCIL LEAD

The Arts Council received its first charter in 1946. A year later the National Health Service was founded. Both offer national services designed to offer benefits to society. The function of the health service is to care for the nation's health; the function of the Arts Council is to help to fund the opportunity to appreciate the arts. Man does not live by bread alone.

The two services were set up on a completely different basis. Aneurin Bevan, a socialist minister, decided on a state socialist pattern of a universal free health service, centralized in the minister. This is the same pattern as that of the health services in communist countries.

Maynard Keynes, who designed the Arts Council, was a Liberal economist. He was concerned to protect the freedom of the arts. His system is one of state grants, administered by independent trusts. The trusts take the artistic decisions; not the minister, not even the Arts Council. As Chairman of the Arts Council, it is not my business to impose artistic opinions.

At the same time he left the operating arts companies dependent upon the box office. In the performing arts, every company has to win a part, usually a large part, of its turnover by pleasing the public, and remains therefore dependent on public support, not simply on state funds. The audiences provide the most important discipline.

In 1946 the phrase 'social market economy' was not in use, and perhaps had not even been invented. Yet this is what the Keynes's design is. It starts by accepting the validity of the market test. If opera goers are not satisfied with the quality of performance they will stay away. Empty seats will lead to a cash crisis. The company will have to raise its quality or close down. This market test comes first. There is a secondary test of satisfying the Arts Council that the company's work deserves support.

At the same time Keynes recognized that the market does not necessarily produce ideal social answers. Mass markets are dominated by mass tastes. The health of society depends upon satisfying minority tastes – not élites but the preferences which smaller numbers share. Sometimes the market will support such minority institutions, as the newspaper market now supports five quality newspapers in London. Sometimes it does not. By British standards there are very few quality newspapers left in the United States. When it does not, cultural diversity becomes a matter of public interest.

Keynes believed, and Parliament has since accepted, that relatively modest public grants would enable the market to support the high-quality minority arts in opera, dance, theatre, the visual arts and music. Literature has seldom been an important part of the Arts Council's work, not because it is less important, but because it has needed less help.

In France the policy went the other way, and a national arts service was created under a Ministry of Culture. The result is that their Ministry directly employs 15,000 people, almost a hundred times the staff of the Arts Council. The French music inspectorate alone – a body to which Britain has no parallel – employs more people than the Arts Council. The average grant processed by each member of the Arts Council staff is about £800,000, so Keynes's design has not led to the creation of a large bureaucracy. The management of money, as the Treasury knows, is the cheapest way of administering state assistance.

Imagine what would have happened if Bevan had been Minister for the Arts and Keynes had established the Health Service. Every artistic performance would be wholly subsidized and free. Every night the queues for free seats for the Royal Opera House would mingle on Waterloo Bridge with those for the National Theatre.

Because the seats were free, demand for the Arts would have proved almost unlimited. Public Arts expenditure would have risen to many times the present level – and there would be complaints on all sides that the Government was failing to meet the demand, that only Ambassadors and Cabinet Ministers could get seats at Stratford-upon-Avon. A vast staff of bureaucrats would have been created. There would be pathetic complaints about the two-year waiting list for *Carmen* in Cardiff.

Suppose Maynard Keynes had designed the Health Service. He would, I think, have accepted the market and diversity of control. Each hospital would have been a small business unit, not subordinate to layers of bureaucratic hierarchy and politicized bargaining.

The state would have given funding assistance to the hospitals, through an independent body, but hospitals and general practitioners would also have been dependent on earnings from private patients, from insured patients and from assisted patients. The old, the young and the unemployed would have been cared for without charge, possibly through a voucher system. Those in work would have been in genuine insurance schemes. The affluent would have insured themselves.

There would not have been the growth of administrators to beds which is one of the striking characteristics of the NHS. In 1948, according to Dr Max Gammon's figures, the clerical and administrative staff in the NHS amounted to 25,000. By 1984–85 this had risen to 106,000, an increase of more than 300 per cent. The number of beds fell in the same period from 544,000 to 335,000, a fall of 40 per cent. The bureaucrat to bed ratio was 1 to 22 in 1948; it is now one to three. Visit a hospital, and imagine the invisible bureaucrat who stands behind every third bed. We do not have a silent bureaucrat behind every third seat at the Royal Opera House.

The National Health Service cannot be put right unless we move from a socialist to a social-market model. The surplus bureaucrats do not only use resources which ought to be spent on patient care, they impose a pattern of decision taking which is slow, politicized and inefficient, everything that Mr Gorbachev attacks.

I would be the last to pretend the Arts Council system is perfect; I am, however, convinced that Keynes was right and Aneurin Bevan was wrong. The three principles of medical reform should be the elimination of bureaucracy, the independence of the hospital and choice for the patient.

7 July 1987

THE COLLECTED WORKS
OF A LITTLE-KNOWN POET

The Romantic movement was one of the greatest revolutions of human culture. It changed every art; it changed human society; it changed man's idea of himself. The Romantic hero dominated politics as much as literature – Napoleon as much as Byron is a Romantic characterization. Nearly two centuries later Romanticism is still a powerful political influence, and still for many people the normal standard by which art is judged.

When one reads the English Romantic poets, it is striking how swiftly the revolution happened. Wordsworth and Coleridge came first, born in 1770 and 1772 and therefore adult by the time of the French revolution of the early 1790s. Byron (1788), Shelley (1792) and Keats (1795) are children of the revolutionary period itself. In a single generation the old order gave place to the new personality, just as Napoleon knocked over the old thrones of Europe.

Almost from the start, the Romantics themselves looked for intellectual and cultural ancestors. Some they fetched from the Elizabethan age, with Keats – against all the odds – trying to persuade people to read Chapman's *Homer*. Others looked for precursors nearer their own time. The French, including Napoleon, admired the forgeries of Ossian. William Lisle Bowles, an amiable Wiltshire rector, was admired for reviving the sonnet.

Coleridge rightly praised Chatterton, the boy genius from Bristol, and wrote a poem to his memory.

Chatterton was born in 1752; in 1753 there was born an almost unknown Devonshire poet, John Bampfylde. Until 1984, when Roger Lonsdale, the Fellow of Balliol, published his *New Oxford Book of Eighteenth-Century Verse*, I thought I was probably Bampfylde's only living admirer. Roger Lonsdale has now produced the first complete edition of Bampfylde's poems. There are thirty-five of them, and they are published in a limited edition of 300 which will no doubt multiply the total of Bampfylde's readers. The introduction records that Coleridge had recognized Bampfylde just as he recognized Chatterton. The Romantics had already seen that here was another poet who felt as they did, but had been born a generation before them.

Like Chatterton, the story of Bampfylde's life was tragic. He was the second son of an old Devonshire family. His brother, though sane, was a spendthrift. At least one sister went mad. Another relative had been King of the Gypsies. John Bampfylde went to Winchester, briefly, when the poet Joseph Warton was headmaster. He went on to Trinity Hall in Cambridge, though he did not complete a degree. He ate at least a dinner or two at Lincoln's Inn. He retired to the Devon countryside. He was pushed by his family into returning to London. It all sounds like a fairly disturbed adolescence.

When in London in his early twenties he had his portrait painted by Sir Joshua Reynolds; Bampfylde had a handsome but over-sensitive face. He fell in love with Sir Joshua's niece, the attractive Miss Palmer – James Boswell's 'fair Palmerina'. In 1788 he published sixteen sonnets dedicated to her, proposed marriage, was rejected and went mad. He broke Sir Joshua Reynold's windows in Leicester Square, banged on the door and was taken away by the Watch. The magistrate bound him over 'to be on his good behaviour to the King and all his subjects, especially towards the said Sir Joshua Reynolds'..

I suppose Sir Joshua did not want to see his favourite niece marry a more or less penniless, mad poet, even one from a good Devonshire family. In the end Reynolds made Miss Palmer his heiress, left her £100,000 – perhaps £5m in modern money – earned by painting portraits. She did marry, a seventy-year-old Irish peer, and eventually became a Marchioness – a classical rather than romantic course of action.

Shortly afterwards Bampfylde – then still only twenty years old – was found starving in filthy lodgings in Holborn. He had gone mad for love, was now insane, and remained insane for almost all the rest of his life. He died aged forty-three, at a private madhouse in Sloane Street. At the end he recovered his sanity, but, like John Keats, was consumptive, and that killed him.

Coleridge commented, no doubt rightly, that 'predisposition to madness gave him a cast of originality – and he had a species of taste which only Genius could give'. The mad genius is an important Romantic concept, and Bampfylde fulfilled it. He was not only a good poet, but a man of artistic nature. Unfortunately none of his music survives, but professional musicians were astonished by his ability as a composer. His pieces are said to have 'seemed as emanations from his own mind, or that instant inspired by the God of music'.

He always found it difficult to control 'his powerful creative temperament' as Dr Lonsdale calls it. He was also, as most of his ancestors were, an intellectual, in some ways of a surprisingly modern kind. He included among his sonnets one 'on learning the Torture was suppress'd throughout the Austrian dominions, in consequence of Beccaria's Treatise on Crimes and Punishments'. He wrote a sonnet attacking slavery and another in defence of the woods at Canon-Teign. He would have been an environmentalist, against apartheid and a supporter of Amnesty.

These are, so far as I can trace, the first sonnets of the Romantic movement, published in the years before the celebrated sonnets of William Lisle Bowles. Are they good sonnets? Not excellent by the standards of Shakespeare, Milton or Wordsworth, but good by the standards of almost any other writer who has written sonnets in English. At any rate, when I first stumbled across them knowing nothing of his tragic story, I found them both musical and moving. My own favourite is the last sonnet he published, with the only too English theme 'On a Wet Summer':

> *Or 'neath my window view the wistful train*
> *Of dripping poultry, whom the vine's broad leaves*
> *Shelter no more – Mute is the mournful plain,*
> *Silent the swallow sits beneath the thatch,*
> *And vacant hind hangs pensive o'er his hatch,*
> *Counting the frequent drop from reeded eaves.*

He is indeed a precursor of the Romantics, but he is more than that. He was a poet who, with some clumsy lines, had a real ear for the music of language and had something to say. I admire the 's' and 'th' line, though I am not sure everyone else will. Yet what a sad, broken life – mad for the love of a girl who would marry a man of seventy to get a title. Let us all break Sir Joshua's windows in protest.

The Poems of John Bampfylde, 1754–1796, Ed. Roger Lonsdale. Published by Perpetua Press, Oxford. Limited edition 300 copies. £30.00.

10 May 1988

CLASSIC LESSONS LEARNT FROM TWO WEEKS IN THE PUBLIC EYE

During the last ten days I have received a ridiculous excess of publicity, more than I have ever had before. I have read long profiles of myself, some of which bring out defects in my personality with which I am uncomfortably familiar, while others show a generous understanding of what I once tried to achieve. Some of the facts are mistaken, but all the portraits are individually recognizable; some are unfriendly, but none of them strikes me as unfair. Seen from that point of view, I can well understand that I appeared in that unfavourable light; seen from another point of view, I recognize the echoes of a common purpose.

What is remarkable is the congruity. The articles written about me closely reflect my view of the person or newspaper that wrote them. I can well imagine the profiles I would write about those who have commented on me. Their reservations about me seem to be the mirror image of my reservations about them.

This appears even to apply to newspapers. The *Observer* never has a good word to say for me, but then – with the odd exception – I do not have a good word to say for the *Observer*. *The Guardian*'s ideology I regard as shallow and sentimental; why should it not see me as severe and authoritarian? I have a deep reserve of loyalty to *The Times*, and *The Times* is kind to me. I have the respect of a lifelong competitor for *The Daily Telegraph*; I understand what Peregrine Worsthorne is doing at the *Sunday Telegraph*, and admire it. The *Daily* and *Sunday Telegraph* show understanding of my position. I have read the *Daily Mail* all my life; the *Daily Mail* behaves like a friendly power. I have long had a reciprocal sympathy with the *Mirror*. I enjoy *The Sun*'s knockabout; *The Sun* enjoys knocking me about.

I find this congruity slightly alarming. It presumably means that every critical judgement each of us has formed is reciprocated. On the other hand it must also mean that the people one loves and admires return in large measure one's affection. Rather to my surprise I find that my old friends, such as John Grant in *The Times*, have understood me more shrewdly than my old sparring partners. I feel grateful for it.

When the Broadcasting Standards Council story was still a well-leaked secret I had the technically interesting problem of continuing to refuse to comment on a subject perfectly well known to the journalists who were asking me about it. I was caught by the Press Association correspondent at an Arts Council press conference, called to unveil our new plans for literature. He asked me whether it was true that I was going to be the chairman of the Broadcasting Standards Council.

I had to reply that there were three answers I could give, 'yes', 'no' or 'no comment'. Each answer would have its own significance. The answer I was giving was 'no comment'. As time went on, even this answer had to be qualified, if only because the press already knew so much of what was happening.

Sometimes the journalists knew more than I did. In the week before the announcement I was in Tokyo; they were ringing from London. In that situation they could provide me with information, including the news of Michael Grade's South Wales speech. I found myself combining 'no comment' with an off-the-record discussion of what was happening. I could not comment on an appointment that had not yet been made, but at the same time I did not want my position to be misunderstood.

In the last three weeks I must have spoken to more than fifty journalists, from national and regional newspapers, agencies, radio and television, most of them British, some foreign. The professional problems for them were considerable. I came through this strange period of over-reporting feeling I had been treated courteously and fairly. That applies to the radio and television interviewers as well; I was not cut so as to make a false point. The case I had to make may or may not be a convincing one. I have only myself to blame if those who have heard it are not convinced by it.

I do not intend to write in *The Independent* about the actual work of the BSC (if we can be called that without receiving multiple orders for slabs of steel). I have not written about the work of the Arts Council, because I do not think the chairmen of quangos ought to confuse their offices with their journalism. As a journalist I like to write about matters on which I do not have official responsibility.

The flood of publicity did, however, show that there is one important confusion. Some journalists describe me as authoritarian, others as liberal. I regard myself as one who believes, as did the framers of the American constitution, in liberty under the law; the survival of liberty depends upon the authority of the law. As a preparation for my new post I have been rereading the classic texts of liberal theory, John Locke's *Treatise on Civil Government* and John Stuart Mill's *On Liberty*. As an antiquarian bookseller I am interested by the coincidence that Mill published *On Liberty* in 1859, the same year Darwin's *Origin of Species* first appeared.

Locke wrote: 'God having given man an understanding to direct his actions, has allowed him a freedom of will, and liberty of acting, as properly belonging thereto, within the bounds of the law he is under . . . The power that parents have over their children arises from that duty which is incumbent on them, to take care of their offspring, during the imperfect state of childhood . . . but when he comes to the estate that made his father a freeman, the son is a freeman too.'

Mill wrote: 'The only part of the conduct of anyone, for which he is answerable to society, is that which concerns others. Over himself, over his own body and mind, the individual is sovereign. This doctrine is meant only to apply to human beings in the maturity of their faculties.'

But Mill also wrote: 'To bring a child into existence without a fair prospect of being able, not only to provide food for its body, but instruction and training for its mind, is a moral crime, both against the unfortunate offspring and against society . . . it is in the case of children that misapplied notions of liberty are a real obstacle to the fulfilment by the state of its duties.'

Of course modern psychology teaches that even adults are not as rational as Mill's doctrine requires. In any case I am afraid Michael Grade will think Locke and Mill unsuitable guides to the problems of broadcasting standards. Neither of them had much experience of broadcasting; both are dead; Locke was born in Somerset. Nevertheless, at a time when my views have been the subject of public curiosity, I wish to declare Locke and Mill among my intellectual luggage at the unforeseen frontier I am crossing.

24 May 1988

THE RICHNESS OF
TRADITION THAT MAY
FALL VICTIM TO PROGRESS

In Japan, one can see the struggle between the old culture and the new. The same struggle takes place in Britain, and we all see it most clearly where we live. The rest of England is not particularly conscious of the culture of my own home region of Wessex – that is the counties of Devon, Dorset, Somerset, Wiltshire and Hampshire (Cornwall and the Isle of Wight are different). We are regarded as an amiable but a rather out-of-the-way people, and our countryside is seen as holiday country, sunny and beautiful no doubt, but not intended for the serious business of life. We have no large cities except Bristol, on the northern edge; and the south coast ports of Portsmouth, Southampton and Plymouth.

Wessex has many beautiful small towns and is visited for the village churches and ancient cathedrals, Winchester, Wells, Salisbury and Exeter. At the dissolution of the monasteries we lost many of our great abbeys, including Glastonbury, the oldest and greatest abbey in Britain. The dominant historic period of Wessex was before the Norman conquest; our greatest king was Alfred, our greatest statesman and saint was Dunstan. In those centuries Wessex was the cradle of English civilization, of the learning as well as the government of England. The culture of Wessex is a Christian culture.

The people do not think themselves better than other people, but they do regard themselves as remarkably fortunate. For most of the region, apart from the great hill features like Salisbury Plain, Mendip or Dartmoor, the climate is mild, and the social climate is mild as well. Wessex saw little of the Industrial Revolution; it has a liberal and Wesleyan tradition but no strong socialist one.

Wessex manners owe something, I think, to the Celtic strain which lies near the surface of the West Country. We are accustomed to talking to each other in an easy-going way in which more is being said than is being stated. Like the Welsh or the Highland Scots, we are not sure that it is either necessary or polite to call a spade a spade. In money matters we tend to be careful but skilful. There was one happy moment when a quarter of the drink trade of Britain seemed to be in the hands of Shepton Mallet.

Thanks to the property boom, there is now a great deal of money in Wessex; there has always been extensive property relative to the people in the West Country, and London prices for houses stretch almost to the borders of Devon. The greatest wealth is naturally in the eastern fringe, where London has the strongest influence.

Of course, Wessex has its problems; unemployment is still high by post-war standards. There is more crime than there used to be, much of it said to be caused by drink. But there is no doubt that Wessex is for most of its people one of the happiest regions of the world in which to live. In Somerset we look back to the Roman period in Bath; we look back also to the early eighth century when King Ina had his palace at Somerton. The Danes, the Normans, the wars of the roses, the Reformation and Monmouth only somewhat disturbed us. Like everyone else we suffered in both world wars. But if any place on earth is a summer paradise, this is it.

It is natural that Wessex people should feel that this good way of life should be preserved. We have a strong environmental lobby. With one or two exceptions Wessex escaped the worst depredations of 1960s development, though the Roman epigram that what the Barbarians left the Barberini destroyed could certainly apply to the Blitz and the developers in Bristol. The centres of most of the small towns have survived, though they have grown to allow for increases in population.

It is national rather than regional influences which most threaten our culture. We have national communications, national television and radio, national as well as local newspapers, national education. Wessex seems to make the best of it, and no doubt rejects much that it is exposed to. Wessex teachers seem still to produce West Country students, as friendly and sensible as ever.

Yet even in Wessex the attack on our traditional culture continues, as it does in the rest of the country, and the defence of culture does not bring people to assert their loyalties in the same way as threats to their environment.

Education ought to preserve and transmit the civilization of a nation. In Wessex we have a particular love of our history. When I moved seven miles, a long way in Wessex, to the village in which I now live, I was taken by a boy to see the church tower. 'That pinnacle,' and he pointed, 'was the one from which they hanged one of Monmouth's men, after they had quartered him.' I am sure he was right and that he knew by folk-memory, some 300 years old. I hope history will be equally well cared for under the new core curriculum.

We should be more worried about English literature. The English teachers I meet are certainly worried by the GCSE. So are their pupils. What they say is that the GCSE in English does not necessarily require any dead author to be taught. One London school apparently teaches GCSE with George Orwell as the sole dead author. How angry he would have been. This is done because it is thought that children cannot relate to authors not of their immediate period. It denies them their cultural inheritance.

No Chaucer; little Shakespeare; no Milton; no Pope; perhaps Gray because the *Elegy* is in the anthologies; no Johnson or Gibbon; with luck a couple of sonnets of Wordsworth; no Keats; no Shelley; Byron as a television personality – the Wogan of his day; no Jane Austen; Dickens merely another name, Thackeray not even that; no Tennyson; not even Bernard Shaw – this is now the blasted landscape of too many children's knowledge of English literature when they leave school.

Yet literature is the great achievement of British culture, probably the richest in the world; something which has helped to shape the mind and personality of the British people, and has been eagerly imported into the culture of other nations.

Our literature is founded on Christianity. Shakespeare was a Christian playwright, in that he was the product of a Christian society and a Christian education. Christianity formed his mind and spirit. If English literature is being taught as something which began in 1945, Christianity is taught with even less confidence, understood as a myth among myths, holding no more real truth than Buddhism now has for the average Japanese child. We care now for the churches – no one without challenge can move a single stone in an ancient Christian monument. We have discarded our sacred liturgies. We do not teach our children the Christian faith. No wonder we fear that our national culture, based from early times on Christianity, is in decline.

31 May 1988

A DISPASSIONATE VIEW OF A CORPORATION AT ODDS WITH ITSELF

One of my minor regrets when I accepted the chairman-ship of the Broadcasting Standards Council was that I thought I would be unable to review Alasdair Milne's memoirs. They would obviously raise issues which I should be dealing with on an official basis. Last weekend I bought a copy at Paddington Station to read on the train to Bath; I bought it for weekend reading, not for purposes of review.

I still feel inhibited from a general review, but, apart from one omission and a small correction of fact, there are two general observations I think do need to be made. The first is what a remarkably honest and dispassionate book it is.

Anyone who wants to know what the issues were which led to Alasdair being dismissed by the present board of governors can read either Michael Leapman's revised Coronet paperback – *The Last Days of the Beeb* – or Alasdair Milne's *DG*. Michael Leapman tells the story as an impartial reporter who is on the whole critical of the BBC's management. Alasdair is writing as the deposed leader of that management.

For much of the period that Alasdair held office I was the leading proponent on the board of governors of the alternative view to his. He brings out clearly, with particular reference to passages in the Annan Report of 1977, the continuing issues of principle which divided us in the 1980s. I would be perfectly content for anyone to read Alasdair's book and decide which of us was right, or how far either of us was right. The central issue was producer power versus the governors' public responsibility.

Alasdair's ability to distance himself from his natural emotions seems to me to be admirable. I do not think Hugh Cudlipp would be happy to be judged on the basis of Cecil King's memoirs, nor Rupert Murdoch on the basis of Harold Evans's.

Of course, I still think that Lord Annan was right when he argued – as Alasdair quotes – that 'it would do worlds for the reputation of the BBC with the public if the governors were seen to govern'. Alasdair still thinks that 'the producers actually make the BBC and the public service ethos what it is'. But I view with renewed respect a man who can handle so fundamental an issue, on which he eventually suffered so painful a defeat, in so fair-minded a way.

The minor correction is that I was not involved in recommending Duke Hussey's appointment, nor was I consulted on it, though I did and do very much welcome it. I was consulted a few weeks earlier on the succession to myself as vice-chairman; I said the new vice-chairman would need to be tough, should have wide experience including finance, and for political balance should ideally come from the left. That was a reasonably good Identikit picture of Lord Barnett, who was given the job, but I did not suggest any individual name.

The story Alasdair does not tell is the first confrontation which defined the issue. At Stuart Young's and my first meeting of the governors in September 1981, the board was asked to authorize the signing of a contract covering sales of BBC television in the United States. Stuart and I asked for more information. I remember going around to his office, where we found we were agreed on the elementary point that we would not authorize any contract unless we had been given the chance to see it.

To my astonishment the Secretary of the BBC told me that it was not usual for governors to read such contracts, or even be allowed to see them, before the board authorized the corporation to sign them. Moreover, he said, Alasdair Milne, as Managing-Director of Television, was unwilling to let Stuart or myself see them, on the grounds of commercial confidentiality. I spoke to

George Howard, who was then the Chairman, and he said that he thought that governors should not press to see such documents. He was clearly impressed by Alasdair's reluctance to show it to us.

I made it clear that neither Stuart nor I was prepared to act as governor if we were not to be shown papers we had to authorize. George Howard reluctantly climbed down; we were shown the contract, though it was too late to amend it. The contract eventually came to very little and had to be replaced by other arrangements.

That was my, and indeed Stuart Young's, first experience of being a governor of the BBC. If, after that, we worked to strengthen the role of the governors it is hardly surprising.

The other general observation is the difficulty of making two-tier boards work together. We are always being threatened with two-tier boards as the European norm for industrial companies. In my experience they are either a recipe for dispute, or involve the abdication by one board or the other of all but nominal authority.

The attitude of the management in the BBC to the board of governors is well put in two sentences of Alasdair's: 'So who are the governors and what do they do? You might well ask.' Alasdair's view was that there could only be one board with real power, and that had to be the board of management. The governors naturally thought that they should exercise at least some broad, ultimate responsibility. The dispute arose from the structure of the BBC's constitution. That constitution sets up the two boards as fighting cocks.

In single boards I have never known the division to arise between management and outside directors which seems to arise frequently in two-tier systems, at least when the two boards have largely or wholly different membership. On other boards there are often arguments about policy, but these are determined by temperament, experience and conviction, not by whether directors are executive or non-executive.

Any well-run board tends over time to move towards unanimity on the big strategic issues. People who find themselves consistently at odds with their fellow directors tend to leave often perfectly amicably. If, however, there are two boards, each anxious to protect its own authority, this very tendency to unanimity becomes dangerous. Each board is united, but it is united against the other.

I regard the BBC therefore as a warning against the wider development of two-board systems. There must always tend to be conflict between the two, just as the American constitution builds in conflict between the Congress and the White House. The inherent ambiguity of the BBC's constitution leaves the corporation permanently under stress. It was his inability to bridge that ambiguity which doomed Alasdair Milne's period as Director-General; with that one can sympathize, for the ambiguity is a fundamental constitutional defect.

DG: The Memoirs of a British Broadcaster, Alasdair Milne, Hodder and Stoughton, £12.95.

21 June 1988

LEARNING FROM THE
PROFOUND PAIN OF THE
GREAT DEAD

have practised most of the professions which the public distrusts. I have never been an estate agent or a stockbroker, but I have been a journalist, a parliamentary candidate and a company director. The one trade I have followed which has a benevolent image is that of an antiquarian bookseller.

The image is not without its drawbacks. Being a bibliophile was an even greater handicap to Michael Foot than being a connoisseur of claret was to Roy Jenkins. And Michael Foot was only a book collector; book dealers are seen as amiable, scholarly, benevolent, but also as unwordly, unbusinesslike and ineffective. In fact, book dealers are not much more unworldly in their approach to business than the publishers – and they have one of the most competitive businesses.

Yet it is true that book dealing is one of those occupations – journalism is another – in which the pleasure of what one is doing is so great that it overshadows the commercial reward. Being on the track of a good story gives an extraordinary pleasure of the chase. It is not entirely an intellectual pleasure, but it is one with intellectual elements, as though one could put together the delights of foxhunting with those of playing chess.

In book dealing there are similar moments. In Pickering & Chatto we had a particularly good day at Sotheby's last week, buying a collection of 2,500 eighteenth-century political pamphlets which was the star lot of the sale. We were in just the mood I remember when we saw the first page proofs of one of the *Sunday Times* scoops of the 1960s. We did what journalists do – opened a bottle of wine and celebrated.

The excitement of the chase is common to politics, journalism and bookselling, but rare books have another pleasure which I have not found anywhere else. It is the constantly deepening acquaintance one has with the authors in whose works one deals.

A bookseller gets to know the authors in a quite different way from that of an academic. Each time he catalogues a book or manuscript is like a brief meeting. Where the academic scholar researches an aspect of the life in depth, the bookseller deals over time with numerous incidents in that life. It is much closer to the way in which one gets to know one's friends, by casual meetings which gradually form links of affection and understanding. An antiquarian bookseller, or a selective book collector, forms an ever-widening acquaintance with the dead, which becomes one of the resources and pleasures of life.

In our business we have this month bought in New York some de Quincey letters (Thomas de Quincey published *The Confessions of an English Opium Eater* in 1822), a letter from Edward Gibbon and a presentation copy of Bishop Berkeley's *Siris*, 1744. We found in Edinburgh a remarkable draft letter of William Cowper, the late-eighteenth-century poet, and in the same Sotheby's sale a book from John Locke's library. It is like going to a club and meeting, for a brief conversation, some of the great authors in history.

I have been reading Locke since Oxford, and I suppose he has played a larger part in forming my ideas than any other thinker. As he also formed the mind of Thomas Jefferson, that is hardly a matter for regret. Berkeley's *Siris* is the most transcendent mystical statement of religion in modern English. To deal with a book Locke owned, with a copy of *Siris* that Berkeley gave to a friend, is to be reminded of my debt to dead authors who have framed my own consciousness. To some extent I am what they thought.

The Gibbon letter apologizes for missing an appointment, and makes another arrangement to meet. 'If the Dean of Carlisle will once more give him the credit to which he is so ill entitled, Mr G will attend him next Tuesday at 10 o'clock in Bolton Street and thence to the Musaeum.' I did not know that Gibbon would have referred to himself as 'Mr G', a Dickensian form of self-address. I might have guessed he would spell museum with an 'a'.

The de Quincey letters are full of suffering, apart from recurrent references to books he has borrowed and mislaid. One, of 1851, is written in the midst of what seems to be a nervous breakdown. 'What I suffer from, if rightly described, is – a two-headed curse, viz a *torpor of the blood* combined with *nervous horror*. All day long for months together I sit motionless upon the floor, or roam for twelve and fifteen miles in mere frenzy of misery upon the public roads.' It sounds like a manic-depressive condition, and it is not surprising that he became addicted to opiates.

Another letter is even more distressing. He is writing to 'My dear Sir William' – which Sir William we have not yet established – and the letter starts: 'We have had the misfortune, which to us is a very heavy one, of losing our youngest child – a boy of rather more than three years old. From his age, he was naturally the plaything and darling of the whole house; and, being of unusually sweet disposition and temper, he was beloved amongst us even beyond the privileges of his infancy.'

Yet the pain of the Cowper letter, written in 1796, is even more profound. It is a draft, subsequently altered, of a farewell letter to his friend, Lady Hesketh, which is now at Princeton. He suffered, as is described in Lord David Cecil's *The Stricken Deer*, from the belief that he was damned. 'I once more address you with the pen of misery dipp'd in the deepest despair. I have nothing left to wish but the wish of many years, that I had never existed. Hunted into this terrible state of mind so long since, what now can I look for? . . . I then knew that I should never see you more, and now I know it, if possible with an assurance of that terrible truth, surpassing what I felt even then.'

This is a letter of farewell, not only for this world, but also for the next. Cowper believed he was damned, but that his friends would be saved. He wrote this letter on the back of a draft sheet of his translation of the *Iliad*, a draft which contains an early version of his translation of the death of Ajax: 'So, nourished

213

once in some well water'd soil, Crown'd with green boughs the smooth-skinned poplar falls.' There is an ironic contrast between the calm beauty of the elegiac lines and the unbearable distress of Cowper's mind.

The great dead did not have any easier lives than the rest of us. Many of them, including Cowper and de Quincey, responded to their suffering with their creativity. Others, like Gibbon, controlled the disappointments of life with a stoic urbanity.

Locke lived an intellectual life which seems to have been emotionally very sustaining. Berkeley lived in the eye of God. Yet what comfort and understanding they offer us: and they ask for nothing in return, save perhaps our compassion.

20 December 1988

A TALE OF MURDER, TREACHERY, SPIES AND INCOMPETENCE

On Thursday, I went to see the Richard Eyre production of *Hamlet* at the National Theatre, which Peter Kemp reviewed in *The Independent* on Saturday. I was impressed by much of the playing, by Daniel Day-Lewis as a romantic Hamlet, and particularly by Judi Dench as Gertrude, the most controlled and yet the most magnetic playing of that difficult part that I have seen. It is a long, full, strong and living production of *Hamlet*, convincing one, if one needed convincing, of Laurence Olivier's judgement that 'it is, without doubt, the best play ever written'.

The production brought out one of the truths about *Hamlet*, which is that it is not one tragedy, but six, perhaps even seven. Until one reaches Voltimand in the cast list – and who remembers Voltimand? – all the characters are real and interesting. There is tragedy of Hamlet, but there is also one of Claudius, one of Gertrude, one of Ophelia, one of Laertes, even one of Polonius. Perhaps there is even a tragedy of Horatio, the honest, good friend who is left alone at the end, to pronounce a melancholy epitaph.

Because I have spent much of my life writing about politics, it is the tragedy of Claudius played by John Castle as a shifty senator which I find particularly fascinating. He is like a number of politicians I have met, plausible, ruthless in pursuit of self-interest, capable of charm, dissembling, treacherous, cunning, yet fatally self-deceiving and weak. He is not, by Shakespearian standards, an exceptionally wicked man. He is about as bad as Macbeth, not as evil as Richard III and nothing like as evil, or as intelligent, as Iago.

Before the play begins, Claudius has already murdered his brother, the elder Hamlet, by pouring poison into his ear. We therefore lose an explanation of how he came to commit that murder such as we are given in the opening scenes of *Macbeth*. The crucial scene of the tragedy of Claudius is Act III, scene 3, when the King tries to repent and fails. 'I am still possess'd of those effects for which I did the murder: my crown, my own ambition, and my queen.' I doubt that sexual attraction was important; the marriage to Gertrude was surely a marriage of state, like King Henry VIII's marriage to Catherine of Aragon after the death of his elder brother, Arthur. It is Hamlet who is obsessed with Gertrude's bed, not 'the bloat King' himself.

The motive that Claudius does not acknowledge is given in the scene between Hamlet and his mother: 'Look here, upon this picture and on this.' Claudius was jealous. He was jealous of his elder brother's throne, of his wife, but above all of being over-shadowed by him from birth. Hamlet's father really did have 'the front of Jove himself' and Claudius really was 'like a mildew'd ear.' Jealousy is often the passion of a weak man, and Claudius was weak.

His political position at the start of the play is also a difficult one. He is threatened by a number of challenges. He seems not to be popular, whereas Hamlet's father was and Hamlet is. He is threatened by an external invasion led by Fortinbras. He has married his brother's widow too quickly, and there were no doubt plenty of Danes other than Hamlet who were critical of that.

He responds to this situation by trying to conciliate everybody. He sends Voltimand off to Norway to persuade Fortinbras's uncle to call off his nephew. He flatters the assembled Lords by pretending to have married because they wanted him to do so. He even flatters Laertes and Polonius.

Throughout the play Claudius uses, or tries to use, spies. He is as spy-addicted as Peter Wright. Polonius, like Burleigh or Walsingham, is his spymaster. It is again characteristic of weak politicians that they become obsessed with spying on their supposed enemies, and with their enemies' supposed plots against them. Polonius is a cunning, but silly and pompous man. Claudius is a cunning man, but foolish to rely on so absurd an adviser. He also, like Louis XVI and the Pope, relied on Swiss guards.

Like most such politicians, Claudius found that his operating methods did not produce the results he hoped for. The Danish people seem to have seen through him from the beginning, despite wine and ceremonial cannon fire. Hamlet despises him even before he knows he has reason to hate him. The only person who is more or less consistently taken in by him, until too late, is Laertes, and it is one of the difficulties of playing Laertes that he is obviously as thick as two planks.

Claudius's attempts to deal with his Hamlet problem are all disastrous. Hamlet is a real political threat, which Claudius – as is true of his kind – sees more clearly than Hamlet himself. Claudius tries to flatter him; that is a ludicrous failure. He spends half the resources of the Danish MI5 on trying to spy on him; that is an even more grotesque failure. He sends agents to have Hamlet killed in England; the agents lose Hamlet and get themselves killed instead. He has his prime minister hide in the Queen's bedroom; the prime minister himself is killed, and Claudius cannot then even find the body.

Finally he arranges for another agent to use a poisoned sword and himself prepares a poisoned wine cup, into which he throws 'an union'. The agent is stabbed with the poisoned sword; Claudius's queen drinks the poisoned wine. Claudius himself is both stabbed with the sword and made to drink the wine. That he manages to have Hamlet murdered in the end is one piece of good fortune in an otherwise remarkable story of incompetence. 'Purposes mistook fall'n on the inventors' heads' is how Horatio describes it, and well he might. Not surprisingly Claudius, having failed to solve the Hamlet problem, also fails to solve the Fortinbras problem, and Fortinbras arrives at the end as the winner who takes all.

Jealousy, cunning, treachery and weakness are not uncommon political qualities. They do not necessarily mean that a politician has no redeeming virtues. I am interested by Claudius's shrewdness, foolish as his policy was. He seems to me to be one of the three intelligent men in the play, along with Hamlet and Horatio. The whole Polonius family is stupid, father, son and even daughter; I wish Shakespeare had given us Mrs Polonius who must either have been very stupid herself or been driven crazy by her family. Gertrude is stupid as well.

I cannot say I have much sympathy for Claudius, but I do have some. He wanted to be king, he wanted to be respected, he wanted to feel safe. He became king, he was never respected, and he never felt safe for a moment. But I think he did probably want to be a good king of Denmark; Richard III probably wanted to be a good king of England too. It is one of the beauties of Shakespeare that he knew that bad men, like good men, are not all of a piece.

21 March 1989

HOW TELEVISION FITS INTO MODERN FAMILY LIFE

I spent last week travelling across Britain. The Broadcasting Standards Council is consulting the public about our draft code. We started at Aberdeen on Monday and finished in Cardiff on Friday, having visited Glasgow, Edinburgh, Newcastle, York, Manchester, Birmingham and Bristol on the way. The form of consultation we are using involves discussion with small groups, usually of ten people. The members of the council do the listening rather than the talking. The groups have been selected by a polling organization to represent different sections of society; young mothers, blacks, police and social workers, teachers, active Christians and so on.

This type of consultation puts flesh on the bones of public opinion polling, which the BSC is also doing. The opinion poll tells you what proportion of the public thinks that something is good or bad; group discussion gives an insight into what they mean by their answers and why they think as they do. I found it very effective and I would certainly use it again.

The message we received about television standards was both clear and surprisingly unanimous. The British public is tolerant, liberal and non-puritanical. It does not want to restrict television to the safe and the innocuous. It wants to be told the truth, whether in news or drama. Equally it can be shocked, and would not tolerate pornography – though the definitions of that would vary – or violent video nasties. It finds rape scenes particularly horrifying. No one argued for wholly unregulated television.

But this is the public's view of adult television, after the children have mostly gone to bed. There is equally a very strong belief that television is a powerful influence on children, and that child-rearing is the parents', and particularly the mothers', job. If television comes into the home as an ally in bringing up children, well and good. If television makes the parents' task more difficult, then the resentment begins. As one father said in Newcastle: 'My role as a television censor starts and ends with my children.'

This explains something which many broadcasters have failed to understand, and I certainly had failed to understand. All the evidence is that the public is particularly concerned about bad language on television and radio, and resents such language when it occurs before 9 p.m. The reason is that language training is regarded as one of the essential tasks of child-rearing in the home.

The mothers know that their husbands are likely to swear in the workplace, and that their sons, and perhaps nowadays their daughters, may swear in the playground. But neither the father nor the children are free to swear in the home. This is part of the respect of the home as a civilized place where violence, including violent language, is excluded. If television or radio bring violent language into the home at a time when children are listening, that is a violation of a central process of the children's education, the learning of the appropriate use of language and of respect for the peace of the family. Mothers do not refer to sexual swear words as shocking, but as 'inappropriate' or 'unnecessary'. The Christians, but only the Christians, are shocked by religious swear words.

These television issues emphasize the central role of the mother in forming the ethical standards of modern Britain. That must be one of the major psychological reasons for Mrs Thatcher's authority. 'My Mam wouldn't stand for it,' said an intelligent student in Birmingham. It was reflected in all the conversations we had.

What will the mother not stand for? She will fight to the limit against anything which threatens the welfare of her children or the peace of her home. She does not want violence brought into the home, though she knows that children from a very early age can tell the difference between fantasy or cartoon violence and violence in real life.

She relies on the broadcasters to help her. The view that parental control can always decide what children should watch is held by very few parents. A teacher in Aberdeen asked her class of twenty-four eleven-year-olds how many of them had television in their bedrooms. Twenty had. Apart from modern homes having more than one set, mothers have to get the meals. *Neighbours*, at 5.30 p.m., is relied on not to contain unsuitable material. In quite a few households teatime now has to be framed around *Neighbours*.

The dominance of this maternal ethic was equally apparent in all parts of the country. The Aberdeen mothers and teachers to whom we were talking on Monday morning shared the same attitudes as the black Bristolians on Thursday afternoon. We are all accustomed to the ideas of the multicultural society, of ethnic differences, of the north-south divide, of Scottish and Welsh nationalism. Yet the overwhelming impression given by our tour was one of a single British culture in which Scottish and English, middle-class and working-class, black and white share the same values to an extraordinary degree. We are more of one nation than we sometimes think.

There is much in this which is very heartening. I have always been an optimist about British culture, but I came back a confirmed optimist. The British are indeed a broadly tolerant, rational, good-hearted nation, and the more you question their underlying beliefs the more admirable they seem. The young were extraordinarily independent and open as well as realistic. The black British were also remarkable. I was particularly touched by the young black boy, with the scars of handcuffs on his wrists, who said to me: 'It must be grand to be a lord.' But I was also very impressed by the young black women with soft West Country accents, with their sense of integrity and their interest in their careers.

I came back therefore with much pleasure, but with three anxieties. First concerns the black–police relationship. All the blacks agreed that they suffer police harassment and prejudice from many individual policemen. 'Hey you, nig-nog, is that a prostitute with you in that car?' was one of the police insults reported by a hard-working middle-aged black man.

The second worry is that one hears much more antipathy to homosexuals than might be expected in a tolerant society. Scenes of men kissing do not seem to promote tolerance; they were invariably commented on unfavourably, sometimes with sharp hostility.

My third worry is that most of the people we met – York and Cardiff excepted – see themselves as living in a violent society. An Edinburgh student goes at night to the fish and chip shop. He is stabbed by a fifteen-year-old, one of a gang, and finds himself in hospital with a collapsed lung. I'm sure mother is bringing up a sound nation. But perhaps it requires more effort by father to civilize the adolescent male.

18 April 1989

RUPERT MURDOCH: HIS RISKS ARE OUR RISKS

A s I grow older I grow fonder of Rupert Murdoch, more aware of his real virtues, more aware of my own cultural biases, less disturbed by his more aggressive attributes. I also like and admire Richard Searby, his long-time chairman, legal adviser and friend. I have known Rupert for almost forty years, since he was a brash young member of the Labour Club at Oxford while I was an elder statesman of the Conservative Association. I have known Richard for ten years, and saw him a week ago at the Commonwealth Press Union meeting in Hong Kong. My affection has not made me admire *The Sun*.

I am sorry that News Corporation has been taking such a slating on the Stock Exchange. I am not worried because I think that the Murdoch empire is in grave danger; indeed I suspect that those who have sold his shares too cheaply may soon regret having done so. I am sorry because it cannot be much fun having a corporate debt of $A10bn (£4.16bn) and a stock price which is, as they say, headed south. Rupert is resilient, but like the rest of us he has to pay for it in the form of anxiety.

The one serious conversation I remember having with Rupert Murdoch at Oxford was held outside a bookshop in the Turl, a narrow street which runs from Broad Street to the High. He told me that he was thinking of buying *Cherwell*, the university magazine – which he never did – and asked me if I would invest

223

in it. I told him I thought *Cherwell* as it then was could never attract enough advertising and declined. He replied that the editorial could be changed, more advertising could be sold and the magazine made a success.

I was right and he was right. *Cherwell* at that point certainly was a bad investment. But that must also have been the first time Rupert saw a truth which he has made the cornerstone of his empire. Changing the operation of bad investments in publishing can create good investments. All his largest profits have come from this type of development. This is true of *The Sun*, Times Newspapers and Wapping, his American television interests, and may be true of Sky, though it has problems.

It is also true of Rupert that he has repeatedly bought more than his finances could support. Every businessman has his own risk ratio and cash ratio. Near one end of the scale is Arnold Weinstock, managing director of General Electric, with his relatively high risk aversion and cash preference; near the other end is Rupert Murdoch, with his acceptance of high risk and his high tolerance for debt. His policies have of course been influenced by the desire to keep family control of the business.

There have been Australian businessmen of his generation who have had an even higher tolerance of debt, and most of them are now on their way out, or are out already. We can regard Rupert Murdoch as the business equivalent of the racing driver who takes his car to the limit of its performance, or the test pilot who approaches the sound barrier. Most importantly, in forty years he has always behaved like this, and has never gone over the embankment. Why has he survived?

I think the first reason is that he is honest. There is obviously a fairly high correlation between risky finance – which Rupert has always engaged in – and dishonest finance, but the combination, as we see from many examples, is lethal. If bankers suspect that some of the assets of overborrowed companies do not really exist, then they have every reason not to extend further credit. But if the assets are good, they should leave the entrepreneur to run things, particularly at a difficult period.

In Rupert's case there is no concern about the quality of his assets. His businesses comprise bona fide assets, and mostly attractive ones, which are truthfully described. His record as a manager of publishing business is unmatched in the past twenty years. Good assets, good management, but overborrowed, is a banking assessment which naturally justifies further support.

That does not mean that Rupert Murdoch has not made mistakes. He probably should not have bought the American *Annenberg* group of magazines for $3bn. It was a high price to pay for a property which left little room for improvement. His skill is to buy cheaply and reorganize. In this case he bought a property that was already more than mature. This purchase used up his borrowing potential, and he is now deprived of the opportunities created by the recession.

It may be true that Rupert Murdoch is a better tactician than he is a strategist. He has been at his best in seizing opportunities. The original purchase of the *News of the World*, the purchase of *The Sun*, the purchase of Times Newspapers were all opportunistic purchases in which he perceived potential values of which the market was unaware.

I think he has exaggerated the advantage to be gained by international grouping. When he has bought the right businesses at the right price he has profited. When he has bought businesses for purely conceptual reasons he has not always done so well. Expansion for its own sake is a dangerous and unrewarding policy.

Of course Rupert Murdoch can at present regard himself as somewhat unlucky. For all practical purposes he is an English language publisher. Unexpectedly the world is passing through an English language recession, common to the US, Britain and Australia, but not being experienced in Germany or the Far East. By far the greater part of the Murdoch business is in the three affected countries. Normally he could expect his three main markets to compensate for each other; now they are singing in unison a song of recession.

There is only one circumstance in which the overborrowing of News Corporation could become intolerable. That would occur if the three recessions were to merge into one depression. That is conceivable, but far from probable. The US, now with a budget settlement and the prospect of lower interest rates, also has the

225

advantage of a cheap dollar. American industry is highly competitive in export markets, and the major European and Far Eastern export markets are not in recession. Of course we do not yet know how the Gulf crisis will end.

It is more likely that the British and Australian recessions will deepen. Interest rates are still high, and in both cases an extreme credit boom is being corrected. There has been no similar expansion of the American money supply, and the American economic outlook is therefore brighter.

There is no such thing as the perfect entrepreneur. Every entrepreneur earns profit by being exposed to risk. If he is betting on red and black comes up three times running he ought, of course, to be able to stand it; six times is more than he will expect; twelve times may be fatal even for the most prudent. Rupert Murdoch is living in a world in which black has already come up six times. If it should come up another six times his business will be in terrible trouble – but so will a great majority of banks and businesses in Britain, Australia and the US. We all ought to wish him well, for his risks are also our risks.

29 October 1990

A SORT OF HAMMER
HOUSE OF HORROR
DEPICTING THE
DISGUSTING RICH

I was one of the fortunate people invited to the *Vanity Fair* launch party, which was cancelled because of the Gulf war. I knew Tina Brown, the editor of *Vanity Fair*, when she was first married to Harold Evans, and I admired the loyal support she gave him during a difficult period at *The Times*. However, I had not seen her in ten years; I was pleased to be invited to the party, and pleased to be sent a copy of the first issue of *Vanity Fair* to be published simultaneously in London and New York.

Although I usually visit New York two or three times a year, I had never read *Vanity Fair* before. I had assumed it was a rather frivolous, sophisticated metropolitan production, with glossy photographs and flattering accounts of the high society of New York. I certainly thought that it was an insiders' magazine, like the *New Yorker*, with the chic glitter that lacquers the writings of the living dead.

Vanity Fair does indeed have all the benefits of skilful modern layout, as one would expect. I do not know Charles Churchward, the art and design director – and I do not like the typeface he uses for the red catchword headings on each page – but he must be the target of every headhunter in the business.

Visually, therefore, *Vanity Fair* conforms to the sophisticated and metropolitan image one might expect. But its content is quite another matter. Article after article is an angry attack on the manners and morals of the world's rich white trash. As objects of attack, the American rich are preferred, but if there should be a shortage, any international rich will do. To judge by the magazine she produces, Tina Brown is an angry young woman, shocked by the morbid sexuality of a society that has acquired great wealth without acquiring any sense of responsibility.

Of course, *Vanity Fair* is a Puritan title. It was first used by Bunyan in *Pilgrim's Progress* to describe the market of worldly folly in which people sold their souls for the trinkets of Beelzebub. It was later used by Thackeray for a novel on the theme of the way we live now. Tina Brown is closer to Bunyan than to Thackeray. Her *Vanity Fair* depicts a city hot with evil, not merely a sharp comedy of social manners.

As with all good Puritans, the sense of the Devils is very strong in *Vanity Fair*. Puritans do enjoy evil; it gets their adrenalin flowing. The most agonizing article in the whole of this issue is Norman Mailer's piece on *American Psycho*. The book, by Bret Easton Ellis, has caused serious controversy in New York publishing circles, although we have not read much about it in London.

Simon & Schuster, which was originally to have published the book, in the end found it too offensive and pulled out – a decision that immediately cost the company the $300,000 (£153,000) advance it had paid to the author. The novel was then taken up by Vintage Books, and is expected to be in bookshops before Easter. I think that I would side with Simon & Schuster.

The book, as described by Norman Mailer, consists of endless descriptions of brand-name goods, interspersed with sadistic accounts of murders of men, women, dogs – any living thing that comes to hand. 'It has a thesis: *American Psycho* is saying that the Eighties were spiritually disgusting and the author's presentation is the crystallization of such horror,' says Mailer.

He quotes some clinically violent passages, but finds it hard to decide between his commitment to free literature and his obvious dislike of the book. He ends by commenting: 'So I cannot forgive Bret Easton Ellis . . . what a deranging work! It is too much of a void, humanly speaking, to be termed evil . . .' The psycho, by the way, is a Harvard man.

One of the virtues of *Vanity Fair* is that the sub-editing picks out the themes of the articles with striking quotes. James Wolcott writing about Hollywood pornography is given a side head: 'Semi-pro athletics in the sack have come to substitute for anything resembling affection.' I agree with that sentiment, but as I first heard a Charterhouse housemaster in the middle of the Second World War argue that love was better than lust, I do not regard it as particularly modern. There is also a profile of William Bennett, a self-promoting Republican politician who wants to be president. The profile contrasts his superficial, public relations approach to the job he held briefly as director of the Office of National Drug Control Policy with the reality he failed to confront.

Mr Bennett argues that drug abuse is, in the end, a moral problem. Monsignor William O'Brien, of New York, comments: 'These kids use drugs to block out the horrors of their lives, because they're so awful.' The contrast between Mr Bennett's egotism and the suffering of the addicted children of poverty is made with deadly force.

Armand Hammer, whom I met once or twice, is now safely dead and can therefore sue neither Tina Brown nor me. *Vanity Fair's* view of him is that he was very rich, very manipulative and very nasty. I certainly thought he was a notable creep, who sucked up to important people – from Lenin to the Prince of Wales – in a most disgusting way. *Vanity Fair* also shows him as a financial cheat, 'conspiring to disinherit his wife's heirs', while trying to buy the Nobel Prize for himself.

There is yet another profile, this time of a Hollywood magnate called David Geffen, of whom I had never heard. He, too, is very rich – he owns Jack Warner's estate, and last year he sold Geffen Records to MCA for $540m. He is described as dressing 'like a hip kid'.

'I date men and I date women,' he said one afternoon in his New York apartment. 'What Woody Allen said was true: "Say what you will about bisexuality, you have a 50 per cent better chance of finding a date on Saturday night."' That, of course, shows that Woody Allen does not understand statistics; if you double your target group, you obviously increase it by 100 per cent, not 50, although I suppose the falsity of the figures does not alter the cynicism of the joke.

What a lot of disgusting rich people there are in the world of *Vanity Fair*. And rich murderers, too. When I was at Sidgwick & Jackson, we published the novels of Dominick Dunne, who specializes in the lethal scandals of American high society. In the tragedy of his own life, his daughter was murdered, and he writes from pain.

Not surprisingly, he is one of Tina Brown's favourite authors. He contributes a most enjoyable article on the Countess of Kenmare, who was a friend and bridge partner of W. Somerset Maugham. She was rumoured to have murdered four husbands but, rather disappointingly, she probably did not. She was, however, a drug addict.

There is something almost humorous about the catalogue of moral dementia that one can read about in *Vanity Fair* – it sometimes reminded me of the Hammer House of Horrors. Tina Brown describes a society of preposterous wealth, but no standards of morality or fidelity. Her strength is that this society angers and fascinates her at the same time.

I started by thinking that her literary ancestor was John Bunyan, and she was obviously both a puritan and an outsider. I now think the apter parallel is John Osborne, and *Look Back in Anger*. I find myself believing that New York, Hollywood and the Hamptons probably do contain the freaks she portrays. At all events they make very good reading. No wonder 800,000 people buy a magazine that tells them about the vile lives led by people much richer than themselves.

18 February 1991

A GENTLE CONCILIATOR
WITH THE GIFT OF CHARM

I probably know the person who wrote the *Times* obituary of Ian Trethowan, for whoever wrote it clearly worked with Ian at times when I was also involved in what he was doing. Indeed, I worked with Ian on no less than four separate occasions. But, of course, *Times* obituaries are anonymous, so the criticisms I have to make may wound an anonymous friend or acquaintance.

The obituary was neither wholly unjust nor wholly unkind, but it was written in the spirit Alexander Pope attributed to Joseph Addison:

> *Damn with faint praise, assent with civil leer,*
> *And without sneering, teach the rest to sneer;*
> *Willing to wound, and yet afraid to strike,*
> *Just hint a fault, and hesitate dislike.*

At each point in Ian's career the obituary awards him guarded praise followed by a put-down. 'He was a respected interviewer and presenter – competent, orderly, courteous, reliable. Those who wanted fireworks went elsewhere.' What a feline touch there is in the use of the word 'respected'; what a damning sequence of compliments is conveyed by the cadence 'competent, orderly, courteous, reliable'. How clear – yet how untrue – the implication is that Ian was a dull broadcaster.

I first met Ian Trethowan when we were both lobby correspondents in the summer of 1954, when he was working for the *Yorkshire Post* and I was a substitute for Paul Einzig on *The Financial Times*. In those days many lobby correspondents worked in pairs, drawn from newspapers which were not in competition with each other; *The Yorkshire Post* and *The Financial Times* had such an informal agreement.

Ian was a much better lobby correspondent than I was, with excellent sources and a strong intuitive feeling for what was really happening in politics. I made up by concentrating on the economic and financial stories, which naturally interested *The Financial Times* most. When he moved to the *News Chronicle* in 1955, Ian was one of the best political correspondents of his time, and could well have made his whole career in that field.

I next worked with him around 1960 when he was at ITN, when ITN was making the running in television news. The anonymous obituarist makes the contrast between Ian Trethowan's style and Robin Day's, and of course that contrast was present. Each approached interviewing from the point of view of their professional experience: Robin as a barrister, sometimes friendly and often formidable in cross-examination; Ian acting as a lobby correspondent, sympathetically eliciting information.

Each was the best early example of his own style, and both types can still be observed in television. Each can be regarded as the founder of a certain school of political interviewing; in police interrogation terms, Ian Trethowan was the archetypal 'Mr Nice', and Robin Day could be the archetypal 'Mr Nasty', although he has mellowed into a particularly cosy 'Mr Nasty' nowadays.

At that time, I was a consultant on economic affairs to *This Week*, which was produced in the same studios as ITN. Geoffrey Cox, Ian Trethowan, and Alastair Burnet were developing ITN's political news coverage, and *This Week* was involved in some of their special programmes.

Together we did the first televised budget programmes, with Ian reading from Press Association tapes the extracts from the Chancellor's speech. It was rather like Ronald Reagan's early days of making sports broadcasts from hastily scribbled telephone reports.

The third time we worked together was at *The Times*. As a new editor – like all new editors – I put together a new team of columnists. Among the first that I introduced to the paper was Ian, who wrote a political column from 1967 until he was appointed managing director of BBC Radio. He enjoyed writing it, and it was an excellent column, always readable, likeable, always well-informed. As a columnist he had the gift of charm.

Ian Trethowan was a political journalist until his late forties. He was a very good one. He was successively at the head of three branches of his profession: a leading lobby correspondent, a leading broadcaster, a leading political columnist. In each role his work combined penetration with an attractive sympathy, and in each he was recognized by his contemporaries as one of the two or three leaders of his period.

Like many professional men he took to administration in middle life. There were some aspects of broadcasting administration at which he excelled; there were others at which he was less good. He had the best understanding of any director-general in modern times of the need for the BBC to have external relations with other centres of power, and these he handled very adroitly.

Those who had to deal with the BBC both liked and trusted him, and welcomed his openness. He had, as the *Times* obituarist rightly notes, an excellent partnership with a strong chairman, Michael Swann.

A fair criticism of his period as director-general, for part of which I was the vice-chairman, is that he was more concerned about keeping the show on the road than with any radical reform. He may have been right. The director-general of the BBC, like the Archbishop of Canterbury or the leader of the Labour Party, has one of the impossible big jobs, in which no one receives a performance rating of 'excellent', and a B grade can put you top of the form.

I concede to the *Times* obituarist that Ian was better suited to the first half of his career than to the second. As a professional journalist he was in the first class; as a professional administrator he was in the second class, though quite high. His successes and failures were determined by his character and temperament.

Although he was born in the home counties, Ian Trethowan,

as his name suggests, had a Cornish ancestry and presumably derived from this his Celtic temperament. Dealing with him was like dealing with one of those soft-tongued, Gaelic-speaking Highlanders who coexist in Scotland with the abrasive lowland culture of Glasgow.

Ian was to the core of his personality both gentle and intuitive. He was courageous – he had been in the Fleet Air Arm during the war – but he was not confrontational. He had the diplomatic skills in their natural form, not learned but instinctive. He would indeed have made a superb ambassador, and might have earned his knighthood in Paris or Washington, as well as at the BBC.

He would have been able to make – as he always did – many genuine friendships with those he had to deal with. His reports home would have been perceptive, colourful and full of understanding.

When such qualities are employed individually, they suffer from no drawback. When they are applied to high administration, they are still much needed, but they are not all that is needed. In the most difficult executive roles, a certain brutality is required by the function. It is the Lord Kings who best hammer crude metal into shape.

Ian, as director-general, was a conciliator rather than a reformer, evolutionary rather than revolutionary. But that was what he was put there to do. If the governors had wanted a revolution they should have looked for a Napoleon and not for a Talleyrand.

17 December 1990

THE TV MONOPOLY OF
THE MIDDLE-AGED MALE

I n my time I have made my fair share of incautious remarks to media correspondents who asked for a quick reply on the telephone. I have, therefore, some sympathy for Alan Yentob, the controller of BBC 2, who last week gave an unwary example of male condescension in a reply to Melinda Wittstock, the media correspondent of *The Times*.

She asked him for a reaction to Anna Ford's request for a BBC women's committee. He replied – and he must wish that he had not – that he would be 'happy to accept a women's think-tank, as long as it represents a range of women's opinions worth hearing'. How well I know from fellow experience what he must have felt as he picked up *The Times* over his morning coffee.

In fact, the BBC, belatedly and sometimes with ill grace, has been improving its reputation as an employer of women. Women such as Jennifer Abramsky, the head of radio news and current affairs, have been given opportunities and have taken them. In the Eighties, when I was a governor, I used to join with the women governors to lobby for better promotion opportunities for women. The opportunities were then noticeably poor. In that effort I was a supporter of Jocelyn Barrow, who is now the deputy chairman of the Broadcasting Standards Council. We made something of a nuisance of ourselves, although we were often outvoted, and on one occasion were given a lunch with the senior members of the personnel department in the vain hope of shutting us up.

I sat next to one of the senior figures in the department, who could not understand why I felt there should be women on the board of management, a level of promotion he could not expect to attain, even after several decades of service. 'I'm only an engineer, so you would expect me to be a male chauvinist,' he said.

Nowadays, John Birt, the deputy director-general of the BBC, has said that the corporation is committed to ensuring that women represent 40 per cent of all employees at each rung of the hierarchy by the year 2000.

Nevertheless, I feel that Anna Ford is entirely right to continue to press for opportunities for women. Much as I shall enjoy watching David Dimbleby, Peter Snow and Peter Sissons on election night, it is at least as odd to have no women on the election-night team as it would be to have a team without men.

The idea of a BBC women's committee also seems a good one. After all, no woman has yet been appointed director-general, deputy director-general, managing director of television, controller of BBC 1, controller of BBC 2, managing director of radio or managing director of external broadcasting. Women at the BBC still have a long way to go in climbing the Himalayas of promotion.

So do women in Britain generally. There has never been a woman editor of *The Times, The Daily Telegraph, The Guardian,* or less surprisingly, *The Independent.* Lady Littler has been the one woman director-general on the IBA or ITC. There has never been a woman Lord Chancellor, Lord Chief Justice or Master of the Rolls. There has never been a woman chief constable. There has never been a woman leader of the Labour Party, the Liberal Party or the Liberal Democrats. There is no woman in the present Cabinet, and there was no woman except the Prime Minister in the last one. There has never been a woman Foreign Secretary, Home Secretary, Chancellor of the Exchequer or chairman of the Conservative Party.

There has never been a British woman ambassador to Washington, Moscow, Paris or the United Nations. There has never been a woman chairman of a clearing bank, although to judge by banks' performances in the past twenty years, women could hardly have done worse than the men. There is, I think, no woman who is chairman or chief executive of any of the top hundred British companies, and most of those companies do not even have a woman director, executive or non-executive, although they have plenty of women customers.

There has never been a woman president of the great majority of professional bodies, including the Royal Society, the Royal College of Surgeons, the accountancy bodies, the Law Society, the Bar Council, and so on. The president of the Royal College of Physicians is a woman, but almost all the highest positions in national life have been reserved for men. We did, for eleven years, have a woman prime minister, and we have often had queens, most of them excellent, but they also are the exception and not the rule.

Britain is worse than most other democratic countries in promoting women to public office. The parliamentary test is not a bad one. Of eighteen West European countries, Britain ranks sixteenth in the percentage of women elected to Parliament, with only France and Greece worse. The British figure is 6.3 per cent, which compares with an average of more than 30 per cent for the four Scandinavian countries. We have forty-one women Members of Parliament, compared with eighty-one in Italy, which has a similar-sized Parliament.

The facts are obvious, and they apply even to national institutions that like to regard themselves as progressive. Since most Oxford and Cambridge colleges went co-educational, several men have been elected heads of what were previously women's colleges, such as Lady Margaret Hall. Not one woman has been elected head of what was previously a male college. Indeed, women have every reason to preserve women-only institutions, because those are the only institutions that give women equal opportunity.

Of course, this is not just an issue of top jobs. The inequity extends all the way down the scale, to middle and lower management, to skilled and unskilled work. At every stage, and in most, though not all occupations, women have inferior employment opportunities, inferior promotion prospects, and are often given the opportunities they do get in jobs that offer inferior pay and conditions.

The reasons are varied, although they include strong cultural resistances. The British Social Attitudes Survey in 1987, when we had already had a woman prime minister for eight years, found that 73 per cent of men thought that the job of car mechanic was suitable for men only. Oddly enough, there were newsreels during the Second World War that showed the Queen, then Princess Elizabeth, training as a motor mechanic in the ATS. Perhaps, however, motor mechanics do have a masculine image, and 62 per cent of women see that as men's work. But bank managers? No less than 31 per cent of men and 26 per cent of women see that as a man's job, too. It is as though frustrated customers were in the habit of saying: 'I shall hit you, if you don't give me an overdraft.'

Women's career ambitions and patterns are not exactly the same as men's, and never will be. Women need provision made for childbirth and child rearing, and often put a higher proportion of their youthful energy into the work of the family. But that can be compensated for by good employment practices. In general, the reason more women do not rise in their jobs is that other people block them, sometimes even other women. Anna Ford is right to demand equal opportunity for women presenters on television, and not only for their own sake: if television assumes that only middle-aged men can discuss serious issues such as a general election, the danger is that the public will think so, too.

18 March 1991

THE SEXUAL AMBIGUITIES
OF OUR FICTIONAL
HEROES

'His nose was as sharp as a pen, and a' babled of green fields.' That is one of the most famous lines in Shakespeare; it comes from Mistress Quickly's description of Falstaff's deathbed. But did Falstaff babble of green fields, and is the line Shakespeare's? I think not.

The first folio, from 1623, is our text authority. There the line reads, mysteriously: 'His nose was as sharp as a pen and a table of green fields.' That plainly makes no sense, and Alexander Pope, one of the earliest editors of Shakespeare, decided to follow the first separate publications in quarto, where the words 'and a table of green fields' do not appear.

'This nonsense,' writes Pope, 'got into all the following editions by a pleasant mistake of the stage editors who printed from the common piecemeal-written parts in the play-house. A table was here directed to be brought in (it being a scene in a tavern where they drink at parting) and this direction crept into the text from the margin. Greenfield was the name of the property-man.'

There is, I think, no other evidence of a property man called Greenfield on the Elizabethan stage, so we can regard him as an invention, a sort of Shakespearian editorial ghost. It was Lewis Theobald, whose edition of Shakespeare was published in 1734, who first suggested 'a' babled of green fields'. This amendment replaced the silence of the quarto editions, the nonsense of the folio, and Pope's implausible ghost of a property man. It was also a poetic amendment, and one feels that Shakespeare would have adopted it, if he had thought of it.

As Theobald argued, 'It has certainly been observed . . . of people near death, when they are delirious by a fever, that they talk of removing; as it has of those in a calenture' – a calenture is a type of delirium – 'that they have their heads run on green fields. To bable, or babble, is to mutter, or speak indiscriminately; like children, that cannot yet talk; or like dying persons, when they are losing the use of speech.'

Some later editors have preferred a less poetic emendation of the first folio that would read: 'His nose was as sharp as a pen on a table of green field.' This requires the change of 'and' to 'on' and the change of 'fields' to 'field', as against Theobald's brilliantly simple suggestion of 'table' to 'babled'. But it has the merit of following the preceding thought more closely. 'Field', in this sense, has the same meaning as 'felt', and the description is of a pen on a green baize table. Just as the dying do sometimes babble, so do they often go green in colour.

I think the odds must be that this was Shakespeare's metaphor, which would mean that Theobald deserves the credit for one of the most striking lines in English literature. If so, he contributed a significant detail to the Falstaff myth – indeed his is the best remembered single line which describes Falstaff. The question of Falstaff's deathbed is, however, acquiring a new poignancy. Am I right in thinking that Falstaff, after 400 years of active life, is now at last dying in real earnest? It is not just that English literature, as a body of knowledge, is dying in our schools, but that we have as modern people, lost interest in Falstaff in a way we have not lost interest in Hamlet.

Fifty years ago he would inevitably have been included in any discussion of those rare characters in literature who have so much life in them that they step off the page and become independent persons in their own right. Falstaff certainly seemed then to be much more alive than the historical characters who surrounded him. Even now most of us would recognize Falstaff if we saw him in the street; we do recognize him instantly when he appears on the stage. We would recognize him even in modern dress, so strong is his image. Yet despite the battle scenes, we should not recognize his real historic contemporary, King Henry V, who could walk from the Tower of London to Westminister Abbey entirely unnoticed unless he was wearing his crown.

There are a number of these living characters in English literature; but they do not live for ever. In our father's or grandfather's generation, Mr Pickwick was one such. People then still read Pickwick for pleasure and laughed out loud at Dickens's jokes. I have not heard the name Pickwick so much as mentioned in non-academic circles in the last five years. Somewhere I am sure there are loyal Pickwickians, but to the general taste he is quite dead. Dickens, like Shakespeare, had a remarkable genius for creating these autonomous characters of fiction. Yet I suspect Fagin and Mr Micawber have survived better than Pickwick.

Fagin indeed is still very much alive, which is strange as he is a caricature of the Jewish pedlar who vanished from the scene a century ago. I do not know what the Jewish Defence League make of him; it seems to me that there is some anti-Semitism in the image, as there is in *The Merchant of Venice*, but some philo-Semitism as well.

The late-twentieth-century concern about Fagin would concentrate on what would now be called his sexuality. Plainly Fagin is quite strongly charged as a sexual figure. It is hard to think that he was not homosexual, in his relationship with Oliver Twist himself, with the artful dodger, with Bill Sykes and the rest of the gang. Yet I do not suppose for a moment that he was a child molester, but more like one of those conscientious homosexual schoolmasters whose attraction to their pupils provides the platonic energy that goes into their teaching.

There is indeed a sexual ambiguity about many, perhaps most, of these autonomous heroes. Peter Pan is an obvious example. If he grew up he would have terrible problems, and there would be a clear danger of him becoming a paedophile in adult life. Yet he lives in our minds, and would certainly pass the test of being instantly recognizable in the street, or in Kensington Gardens for that matter.

Falstaff may have been a closet gay as well. We have all known men who spend most of their time in male company, drink a good deal, affect an exaggerated masculinity, and pretend to want to seduce every barmaid that they meet. Sometimes at least, it is all a cover for their real sexual preference. It may be that some element of sexual ambiguity is essential to the hold that these personalities have on us – though Mr Pickwick seems almost sexless, and he lasted for over a hundred years. Perhaps it is because we see him as sexless that the late twentieth century has lost interest in him.

There is, of course, the supreme example of Sherlock Holmes, so famous that his name is known to thousands who have never heard of Conan Doyle. We now find it very difficult to understand the Victorian bachelors and try to fit all of them into sexual categories that belong to our post-Freudian culture, but not to theirs. We still understand the close friendship of women, and do not automatically regard it as lesbian. We have become far too wary of the close friendship of men, particularly if they share lodgings.

Yet that formidable logic, that chilly exterior, that noble brow, do remind one of another late Victorian persona, though I am sure Conan Doyle did not have him in mind. Sherlock Holmes follows a clue with all the logic that A. E. Housman employed on correcting a classical text. I suspect that Holmes, apart from the evidence of frustration suggested by his cocaine habit, may have been in love with Watson, as Housman loved his heterosexual friend. It would make his career, and his irritation that Watson never understood him, all the more poignant. It would strengthen rather than weaken the astonishing grip that Sherlock Holmes has on the public imagination.

30 September 1991

A NATURAL MAN, BUILT
ON AN UNNATURAL SCALE

B ritish newspapers have taken the view that Robert Maxwell's death was a more interesting event than all the
others things – such as the war in Yugoslavia – happening
in the past five days. As so often, the news editors were right so
far as their readers were concerned. Death is always interesting;
mystery adds to the interest of death; Robert Maxwell had great
wealth and great debts; his personality had the force of an
articulated lorry, and his enjoyment of luxurious display was
equal to that of the Roman emperors.

There are some historic figures – Cardinal Manning (the
prominent convert who was so unpleasant to Newman) comes to
mind – whom one naturally thinks of as bad good men. Their
virtue is real, but it is alloyed with a certain coldness and
calculation which destroys the affection one might otherwise feel.
In the Gospels, Jesus found this in the Pharisees. In the same
way, Robert Maxwell was a good bad man; he could properly
refer to himself as a rogue, he did deals that would not stand the
light of day, he was a bully and had no idea of the duty a director
owes to his shareholders, yet he had geniality, vitality, a creative
instinct and a love for his family which offset these bad qualities.
He was one of the publicans and sinners.

People will always contrast his destiny with that of Rupert
Murdoch, parallel figures down to their initials, yet so extraordi-

narily different in temperament. Both owned mass circulation British tabloids, the *Daily Mirror* and *The Sun*. Both built large international media businesses. Both made fortunes in Britain, and then turned to the larger markets of the United States. Both came to Britain as outsiders, one born in Czechoslovakia, the other in Australia. Both started as men of the left – *The Sun* still supported the Labour Party in the early Seventies. Both borrowed hugely to finance their empire building, and both ran into financial crises in the recession.

No doubt Rupert Murdoch has proved the better businessman. His record has been one of much more consistent business success, crowned now by bringing British Sky Broadcasting to the verge of profitability. His calculation of risk has been precise. If anything, Rupert Murdoch has been the more ruthless in the exploitation of markets, but his financial reputation has deservedly stood much higher. In Simpkin Marshall, in Pergamon, Leasco and then in MCC, Robert Maxwell involved himself in difficulties Rupert Murdoch has been able to avoid.

Yet despite the similarity of the two careers, the two personalities could not be less alike. Rupert Murdoch is a quiet man, with no desire to dominate in company and an ego of perfectly normal dimensions. He is rather a shy man. Robert Maxwell had this vast extrovert personality of a bravura style, apparently thick-skinned, always drawn towards the limelight. One built his empire from the head, the other from the heart. Bankers, who live in a largely abstract world, find more comfort in rational empires.

Robert Maxwell's death was an extraordinary piece of drama. We do not yet know, and perhaps never will know for sure, whether he died from sudden illness, accident, suicide or murder. He died in the perfect stage setting of his luxury yacht when his business affairs were in crisis, shortly after allegations that he was an associate of Mossad. The scene was as though his death had been plotted by a novelist, and Dominic Lawson wrote a brilliant piece in Saturday's *Financial Times*, drawing out the comparison between Maxwell and Melmotte, the financier in Trollope's *The Way We Live Now*.

I found myself thinking more of Samuel Johnson's poem, 'The

Vanity of Human Wishes'. Robert Maxwell did seem to have 'a frame of adamant', if not quite 'a soul of fire'; one could fairly say that 'No dangers fright him and no labours tire'. There is also about his death a strong sense of the futility of worldly achievement. 'His fall was destined to a barren strand, A petty fortress and a dubious hand; He left the name, at which the world grew pale, To point a moral or adorn a tale.'

His would, in the end, be a melancholy story, but for the strength of his family and his late reconciliation with his Jewish roots. After all the bother and trouble of his life, after surviving the Holocaust and the war, after overcoming hundreds of business crises and having controlled billions of pounds of assets, what is there left that makes the world a different or a better place? Even the *Daily Mirror* probably owes more to the editorial skills of Hugh Cudlipp than it does to the management skills of Robert Maxwell.

'*Quam cite transit gloria mundi*', Thomas à Kempis wrote about 600 years ago – 'How quickly passes the glory of the world'. Robert Maxwell devoted his life to his version of the glory of the world, and enjoyed it while he had it. He enjoyed the private jet and the yacht, the caviar, the champagne, and the company of famous people. He enjoyed the sensation of power, and the access to vast funds. He enjoyed his own birthday parties, and fireworks over Oxford. He enjoyed publishing newspapers, and owning football teams, and standing on a dais next to the Queen. These are all simple pleasures, and the visible enjoyment of simple pleasures is always endearing. But, apart from his genuine love for his wife and family, he paid highly for them. The last hours were almost certainly an agony, the dark night of his worldly hopes.

The moral of Robert Maxwell's life seems to be that Thomas à Kempis, whom I do not suppose he had ever read, was right. Not only in the view that the glory of the world passes quickly, but also about the vanity of the ambitions of the natural man. Chapter 54 of *The Imitation of Christ* describes them.

> Nature is crafty and draws, ensnares, and deceives many,
> and has always itself for its end. Nature labours for her own

advantage, and considers what gain may reach her from another. Nature willingly receives honour and respect. Nature is afraid of shame and of contempt. Nature seeks to have things which are curious and fine, and abhors things which are cheap and coarse.

Nature has regard to temporal things, rejoices at earthly gain, is troubled at losses, and is provoked at every slight injurious word. Nature covets to know secrets and to hear news; likes to be seen abroad, and to make trial of many things by the senses; longs to be noticed, and to do such things as may procure praise and admiration.

Robert Maxwell was the natural man, built on an unnatural scale.

His gifts, his energy, his gigantic way of living were outside the ordinary, but what he aimed for was what other men aim for; it was very ordinary indeed. If the natural vanities inevitably lead to disappointment for other men, they were bound to do so for him as well, but to the power of ten. The reason we are all fascinated by his death is that he was a sort of elephant of human nature, larger than life in his vanities but absolutely natural none the less. I am glad he was buried yesterday on the Mount of Olives, which is a place of grace. I shall remember him with affection; for all his faults, he was always generous to me, and I was always suspicious of him.

11 November 1991

PART FIVE

AIDS: APOCALYPTIC ARITHMETIC

n the 1950s I worked for *The Financial Times*. The newspaper was full of intelligent investment analysis, and I benefited from discussions in which I was an inexpert participant. In the early 1960s, when I moved to *The Sunday Times*, I wrote a weekly investment column for about two years.

This elementary financial analysis taught me the power of simple arithmetic. Investment is concerned with addition and substraction, with ratios, with percentages, with compound interest, forms of arithmetic which will have been learned by an intelligent child by about the age of ten. If one has thought seriously about investment, one will instinctively apply these simple methods to other matters which have investment characteristics.

One such matter is epidemic disease. A new disease spreads through the world like a new invention, like Xerox copiers, or Polaroid cameras, or colour television or computers. It expands until it has saturated its market.

It was from this point of view that I first wrote about the Aids epidemic. I could see that Aids had the equivalent of a marketing strategy. It was reaching out through certain specific communities, the central African community, the homosexual and drug-injecting communities of North America and Western Europe. Its initial growth rate was very high, but that tended to fall away as the limits in each target community were reached or people changed their habits. The arithmetic was that of compound interest.

Nobody who has studied investment can fail to be aware of the awesome power of compound interest. A rule of thumb is that factors of seventy will double – a 7 per cent compound rate of interest doubles in ten years and a 10 per cent rate doubles in seven years. In some areas HIV infection in the 1980s was doubling in a year, and in many particular groups it was doubling every two years.

Yet doubling is immensely potent. There is the old story of the Emperor who agreed to give a wise man one grain of wheat for the first square on the chess board, two grains for the second, four for the third, and so on. By the time he reached the sixty-fourth square, he had given away many times the wealth of his whole empire. HIV infections are now estimated to be doubling every five years, and in 1990 there were already about ten million people infected.

If HIV continues to double every five years, there will be forty million infected by the year 2000 – the current World Health Organization estimate. By 2010 there would be 160 million; by 2020 there would be 640 million; by 2030 there would be 2,560 million; by 2035 there would be more than five billion which is the current population of the whole world. Obviously the HIV infection will not be able to maintain a 15 per cent compound rate of expansion for the next forty-five years. It is currently infecting the most vulnerable groups, and will make much slower progress, if any, among less vulnerable groups. Nevertheless the fact that the current rate of growth of the epidemic would infect the whole of the present population of the world inside forty-five years shows the scale of the threat. In some central African countries, a third of pregnant women are HIV positive when tested in hospital.

The other simple arithmetic which impressed me was the effect of doubling on the risk of infection to the individual. I later used a quotation from an African expert, Dr Konotey Ahulu, which put this point very well. He compares having sex with a village prostitute, which he regards as 'equivalent to having sex with ten to twenty strangers', with having sex with an international prostitute, 'equivalent to having sex with 10,000 to 20,000 strangers'.

Sexual networks grow like the grains of wheat on the chess board. If one assumes that each partner has had the same total number of partners, one partner in a lifetime creates a network of two people, and zero risk. Two partners creates a network of four; five partners, thirty-two; ten partners, over a thousand; twenty partners, over one million; thirty partners, over one billion. Some African prostitutes, and some American homosexuals, are recorded as having 1,000 partners in a year. Such networks have virtually unlimited potential for the transmission of disease, and African prostitution and American homosexual bathhouses have been potent in organizing transmission of the virus.

This arithmetic of Aids still seems to be very important. I went on to use the methods of journalism to establish what the best available authorities considered the situation to be. I found that there was hope that a mixture of anti-viral drugs would help to prolong life in those infected, but that these drugs would be expensive, and would probably contain but not destroy the virus. I did not hear much optimism about the early development of a vaccine that would knock out HIV as polio was knocked out.

The more I learned, the more apparent it became that Aids is an environmental disease. Mankind creates environments which are not viable for human beings. They do not sustain social life in a way which allows normal human development. These environments are produced by overpopulation, overcrowding, poverty and lack of economic and social opportunity. They result in disease, drugs and crime.

The big cities become traps for large numbers who form an underclass. The conditions of overcrowding, bad housing and malnutrition are favourable to the spread of all sorts of communicable diseases. The underclass has low resistance and health care is inadequate. This is true of the big cities in wealthy countries, such as the United States, as well as of big cities in poor countries.

Such cities have always suffered from high levels of sexually transmitted diseases. In such environments, and when it was still a fatal disease, syphilis characteristically reached 10 per cent of the population. The social destruction of these cities disrupts family life, and large numbers turn to promiscuous heterosexual or homosexual activity either for money or as an addiction, comparable to drugs.

In the West many people have comforted themselves with the belief that Aids is a 'gay plague'. In fact at least 70 per cent of HIV infections are heterosexually transmitted; Aids is no more a homosexual disease than syphilis. They have also believed that Aids would remain confined to narrow areas. The HIV infection is now spreading from Africa, and the Western infected countries, into the mass populations of Asia, including India and China. Those two countries alone contain 40 per cent of the world's population, over two billion people. In some of the large Indian cities, HIV infection among prostitutes is already as high as it is in Central Africa, and India is at the stage of the epidemic Africa had reached in the early 1980s.

The scientific culture of the modern world naturally, and rightly, looked for a scientific answer to the HIV infection, for a drug to kill the virus, for a vaccine to prevent it, for condoms to insulate multi-partner individuals from the disease. So far these scientific responses have not proved effective, though they are obviously desirable in themselves. The disease is an opportunistic infection of a larger sociological disorder – the disorder which resulted from creating overcrowded cities with underclasses which have lost hope.

The spread of tuberculosis, a familiar disease which seemed to have been conquered, suggests that this sociological analysis is correct. About half the people who are HIV positive in sub-Saharan Africa are also suffering from tuberculosis. That is partly because the effect of HIV on the immune system reduces the resistance to all other infectious diseases, and partly because the conditions which help to spread HIV help to spread tuberculosis as well. The same thing is happening in New York, where strains of tuberculosis which have become resistant to antibiotics threaten to create a new epidemic.

Historically, mankind has turned to religion to strengthen the reaction to sociological problems of this magnitude. The development of Puritanism in the sixteenth century followed the introduction of syphilis into Europe in the 1490s. The sociological collapse of the Roman world was accompanied by the rise of Christianity. Even in studying the prevalence of HIV, one must be struck by the contrast between the low rates of infection in Islamic North Africa, and the high rates in sub-Saharan Africa.

At the simplest level, religion is the one discipline which has proved powerful enough to control sexual appetite. Even in a sexually obsessed age, the Roman Catholic clergy has remained celibate; the great majority of them successfully so. The claim of the Roman Catholic Church to be able to substitute religious faith for sexual activity has been maintained for nearly two thousand years, despite the urgencies of human nature. In the 1960s, the birth control pill and penicillin, with permissive abortion laws in reserve, seemed to free sexual promiscuity from the twin risks of pregnancy and disease. Aids has brought that phase of the sexual history of mankind to an end.

What is needed is not just sexual restraint, but better societies. The hell-holes of the big cities need to be changed. The churches may be very imperfect, but they are one voice of civilization that can still be heard in person in these living tombs of human misery. If these places of horror are to be enlightened, there is no cultural force except religion which is at all likely to achieve that.

WHY THE ONLY DEFENCE AGAINST AIDS IS A CHANGE OF SEXUAL HABITS

The mathematics of the chain letter are quite simple. A single letter sent to a single person who copies it to one other person will reach five people in five cycles; sent to five people, each of whom copies it to five people, it will reach 3,905 people in five cycles; sent to twenty people, who copy it to twenty people each, it will reach 3,368,420; sent to one hundred people, it would theoretically reach more than ten billion people in five cycles.

The arithmetic is simple, but it is to some extent counter-intuitive. Every investment analyst knows that the ordinary investor always underestimates the significance of compounding, and the explosive character of compound interest. This simple arithmetic is important at present, because it is the basic arithmetic of all sexually transmitted disease, including Aids.

The rate of infection of sexually transmitted diseases varies widely, but in proportion to the total number of opportunities for infection. The main aim of public health warnings must therefore be to reduce the number of opportunities for infection by persuading people to reduce the number of separate sexual contacts they have. In Western homosexual communities a change of conduct has already reduced the growth rate in Aids cases.

Aids has been spread by blood transfusions and dirty hypodermic needles. In the main, however, it has been spread by heterosexual intercourse in Africa and by homosexual intercourse elsewhere. There is dispute about the likelihood of a heterosexual Aids epidemic outside Africa, though there has been a considerable number of recorded cases of heterosexual transmission.

What is certain is the arithmetic. Fidelity to a single partner involves no risk. Five partners a year – a fairly rapid rate of change – potentially creates a network of 3,905 inter-related contacts over five years. Twenty partners, a network of more than three million.

Multiple partners are found in the sexual cultures of the worst-infected places. East African prostitutes are thought to average well over 100 partners in a month. Similar rates of contact were known in the homosexual bathhouse cultures in the United States. The sexual networks of highly promiscuous cultures will transmit to a high proportion of participants any disease that enters them.

Of course, this arithmetic is an oversimplified model. Someone who has sex with an infected prostitute may have only one sexual contact, but that could be sufficient to catch the disease. He would have linked himself to a very large infectious network. But what the model shows is the explosive increase in the risk of catching Aids matching the increase in the number of sexual partners. For obvious reasons, these risks are greatest in large cities, which are travel centres. This makes me doubt the wisdom of the condoms campaign.

The implied suggestion of that campaign is that condoms make promiscuity safe. In so far as the campaign encourages promiscuity it offsets the reduction in the risk of infection that the use of condoms would offer. The campaign has the same message as the jocular farewell of the Second World War: 'Be good, and if you can't be good be careful'. It is the implication which is remembered.

I doubt whether morality can be taught conditionally. All successful moral codes are absolute, and have been taught absolutely. The world, and human nature, will whittle away all too much of even the clearest commandments; they will obliterate altogether merely relative advice. In this the conservative theologians are right, and one has to side with the Pope, the Chief Rabbi and the Bishop of London against the moral relativists.

Aids is not the first new disease that mankind has had to face, nor is it likely to be the last. According to the American epidemiologist Hans Zinsser, the first epidemic of polio was recorded in 1840; the first epidemic of encephalitis was observed at Tubingen in 1712; the lethal influenza epidemic of 1917 and after was a new strain of the virus. In some cases, diseases were probably lurking in the regions waiting to infect the European discoverers who first recorded them. Yellow fever was unknown to Western medicine until Dutestre described the outbreaks at Guadeloupe and St Kitts in 1635.

The historic new disease which most closely resembles the social impact of Aids is syphilis. It is still not certain whether Columbus brought syphilis to the New World in 1492, or brought it back from the New World on his return. It is certain that it was unknown in the ancient world – there is no description in Hippocrates, or reference in other literature. There are scattered medieval cases which could be syphilis.

The first great epidemic of syphilis occurred in Naples in February 1495, following the capture of the city by the French army under Charles VIII. Hence its widespread name as the 'French pox' or the 'Neapolitan disease'. It is also known that its first appearance was particularly virulent. Fracastorius, who named the disease, published the classic description in 1546, including an account of the methods of transmission and course of the disease. He writes: 'I use the past tense in describing these symptoms, because though the contagion is still flourishing today, it seems to have changed its character since those earliest periods of its appearance.'

Until the twentieth century there was no cure for syphilis, though mercury was early discovered to be of use in treatment. Dr Salmon, in the late seventeenth century, recommended the application of a roast turnip to the affected part, 'as hot as the patient can bear'. In the absence of a remedy the only defence was a change of sexual habits. The number of occasions of infection had to be reduced to a tolerable level.

This can be regarded as having been successful. For 400 years syphilis was a highly contagious fatal disease. It was never eradicated – it has not been eradicated now – but it was contained. From about 1550 onwards it was kept in most of the world at a low endemic level, rather than an epidemic level, except in time of war.

This was largely achieved in Western society by the spread of puritanism both among Protestant churches and in the Catholic counter-reformation. Puritanism undoubtedly increased the proportion of the population who practised strict monogamy, and it probably reduced the number of sexual partners in the non-monogamous population. Penicillin and the pill seemed by the 1960s to have killed puritanism by removing the fears of disease and pregnancy. We now again realise that there is a Darwinian struggle for survival between each infectious agent and its human host community, a struggle that turns on the number of opportunities for infection the disease is given.

23 February 1988

FOR THE PURE SHALL
INHERIT THE EARTH

P uritanism has been an historic world response to the spread
of sexually transmitted diseases and the breakdown of
order. It makes the ascetism present in almost all religious
systems the focal point of a new spiritual discipline. Two great
Puritan theologians of the Christian tradition are St Augustine
and John Calvin. St Augustine wrote at the time of the sack of
Rome and the collapse of the Western Roman Empire.

John Calvin was born in 1509, within fifteen years of the first
syphilis epidemic, which occurred at Naples in 1494; the disease
had probably been brought back to Europe by Columbus's sailors
after the discovery of America in 1492. Syphilis caused the same
widespread anxiety in sixteenth-century Europe as Aids does
today. Indeed, the two diseases are very similar. They are
sexually transmitted; they are fatal; they have a long latency
period. Syphilis is now curable, but in the sixteenth century it
was not.

Last week, Dr Hiroshi Nakajima, the director of the World
Health Organization, said: 'Sexually transmitted infections have
reached epidemic proportions globally. If sexual behaviour is not
modified, the resulting disease and mortality rates will be even
more staggering.' This is supported by WHO's statistics.

In 1990, 250 million new cases of sexually transmitted diseases
were reported across the world. Most of these cases were not life-

threatening, although many could cause sterility in women or open the way to the Aids virus. Yet the figure of 250 million is a horrifying one. There are about 1,000 million people in the fifteen to twenty-nine age group which is most at risk. That means that up to as many as a quarter of all young people in the world caught at least a minor sexually transmitted disease in 1990. Many, if not most, of the 250 million incidents in which a disease was transmitted could have transmitted Aids if the virus had been present.

Aids itself, however, only accounted for one million of these cases, with syphilis accounting for 3.5 million. But a million new cases of Aids, one in a thousand of the group most at risk, is tragic enough. We may soon reach the stage at which the annual deaths in the world from Aids exceed those from famine.

In the US, crime figures have also reached epidemic levels, and in many other countries they are rising alarmingly quickly. At present rates, one American baby in 140 can expect eventually to be murdered, and in the larger cities, one black baby in fourteen. The drug epidemic is similarly lethal. In the largest cities of the US, drugs, Aids, murder and destitution make the life of young men and women as dangerous as it was for the troops sent to Vietnam. 'Hell no, I won't go' is not an option available in the Bronx.

Human society has always had to deal with the instinctual forces that lead to drugs, sexual variety and murderous conflict. The control of such strong forces requires a stronger force. That has, historically, been found in religion, and in certain highly motivated forms of social order, but the weaker the religious faith, the less effective it has been.

The necessary motivation to control the instinctive behaviour of human beings does not seem to be provided by modern capitalism, even when it is at its most successful. Historically, the highest capitalist culture has been that of the United States, now in a crisis of social disorder. The two most successful capitalist economies of our age are Germany and Japan. Neither is producing enough children to maintain its population. There are at present twice as many Germans as there are Poles. In fifty years' time, if present trends do not change, there will be twice as many

Poles as there are Germans. At the latest count, there are 124 million Japanese; on unchanged trends there will be about 75 million in fifty years. Demographic trends do change, but there is no better indicator of human confidence than the decision to have or not to have a baby. Germany and Japan are conspicuously successful in producing goods, but conspicuously reluctant to produce people.

What signs are there that a New Puritanism is actually coming into existence? One should look at the Puritanism of the young, with its radical sympathies, and not that of the old, which has always existed and reflects both conservatism and the waning of sexual energies. The old may or may not develop wisdom, but they cannot be the leaders of the future.

In religion, Puritanism has usually been connected with fundamentalism; indeed the word 'puritan' itself referred to purity of doctrine rather than to purity of mind. There is evidence of the growing strength of fundamentalism in major world religions, notably in Islam, but also in Hinduism, in Judaism and in Christianity. This fundamentalism is often very disturbing, although that is also a sign of its energy.

The Pope himself, in his message for World Peace Day tomorrow, has warned of the need to reinforce religious tolerance. 'A serious threat to peace is posed by intolerance, which manifests itself in the denial of freedom of conscience to others.' Intolerance, in his view, can result from the temptation of fundamentalism.

Yet this very aspect of fundamentalism makes it attractive to many people. The certainty that one has found the only true way is a source of strength to the believer. So is the division of the world into the elect and the rejected, which appears in the teaching both of St Augustine and of Calvin. Catholics themselves used to believe that there was no salvation outside the Church.

There is, however, also a gentler form of Puritanism which is very influential among the young in the advanced industrial countries. It is an ideology which links some of the concerns of the Green movement, of the women's movement, of rights for ethnic minorities, with respect for animal life and, often, a nondogmatic spirituality. This ideology tends to reject modern materialism and to cultivate a simple lifestyle, a plain unworldliness which would have been attractive to the plain-living Puritans of New England in the seventeenth century. Many of its adherents are vegetarian. There is more natural Christianity in this ideology than dogma, and the respect for all life has a Franciscan character.

These two types of Puritanism, the tough and the tender, the rigorous and the quietist, both offer world answers. The four Horsemen of Death in New York are drugs, Aids, murder and destitution. All relate to addictions: the addiction to drugs and alcohol, the addiction to sex, and the addiction to violence. Both in its tough and in its tender form, Puritanism offers an alternative to these addictions.

The convinced Puritan will be set free from the primal addiction to the world by the acceptance of a higher order of values. There are no drugs that offer the ecstasy of prayer; there are no physical goods with the appeal of the goods of the spirit; there is no sexual diversity as satisfying as bonding to another person, or, for the celibate, of bonding to the divine; there is no thing man has made as worthy of love as the animals and the people that God has made.

As a bonus, the Puritan is free from the universal material fears of our time. Faithful couples do not catch Aids. People who do not take drugs do not die of overdoses. Plain living does not depend on hire purchase. We may or may not like Puritanism, but the world faces a multiple challenge of crime, addiction and disease, which is already destroying the world's greatest commercial city, New York. Puritanism, in one of its forms, is mankind's traditional answer to such challenges.

30 December 1990

THE CLEAR LINK BETWEEN POVERTY AND THE SPREAD OF AIDS

I admire the people who are fighting Aids, whether they are doctors or nurses or patients or health administrators. It takes compassion to deal with so many personal tragedies. It takes courage to look into that furnace.

Some of the most compassionate and bravest people come from the homosexual community that has been scarred by the onset of the epidemic in the United States and Europe. Aids is not a gay plague – 60 per cent of cases in the world now come from heterosexual contact – but the gay community has been among the first to make a coherent response.

There is a strong resistance to thinking about Aids; people need to know the facts, but they do not wish to face them. As a journalist I am aware that the word 'Aids' in the first sentence of an article will mean that many readers will skip what is underneath. The people who are dealing with Aids have all had to break through that barrier for themselves. In learning about the epidemic the people one meets have had the strength of character to overcome a personal resistance of their own, and they have to live with their knowledge.

I had become so confused by the various projections of the epidemic that, after talking to some British experts, I went last week to Geneva to find out from the World Health Organization

(WHO) what its best information was. It speaks of a world pandemic, with at present about 1.3 million Aids cases, and at least eight to ten million people infected with the HIV virus.

The WHO does not have a wholly reliable projection for the rate of increase to be expected either in Aids or HIV, though it does know that half those infected with HIV will have developed Aids inside ten years, and it suspects that almost all the other half will develop Aids in the subsequent ten years. The most recent projection suggests that there will be twenty million adults and ten million children infected with HIV by the year 2000, but that is already thought to be too low an estimate.

There is only one piece of good news. Homosexuals in the United States and Europe altered their conduct in the early-Eighties, practising safer sex and changing partners less often. As a result the exponential growth in HIV infection that was expected among these homosexuals has been avoided. That, however, has given a false reassurance so far as the world heterosexual pandemic is concerned.

Even in North America and Europe heterosexuals and intravenous drug users did not alter their conduct. Nor have they done so in the rest of the world, where HIV has mainly been a heterosexual infection from the beginning.

Britain has suffered a relatively small epidemic by American or southern European standards, but along the American pattern, with most early cases homosexual in transmission. At the end of 1989, for which reporting is not complete, the British rate of reported Aids cases was 1.5 per 100,000 population. The United States figure was 13.9; Switzerland was 7.0, Spain 5.5, France 5.0 and Italy 4.1.

Southern Europe has experienced a far worse epidemic of HIV infection from sharing drug needles than we have. Yet even in Britain it is possible that by 1993 two-thirds of new Aids cases will come from heterosexual contact or injecting drug use. Probably about one young adult in 600 in Britain is now infected with HIV, but we do not yet really know.

The really bad news comes from Africa and Asia. In 1987 the WHO estimated that there were about two and a half million HIV infections in sub-Saharan African countries. By late 1990 a further estimate of at least five million was described as 'very conservative'. The estimates are doubling every three years.

The number of infections is about equal among men and women; apart from contaminated blood products, which account for about one infection in ten, the great majority of cases arise from heterosexual contact. The HIV infection rate is already about one in forty of adults in these countries.

This produces a devastating effect on the children. At the end of last year 500,000 children were estimated to be infected with HIV in Africa; all are expected to die inside five years. Children die faster. The WHO forecast is that during the Nineties ten million African children will be infected with HIV, and ten million more will be orphaned.

The disease is spreading from the African towns to the villages, and from east to west Africa. In 1985 the developing countries accounted for about half the world total of infections. By the year 2000 it is expected to reach 75 to 80 per cent and 80 to 90 per cent by the year 2010. In some cities of central and east Africa, the rate of HIV infection has reached 25 per cent of adults. At that level, society itself is being destroyed.

This heterosexually transmitted epidemic is now reaching Asia. Spread by drug practice, it is rife in the brothels of Thailand; it is a growing problem in India, and there are disturbing reports from China. So far, the masses of Asia have been spared, with 60 per cent of the world's population producing less than 0.5 per cent of reported Aids cases. That reprieve seems to be at an end.

The epidemic is already severe in the Caribbean, with Bermuda, the Bahamas and French Guyana reporting more than 60 cases of Aids per 100,000 in 1989. It is spreading in South America, where there are a million estimated HIV infections. Infected blood donors are still a significant cause of infection in developing countries.

What do these alarming figures mean? There are about five billion people on earth; around two billion of them fall into the family-forming age and they are the group most at risk.

The best estimate of current HIV infection is eight to ten

million. If one takes the lower figure, that probably means that one in 250 of the human breeding group is infected.

Both reported Aids and estimated HIV infections doubled repeatedly in the Eighties, but faster in the earlier years. Present opinion seems to be that HIV infection will double most frequently in the regions now largely free of infection, which cover 70 per cent of the world's population; it will perhaps double less frequently in Africa, and probably less frequently again in America and Europe. Good medical systems and adequate resources are essential in limiting the spread of infection.

The most recent WHO forecast suggests that HIV infections may double every seven years. That may be right, or even pessimistic, for America and Europe, but it is likely to be too low for Africa and much too low for Asia. Few informed people would be surprised if HIV infections worldwide were to double among young adults every five years – or less.

That would give this sequence: 1990, 1 to 250; 1995, 1 to 125; 2000, 1 to 63; 2005, 1 to 32; 2010, 1 to 16. If this deadly progression is to be slowed, HIV infection has to be prevented in the heterosexual population of poor countries, where there are limited resources, weak medicine, and usually high existing rates of sexually transmitted diseases.

The pandemic's rate of increase will probably not be affected by any of the fifty or so anti-viral agents now being tried; though they offer hope of prolonging life and slowing the disease, they will not kill the virus, nor offer a cure.

The rate could be affected by the successful development of a vaccine, though a vaccine might only give partial immunity, or immunity for a limited time, or immunity from particular strains of the virus. The discovery, testing, manufacture and distribution of a vaccine is likely to take at least ten years. It is perhaps the best hope for the twenty-first century, but not for the twentieth.

Most of this is not in dispute, though experts offer different projections, and some past projections have already proved inaccurate. In all countries, the HIV pandemic already is, or will be, a very grave medical problem, the cause of countless individual tragedies. But the link between poverty and the spread of

Aids is already very clear in Africa, Latin America and even in the inner cities of North America and Europe. The pandemic threatens every country, but most of all it threatens those least able to help themselves.

4 February 1991

FIVE ACTS IN AN
EXTRAORDINARY
TRAGEDY

The ingredients of tragedy can often be quite ordinary. A Scottish housing estate, run-down in parts but no worse than other such estates and better designed than many; social class four and five children with no prospect of industrial work and no skills training; families broken by drink and a pattern of delinquency; prison and the dole providing background institutions as familiar as the Garrick and Lord's are to a London subculture; the grind of poverty on mothers with too many children; the double devaluation of the low self-esteem of the individual and the low self-esteem of the community; the sense of despair reinforced by old graffiti and decaying walkways – these are the conditions of life in the Muirhouse Estate in Edinburgh.

Such conditions can be found in some areas of most, if not all, of the larger cities of Britain, and Edinburgh is not a very large city. In Edinburgh, however, they have produced a double tragedy, which so far has not been found in the rest of Britain, except possibly London; it is common in cities in the United States and southern Europe, including Madrid, Milan, Turin and Zurich. As it happens, we know a great deal about the Edinburgh tragedy; it has a unique record.

Muirhouse Estate has one institution that was, and is, exceptional. It is the Muirhouse Medical Group, a large practice of one part-time and six full-time doctors who have a particular interest in medical research and were given the support to carry it out. In 1979, they became concerned about the numbers of their young patients who were developing drug dependence problems.

This was not the Sixties, and these new drug users were not hippies or students interested in expanding their consciousness. They were local young people, from the Muirhouse and the adjoining Pilton estates. Pilton is architecturally much grimmer than Muirhouse and is due for demolition. In the middle and even the late Seventies this area had only a very small drug problem, probably no more than forty individuals out of a practice covering 12,000 – less than 1 per cent of the risk group, who were aged about twenty.

By 1980 several of the Muirhouse GPs had become aware that a growing group of adolescents and young adults were asking for unjustified amounts of strong pain-killers. Questioning established that most of them were injecting heroin. Since 1981, 352 drug users have been identified in the practice, about 70 per cent male. A similar epidemic was occurring on other estates.

The doctors' growing awareness led to a research project, which was funded from 1984 by the Scottish Office, to study the development of the drug epidemic. About 200 of the Muirhouse drug users have been monitored since that time. The project was conceived in 1979 as research into drug use, its consequences and treatment. It began before the Aids epidemic had started, and before the HIV virus had been identified.

However, in 1983 the HIV virus did, in fact, reach Edinburgh. The infection – which had not yet been identified – spread suprisingly quickly among the drug-injecting group. It was spread by shared needles, and at that time the Edinburgh police were cracking down on anyone who sold new hypodermic syringes to drug users. The sharing of needles was also part of the drug ritual, something that gave people taking heroin, or other drugs, a warm feeling of comradeship, like taking part in a round in a pub.

By the middle of 1984 about half the drug users were infected; nobody knew it at that point, but blood samples were being taken to study an epidemic they did know was spread by needle-sharing, that of hepatitis B, a sometimes fatal virus that attacks the liver. The Muirhouse study, therefore, became one of the few scientific accounts we shall ever have of a community at risk from HIV at a point when the risk was not yet known.

I was taken around the Muirhouse Estate last week by Roy Robertson, one of the partners in the Muirhouse Group practice and one of the co-authors of the reports on this research. He introduced me to one of his young patients, who has full-blown Aids. Before that I had been speaking with clinicians, doctors and administrators who are trying to manage the Aids epidemic in Edinburgh.

What is happening now is that the disease is marching on. As a result of the experience of the drug injectors of 1984, the drug community has adjusted its behaviour, just as the homosexual community has changed its conduct. Many drugs users are following rules of safe drug use, just as homosexuals are practising safe sex. There is less injecting, and those who do inject are less willing to share needles. Clean needles have been made freely available.

As a result, the rate of new infections among drug users, who are now mainly using pharmaceutical drugs such as dihydrocodeine, has fallen. The 1983/84 experience, of a drug group going from zero to 50 per cent infection in a year, is not likely to be repeated in Britain.

Yet most of the infected drug users from that period have not yet reached the stage of full-blown Aids. The average period between infection and full Aids is ten years. It is known that most of this group were infected in 1983/84. Some are already being treated with AZT or other anti-viral drugs, which can delay the onset of the disease. The largest number of deaths is likely to occur in the mid-Nineties; they are only now starting.

Yet the virus is winning, and the infected group is showing a consistent and progressive reduction of the cells vital to the immune system. There is some probability that this later phase of the HIV positive stage of the disease, when the CD-4 count – which measures the strength of the immune system – has fallen to or below the critical 200 level, is also the most infectious. At that stage, the virus is multiplying most rapidly. And the evidence is that the infected drug users, although they have changed their drug practices, have not changed their sex practices. They are not abstaining from sex, and they are not using condoms.

The Edinburgh drug users are almost exclusively heterosexual – their masculine culture does not tolerate homosexual conduct, even in prison. They are not particularly promiscuous and tend, in the main, to have long-term stable relationships with wives or girlfriends. About 25 per cent of these relationships lead to infection of the partner, who is often not a drug user. There is also evidence of transmission to further heterosexual partners of those who have been infected by Edinburgh drug users.

I spoke to a young registrar at an Edinburgh hospital. She is treating a stable and cheerful seventeen-year-old patient whose first and only sexual experience was with an older boyfriend. That transmitted the HIV virus. In another case a young male student went with a girl at a student party. In the morning he could not remember her name. She had infected him with the virus. Heterosexual transmission seems to be taking over from injecting-drug transmission; the spread will be slower, but potentially much wider.

This is the plot of the tragedy. Act I is the decay of a valid working-class culture, a failure of employment, of education, of housing, of social function. Act II is young people, in a group, contracting out of society and into an injecting drug culture. Act III is the spread of HIV infections as the result of needle-sharing by this group.

Act IV will be a peak of Aids deaths in Edinburgh, probably in 1994 to 1996, a crisis that will strain the city's medical resources and an already weakened local community. Act V will be the spread of the infection by heterosexual contact to subsequent non-drug-using partners of non-drug-using partners of the original victims of the disease. That process has already begun. When the seventeen-year-old girl was tested, she thought it impossible that she could be infected after her first experience of sex with a young man who was neither a drug addict nor a homosexual. Unfortunately, she was mistaken.

25 March 1991

ONCE A SPIRITUAL NEED, NOW A MATTER OF LIFE AND DEATH

Last Thursday, I visited the offices of the Salvation Army in Queen Victoria Street and talked to Dr Ian Campbell, a captain in the organization and the medical adviser at its international headquarters. He is the co-ordinator of the International Aids Conference the Salvation Army has called in Switzerland next month, and has recently visited Brazil, central African countries, Haiti and India. He is an important observer of the world HIV epidemic.

The same day, the Department of Health published the first results of its anonymous screening programme for the HIV virus, the first reliable information we have on the spread of the infection in England and Wales. Sir Donald Acheson, the Chief Medical Officer at the department, said the news was 'disappointing, but not unexpected'. We now know that the HIV virus is well established in the heterosexual population of London.

England is not, by international standards, an advanced case of the world epidemic. Our figures are below the average of the European Community, and well below those of the United States, sub-Saharan Africa, Brazil and the Caribbean. Yet they are rising, and there is no sign of the epidemic being brought under control.

The average rate of HIV infection among pregnant women in inner London is one in 500, and that rises to one in 200 in some districts. The comparable figure outside London is still only one

271

in 16,000. Another survey, published in *The Lancet*, suggests that these London figures are rising rapidly. Last year, 18 out of 4,106 women (1:230) who gave blood for rubella testing at St Thomas's Hospital were HIV positive; in 1988, the number had been two out of 3,760. That is an eight-fold increase in only two years.

Dr Campbell was able, from his recent experience, to fill out for me the statistics of the World Health Organization; they show that the HIV virus is making rapid progress throughout the world, but is still at its worst in Africa. He has recently been in Uganda, probably the worst-affected country in the world, with rates of HIV infection in some cities reported as high as one in two of the sexually active population.

In Uganda, Dr Campbell found a society being destroyed by the HIV virus, even though only a small proportion of those infected have progressed to full-blown Aids. There are homes being run by eleven-year-olds; the parents are dead, some of the younger children are dead or dying and grandparents can no longer cope. There are secondary epidemics of diseases such as tuberculosis, and social epidemics – poverty, unemployment and malnutrition.

Dr Campbell divides the world into countries such as Britain, which have the luxury of time, and countries in which 'you have the Uganda scenario in front of you'. In this group he puts many other African countries, as well as India and Brazil, and also several large cities in the United States, such as Miami, San Francisco and New York. In New York's borough of Queens, 23 per cent of outpatients at a Salvation Army hospital have tested HIV positive – that is a rate of one in four.

The Salvation Army is a Christian body dedicated to finding a compassionate Christian response to social evils; they first fought the poverty and degradation of the Victorian slums. They do not believe that science or technology can, on their own, prevent the further spread of the disease, although they are entirely supportive of scientific and technological measures. They regard a change of behaviour as far more important than condoms, or even medicines or vaccines, although they approve of the use of condoms as a protection against infection. The best current view

272

is that an effective anti-HIV vaccine is still ten years away, and may then offer only short-term immunity.

They do not believe that a change of behaviour can be imposed from the top downwards, but that it has to develop from communities affected by Aids as the community's own response. They also believe that the lessons learnt by one community can be transferred to another, and they use their experience in Africa to help their work in Brazil. The Salvation Army believes that the poor can teach the poor, and that the poor may also be able to teach the rich.

I have in front of me a community counselling document prepared by village people in rural Zambia, in the area of the Chikankata Hospital, more than a hundred miles from the capital, Lusaka. This states, as a community conclusion, that high-risk activity includes unfaithfulness in marriage, and pre-marital and extra-marital sex. The proposed responses are faithfulness in marriage, abstinence until marriage, and the adoption of a Christian lifestyle. The Salvation Army claims that these are community responses to a crisis that threatens the survival of the community, and not merely responses imposed by Salvation Army counsellors from outside.

This is, in some ways, a similar approach to that of Alcoholics Anonymous, which is also prepared to accept the logic of abstinence and the need for community support. It is not easy for alcoholics to give up drink, and it is not easy for partner-changers to give up pre-marital or extra-marital sex. Without community support it may be impossible.

In Europe and America, we have a particular cultural problem that stands in the way of such a community response. Before the invention of the contraceptive pill and the availability of easier abortion, a mainly monogamous culture was supported by the fear of unwanted pregnancy outside marriage. Those of us who were born before 1940 grew up in this culture, which was based on what the Zambians call 'a Christian lifestyle'.

In the period between the introduction of the Pill and the onset of the Aids epidemic, a counter-culture was established in which high sexual activity with multiple partners was put forward as good in itself. Many people born after 1940 have been strongly influenced by this culture and they are likely to remain as cultural leaders until they start to retire in the next century. To them, the advocacy of the Christian lifestyle is genuinely shocking.

Fortunately, most people in Britain have continued to follow a lifestyle of relative sexual restraint with at least prolonged periods of fidelity. Studies suggest that about a third of young men and women do not have full intercourse before the age of twenty and that most of those who are sexually active at that age had only had a single partner in the last year. Rapid and frequent changes of partner remains a minority lifestyle, and in the case of young women, the minority is a small one.

Perhaps because I am a member of the pre-1940 age-group, I find the Salvation Army case convincing. The 'unzip a condom' approach to the HIV epidemic reminds me of the filter-tip response to the issue of cigarette smoking and cancer. It is not wrong, but it is a distraction from the real issue. The Judaeo-Christian sexual code has a function to provide for the care of children and also, like the Jewish dietary laws, to prevent the spread of disease. In Christian terms, sexual morality is determined by spiritual needs, but in Darwinist terms, Christian morality is a strategy for survival. We have had twenty-five years in which the security of faithful marriage seemed to be unnecessary. That period has come to an end.

20 May 1991

A SPECTRE OF DEATH
HAUNTS US CITIES

I n late May I went to Atlanta, Georgia, to visit the HIV-Aids division of the Center for Disease Control, which is part of the US Department of Health and Human Services. They are the people who have the greatest knowledge of the Aids epidemic in the United States. Some of their information is relatively reassuring; some of it is very alarming.

As in Europe, but earlier than in Europe, the HIV epidemic in the US started with homosexual transmission, progressed to transmission by needle sharing among drug users, and is now expanding to heterosexual transmission. That pattern is the basic one for the HIV epidemic in North America and Europe.

The most reassuring news from the US is that the annual growth rate of new Aids cases has fallen to 10 per cent. Latest reports for the year to the end of April 1991 give 42,333 new cases as against 38,517 in the year to the end of April 1990. These people were of course infected in the Eighties, many of them in the first half of the decade.

The best estimate of the number of Americans infected with the HIV virus is between 800,000 and 1.2 million, although some experts offer a wider range of possibilities. The CDC estimate is one million, which is 1 in 250 Americans. If the HIV epidemic were stable, one would expect about 5 per cent of the infected population to reach the full Aids stage each year. The presently reported rate of Aids would therefore account for an HIV-infected community of about 850,000, if the epidemic had stabilized completely. When new HIV infections are no higher than Aids deaths the epidemic will be in a steady state.

Nevertheless, Aids is now one of the leading causes of death among young adults. By 1989, Aids was the second largest cause of death among young men aged twenty-five to forty-four, having overtaken heart disease, cancer, suicide and homicide. In 1988 Aids was eighth among the causes of death of young women, and by 1991 it is expected to have risen to fifth place. Even if the epidemic is stabilizing, it is doing so at a horrifying level.

If one looks at the big cities – and in the US, though no longer in Africa, Aids is still largely a big-city disease – one sees a very wide range of infection. The lowest rate reported in 1991 is 3.7 per 100,000 in Lake County, Illinois; the highest rate is 130.7 per 100,000 in San Francisco. There is relatively little Aids infection in the Midwest states; even Chicago has a rate of only 15.7, a ninth of San Francisco's.

Figures per 100,000 seem reassuringly distant. Yet we would have to convert these figures by a multiple of fifty in order to estimate the proportion of the sexually active population that is infected with the HIV virus. That factor assumes that each Aids case reported in a year is represented by twenty-five people infected by the HIV virus, and that not more than half the population is sexually active, other than with a single partner.

Of course this is only a rough estimate, but until there is widespread testing, it is a reasonable one. When one applies it to US cities, a number of the big ones show outstandingly high levels of probable HIV infection. On this basis there are no fewer than twenty-seven metropolitan areas where the HIV rates among the sexually active population exceed one in a hundred.

This calculation is not made by the CDC, but it is based on their latest figures. It might be wrong if the estimate of twenty-five HIV cases to each new Aids case were mistaken. Seven Aids cases in eight are male. Obviously, the proportion of sexually active males, including homosexuals, who carry the HIV virus, is higher again.

On these calculations the ratio of HIV infection among sexually active males in Atlanta, Georgia, itself is likely to be one in thirty.

The same ratio would apply in West Palm Beach (Florida) and in Houston (Texas). The ratio rises to about one in twenty in Fort Lauderdale (Florida), Jersey City, Miami (Florida), San Juan (Puerto Rico), and Newark (New Jersey). In New York City it is one in fifteen. In San Francisco (California) it is one in nine. A number of other big cities, including Dallas (Texas) have a ratio of one in forty.

Set against an estimated US-wide ratio of one in seventy of sexually active American males currently infected with the HIV virus, the big city figures are very bad, but not unbelievable.

Yet they are catastrophic estimates, even if one takes the optimistic view that the disease has stabilized. Dr Ian Campbell of the Salvation Army gave me his rule of thumb that anything in excess of 5 per cent represents a social disaster. Yet the 5 per cent level has been reached, so far as one can tell, by sexually active males in seven big US metropolitan areas, and surpassed in New York City and San Francisco. The level of HIV infection may be stable, but it is also lethal.

Aids, like other sexually transmitted diseases, is particularly a disease of the urban poor. That has always been so. In Victorian London you could find cases of syphilis in Mayfair – including Lord Randolph Churchill – but a much higher proportion in the East End. In New York there are many more cases of HIV infection in the Bronx than in Manhattan, and that is true of syphilis as well.

Aids discriminates by poverty, by class, by gender, by ethnic group, by sexual preference and by lifestyle. It is not an equal opportunities infection.

The great fear of Middle America is that HIV infection will spread among women and students. Inner-city tests on pregnant women show some very high rates of HIV infection, much higher than the 1 in 200 shown in recent anonymous surveys in parts of London.

But this still seems to be an inner-city spread of the epidemic, often the result of prostitution, sometimes associated with other sexually transmitted diseases and drug abuse, including crack.

Exchange of sex for drugs among inner-city teenagers is one of the important transmission routes for the disease.

The US middle class is not yet having to face many cases of women being infected with the HIV virus by heterosexual intercourse with men who are neither bisexual nor drug users. In universities a recent survey, reported in 1990, showed that 1 in 200 males but only 1 in 5,000 females in higher education were infected with the HIV virus. That rose to 1 in 100 males older than forty.

This suggests that homosexual transmission is still much more important than heterosexual on US campuses, and that academics have about the same lifetime risk of being infected as American males generally.

The three chief methods of transmission have different social implications. The US homosexual and bisexual community crosses class boundaries. There is therefore a risk of infection between upper and lower socio-economic groups. The needle-sharing community belongs mainly to the lowest socio-economic groups. The United States has no common social habit of upper-class heterosexual men consorting with under-class prostitutes.

Women in middle-class communities are therefore still relatively free of the HIV virus, even when they live in high-risk cities such as San Francisco, New York City or Miami. They are also relatively free of hepatitis B, a more infectious virus spread by the same forms of transmission. Female students have very low rates of infection. The final breakout of Aids infection from the homosexual community and the inner-city ghetto has not yet occurred and may not occur. But in New York City one man in fifteen aged between fifteen and fifty is already infected with a fatal disease.

3 June 1991

MONOGAMY WILL BE OUR
PATHWAY TO SALVATION

The historic question about Aids is which side is going to win, the virus or the human species. If HIV had spread in any earlier century, then the virus would probably have conquered, if only because of ignorance. There is now a possibility, but no more than a possibility, that the human species will prevail. Yet myxomatosis did win the war against rabbits.

I do not mean by victory for the virus that the whole human race would be wiped out. That is unlikely to happen. Very few infectious diseases are fatal in every case; rabies is an exception, but rabies is not a disease endemic to our species. Nor would such a total victory be a success for the virus, since it would have wholly destroyed its host community. A successful virus has to be a farmer and not merely a butcher; it must not destroy the herd on which it lives.

There are many species of monkey which co-exist with the Simian Immunodeficiency Virus (SIV) without symptoms. It is probable, but far from certain, that there are some members of the human species who similarly have a natural immunity to the Human Immunodeficiency Virus. That will not be known for another ten or twenty years, when it will be possible to determine whether there are any long-term survivors of the infection. Already, however, there is a report of a family in California where three generations are HIV positive – grandmother, mother, daughter – and none shows symptoms. It would be normal to expect natural immunity in perhaps 5 per cent of a host community.

There is some genetic evidence that the human species has had previous encounters with retroviruses which did become universalized. If HIV were to succeed in this way, the whole human species would eventually be descended from the 5 per cent or so who may have a natural immunity which they can pass on to their descendants. The situation of the human species would then be like that of the monkeys which have a natural immunity to any adverse consequences of SIV.

At present it seems unlikely that the spread of the virus will be prevented by medicine, whether by drugs or vaccines. New drugs certainly offer the promise of longer life for those infected and better life, as well, but there is no reason to expect a curative drug to be developed. Vaccines face the extreme variability of the virus, and some probability that any vaccine would offer only short-term protection. A vaccine which protected only against some HIV strains, and perhaps only for a year or so, would not alter the course of the pandemic.

The estimates of the World Health Organisation, given last week, are that there will be 30 million to 40 million people infected by HIV, and 12 million to 18 million with active Aids, in the year 2000. These estimates have been revised upwards as the disease spreads into Asia. Mathematical models suggest that the disease will not reach a steady state until the middle of the next century. By that time, unless there is an unforeseen medical breakthrough, the disease will have reached its local natural level throughout the world. That level will vary according to a number of factors: economic, cultural, social and perhaps also genetic. The annual death rate worldwide could reach the hundreds of millions.

Aids is very much a social disease; it feeds off poverty, poor health care and overcrowding, not only in the American pattern where homosexuality and drug-taking have influenced the spread, but also in the African and Asian pattern where prostitution and migrant labour provide a rapid transmission system. Aids is a sexually transmitted disease, and the best predictor of the risk of infection for an individual or a community is the number of sexual partners.

We do not have very reliable figures for variations in partner change, but it is clear that there is a wide range among individuals and among nations. High partner change nations are obviously at much greater risk than low ones, and homosexuals are at risk because they have formed a high partner change subculture. The puzzling question is why the human species is not universally a high partner change species. In genetic terms, it is monogamy that has to be explained. Part of the explanation may be the impact of the previous sexually transmitted diseases.

The natural assumption for a dominant male to have the best chance of transmitting his genes would be to fertilize as many females as possible, forcing less dominant males out of the genetic chain of succession. This is a common pattern among the other primates and in many other species. Other primates experience pair-bonding, but do not attempt to limit the dominant male to a single sexual partner.

As it is common in the other primates, this may indeed be the best strategy in favourable climates. Most monkeys live in moist, hot climates with an abundant food supply matched by an abundant supply of infectious diseases. During man's hunter-gatherer period, food would not have been a problem in such regions, but deaths from infection in infancy would have been very high. Maximizing conceptions would, therefore, have paid off as against maximizing food supplies.

Man is, however, the only primate to have successfully colonized extensive areas of desert and frost. There the problems for the hunter-gatherers would have been quite different. Food was always in short supply, but so were infectious diseases. So long as man was continuously on the move, infectious germs would have been relatively rare in the frost zone. The strategy for successful survival depended, therefore, on a much more arduous business of feeding a smaller number of children. In these circumstances, monogamy would have been an efficient strategy for survival as it certainly is against HIV infections.

The variation in the rates of HIV infection is very wide, even inside countries which had already experienced cases of Aids by

1980. If one looks at the Aids map of North America, there are relatively few cases outside the big cities and away from the coasts. The HIV risk in the rural Midwest remains low. In Britain, a pregnant women is eighty times more likely to be HIV positive in south London than in the rural counties. These figures have been shown to be influenced by African women, formerly infected in sub-Saharan Africa, who have their baby in London. In Uganda and Tanzania, 30 per cent of pregnant women have been found to be HIV positive. Those are potentially wipe-out figures.

The monogamous communities of low partner change countries provide a solid reason for believing that Aids will not become a universal disease. There is a level of low partner change below which the HIV infection cannot sustain itself in the community; 70 per cent of British people probably fall below that level. Unfortunately, 30 per cent of the British population is responsible for 70 per cent of partner change, and in that 30 per cent there is a very high partner change sub-group probably amounting to some 5 per cent of the whole. These high change groups will sustain the virus and will inevitably infect some individuals from the low partner change majority.

How far the human species can rebuild a monogamous culture, which has itself never been universal, must be in doubt, particularly as polls show how reluctant people are to change their habits. Yet for the majority of people in this country sexual fidelity is still the norm, and partner change is often motivated by the search for the ideal partner.

Until the late Fifties this norm of monogamy was enforced by the fear of pregnancy; the question is whether in the Nineties or later it will be restored by the fear of Aids.

2 December 1991

AIDS AND THE GRIM
ARITHMETIC OF DEATH

I n recent weeks I have given three lectures on Aids to the Bath Clinical Society, developed out of articles I had written for *The Independent*. My approach has been journalistic. I have tried to report what the best available authorities are saying about the spread of the epidemic. Certain points have emerged clearly.

The first is that there is unlikely to be a quick medical solution to the disease, comparable to the defeat of polio by vaccination, or of syphilis by penicillin. Some anti-HIV vaccines may be developed inside the next ten years; but the virus is highly variable and the vaccines are likely to provide immunity only to some variants. They may require repeated revaccination, and are bound to be quite expensive. Anti-viral drugs may delay the onset of clinical Aids, but are unlikely to destroy the virus itself.

Medicine is now in the same position relative to HIV as it was in the nineteenth century to syphilis. Doctors confront a sexually transmitted and lethal disease with a long latency period, without having a direct way of destroying it.

The second conclusion is that Aids is a social disease, and must be confronted with social as well as medical policies. An Aids map of the world, with its dark clusters in central Africa or on the coasts of the United States, shows that the disease thrives in the conditions of the big city. These conditions include female and male prostitution, travel links, poverty, overcrowding, homosexual communities, intravenous drug abuse, contract labour, inadequate health services and the collapse of family life. Stable families provide the basis for stable sexual relations in adult life.

Big cities also create extensive networks for potential infection. Dr Konotey Ahulu has produced an excellent clinical book, *What is AIDS?*, written for Africans. He compares having sex with a village prositute, which he regards as 'equivalent to having sex with ten to twenty strangers', with having sex with an international prostitute, 'equivalent to having sex with 10,000 to 20,000 strangers'. The figures may be on the low side, but the comparison is valid. The risk of Aids infection is determined both by the number of partners of the individual and by the size of the network from which the partners are taken. Aids is a disease of crowds.

There has been correspondence in *The Times* about the threat of Aids to the heterosexual population. There is no doubt that Professor Michael Adler, of University College, is right and that Dr James Le Fanu's original *Times* article overlooked the fact that, 'vaginal intercourse accounts for 70 per cent of HIV infections in the world'. In Britain 'up to 1985, 2 per cent of all HIV infections were as a result of sexual intercourse between men and women; by 1991 this had increased to 24 per cent.' Of course, many of these cases involved high-risk groups, including bisexuals, drug abusers and people from the worst HIV areas of Africa, but the growth of heterosexually transmitted HIV is established in Britain as in other countries.

Past projections of the number of Aids cases have often proved incorrect; indeed Aids forecasting is even less reliable than Treasury forecasting. The World Health Organisation forecast of forty million HIV cases by the year 2000 is no more than a good collective guess. Nevertheless, Aids is spreading from Africa, where the infection rate in the worst instances has reached a third, to the mass populations of India and China, which come to two billion between them. Worldwide, the present level of HIV infection is probably about 1:500. By the year 2000 that may well have risen to 1:125. That means a projected growth rate of 15 per cent compound, which doubles every five years.

What will happen then? Late Victorian surveys showed that as many as 9 per cent of the population of major European cities had syphilis. In the Thirties, hospitals in the US found admission rates of between 5 and 25 per cent, and prisons recorded rates of 15 to 35 per cent. That was the prevalence of an earlier sexually transmitted disease. Will HIV, worldwide, move up to the 5 or 10 per cent level by 2010 or 2020, or can it be halted at around the 1 per cent level it is expected to reach by the year 2000? These are, of course, percentages of the total world population, and must be increased to approximate to infection rates for the sexually active group.

The medical weapons are not very strong. The advocacy of condoms is at best a second line of defence. Few people use them invariably, particularly in marriage; there can be considerable resistance to them; in poor countries they are very expensive relative to local wage rates. In addition, advertisements advocating condoms may be taken as giving the misleading reassurance that promiscuity can be made safe.

Equally, people are not likely to change their conduct because of preachers or posters advocating marital fidelity. Cultural patterns are changed by deep cultural forces, if at all. Fifty years after the introduction to Europe of syphilis in the 1490s, there came the wave of puritanism of the 1540s, which was a dominant social influence that lasted for a hundred years.

The major world religions, and traditions, with the possible exception of Hinduism, have sexual codes that seem designed to protect children in the family, and incidentally to prevent sexually transmitted diseases. A fully observant Christian, Jew, Muslim, Confucian or Buddhist would be at little risk from HIV; Islamic countries in North Africa have very low rates of infection compared with central Africa. Religions have more influence in the poor countries where HIV is the greatest threat; religious rules may be more important than anything that governments or advertisements can achieve.

Governments do, however, have a social responsibility. Obviously they should provide the best health service their countries can afford. More generally, social failures, such as the catastrophes of the American inner cities, will also prove to be focuses of disease. An underclass heavily infected with HIV will transmit that infection to the rest of society.

In the Sixties, the wealthier countries adopted a new attitude towards sex. The old doctrines of restraint before marriage and fidelity in marriage were replaced by a post-Freudian belief that promiscuous infertile sex was necessary for the full enjoyment of life. Those attitudes will not be reversed by arguments or by people saying that the old standards were better. If a shift of attitudes does occur, it will be because the public generally has become aware of the danger of changing partners.

In the next century the best measure of the lifetime risk of dying of Aids will be the individual's lifetime number of sexual partners. There will be virtually no risk for those who have only one partner, or none. Yet even at what might be regarded as a normal number of partners, the risk will become significant.

The WHO forecast for the year 2000 implies that about 1:80 of the sexually active will be infected worldwide. The rate will be far higher in the worst-hit countries. Even on these figures, someone with five lifetime partners would run a 1:16 risk of having an infected partner. By 2010 that could have risen to a risk of 1:4.

A promiscuous person, with say, ten partners a year, could by 2010 have a 1:2 chance of sleeping with an infected partner each year and therefore would be more likely than not to be infected sooner or later. The growth of the risk of infection, with few partners or many, is the grim arithmetic which may change sexual attitudes in the twenty-first century if the disease follows the WHO projection.

17 February 1992

PART SIX

THE PAST: PLEASURES AND INSIGHTS

I was born on 14 July 1928. My mother had been a classical actress in the United States, and had acted with players such as Margaret Anglen, Sarah Bernhardt, Alfred Lunt and Lynn Fontane in Greek tragedy, in Shakespeare and in modern dramatists such as Somerset Maugham. My father was a Somerset landowner with an estate of about 1,000 acres and a country house, Cholwell, built by his grandfather in the early 1850s. The Mogg family, which became Rees-Mogg at the beginning of the nineteenth century, had lived in Somerset since the reign of Henry III and can trace their ancestry at least to the reign of Henry VIII.

Both my parents had been born in the reign of Queen Victoria, my father in 1889 – the same year as Adolf Hitler – in the village of Hinton Blewitt, where I now live, and my mother in the New York village of Mamaroneck, on Long Island Sound, in 1892. They met when my mother came to England to join the Old Vic company for the autumn season of 1920, and they married on 11 November 1920, the second Armistice Day, which was my father's thirty-first birthday. It also happened to be the day when Roy Jenkins, now the Chancellor of Oxford, was born.

My Rees-Mogg family circle went further back into the nineteenth century and indeed seemed almost to touch the eighteenth. Two great-aunts and a great-uncle lived in St James's

Square in Bath and had a house they had built for the summer in the same village as Cholwell. My grandmother lived in comfortable rooms in Kensington, but she, with an interest in theosophy and the poetry of W. B. Yeats, was a figure of the early twentieth century, where the Miss Rees-Moggs had stayed firmly in the nineteenth. They talked of the railway line from Paddington to Bristol – Brunel's line – as a new event, and remembered the people of their parents' generation discussing the stage coaches from Bath to London.

The life I led as a child was indeed little changed, except for the presence of motor cars, from the nineteenth or even the eighteenth century. We were the only landowners in our village, the summit of a little local hierarchy, which included the Rector of Temple Cloud, Mr Westhead, and the local doctor, Dr Vaughan. Apart from one or two clerical jobs in the local government office, and jobs in the new garage, the work in the village was provided by farming, the roads, or the North Somerset Coalfield, which my ancestors had developed. By the 1930s we were no longer in coal, apart from some slender royalties, but we had been coal developers from 1635 to about 1900.

At Cholwell we had a small staff, reduced by the Depression, of a housemaid, a parlourmaid and a cook. I shared my middle sister's governess. We were entertained as children by the two or three gardeners – my father also ran a small apple and fruit orchard. We were not a very rich family – my grandfather's business in America had gone under in the panic of 1920, and I suppose my father's net income in the early 1930s was about £1,500, well below the supertax level. But we were living the familiar life of a landed family in a traditional manner. My father did not have any interest in horses or field sports, so that part of it had dropped away.

In this setting the past was always very close. My mother was drawn to it by the tradition of England and by her own knowledge of Shakespeare. Her family – unusually for an Irish-American family – were anglophile. Although they were Roman Catholic, they came, as the name Warren suggests, from English settlers in Ireland who were ultimately of Norman descent.

My birthday also gave me a certain feeling for history. In 1928, or in the early 1930s which I can first remember, the French Revolution did not seem all that far away, any more than the 1850s do now. We were then no further from Robespierre and the execution of Louis XVI than we now are from Florence Nightingale or Charles Darwin, almost modern figures. I was flattered to think that my birthday was also a holiday in France, but I knew from an early age that I had no sympathy with the French Revolution.

As a child I saw the Fall of the Bastille as bringing to an end an age of gold. There are two dates in European history which seem to rule off a particular period of civilization, 1789 and 1914. It was the earlier date which I most regretted. When I started to read English literature it was the eighteenth century which captivated me, Gray's 'Elegy', Boswell's *Life of Johnson*, Johnson's *Lives of the Poets*, Walpole's *Letters*, Gibbon's *Decline and Fall of the Roman Empire*. Later came the poetry of Alexander Pope.

With these authors I have enjoyed a lifelong friendship which has framed my mind. Gray's 'Elegy', with its gentle and urbane melancholy, consoled me in the depressions of adolescence, Boswell's *Johnson* gave me, as it gave Boswell, a second father figure. I have never fully adopted the moral principles of Samuel Johnson, but his morality, based on his robust realism, helped to form my character. Walpole developed in me a taste for antiquities, that alliance between the collector and the historian, and Gibbon started a lifelong interest in historicism and the causes of national decline.

My passion for the eighteenth century, and it was nothing less, came from the feeling that it was a land of lost delight, that the twentieth century was a decadence, relieved only partly by the advance of science. As a child I hated the industrial revolution for having replaced so much beauty with so much ugliness, with an ugliness of physical things but also with an ugliness of society. My only full-blown psychic experience, which lasted perhaps for seconds, took me back in a retrospection of an eighteenth-century Somerset funeral. I do not believe that I had lived in the eighteenth century, but I am sure that I have always had some access to a memory which covers the years 1720 to 1780, and that an important part of my nature has been shaped by that elusive but powerful influence. I have even always felt a strong impulsion to live in eighteenth-century houses and in eighteenth-century streets.

I do not know how far other people feel this pull towards a particular period of history. I know that many do not, but I suspect that some do. It is both limiting and strengthening. It certainly limits one's taste. I enjoy composers down to the death of Haydn, but have little feeling for nineteenth- let alone twentieth-century music. I have no feeling for the modern school in music, in painting, in literature, and rather envy people for whom mid-period Picasso has meaning as well as a sort of despairing energy.

On the other hand I have a more direct access to my heroes. In my dining room in Somerset, a panelled room constructed in 1990, there hang four portraits, one of John Locke, from about 1670, one a beautiful and tender Kneller of Alexander Pope when he first came to London at the age of sixteen, one a studio copy of Sir Joshua Reynolds' last self-portrait, given by him to William Mason, his friend and executor, and the fourth Brompton's sketch from the life after which he painted his formal portraits of William Pitt, the great Earl of Chatham.

Of these, Alexander Pope has been my closest eighteenth-century friend and mentor. Samuel Johnson, as is clear in the *Lives of the Poets*, admired Pope as a poet, but did not really approve of him as a man. He was unable, as a moralist for whom truth was the central value, to appreciate the stratagems which Pope sometimes delighted in. He was offended by the intensity of Pope's satire. Yet he understood Pope's greatness as a poet.

For me Pope has, quite simply, been a friend, someone I love and admire, someone from whom I have learned much of what I know. I neither believe Pope to have been perfect, nor think he ought to have been. He is not Christ. Yet for anyone whose trade has been to write English, he is the supreme Professor, and for anyone who cares for human beings he combines affection with suffering, the two most endearing qualities.

I write, of course, in a subdued copy of an eighteenth-century style, and it has served me well in twentieth-century journalism. I have read more eighteenth- than twentieth-century literature. Eighteenth-century English prose owes its highest qualities to the poetry of Pope. They are the condensation of energy, the balance of antitheses, the lucidity of every word and the harmony of the sound. These are such great virtues in a prose style, and are so crystallized in the poetry of Pope, that anyone who wishes to write English which is both forceful and harmonious should keep Pope's works always on his bedside table.

I am not as close to Joshua Reynolds as to Pope, and have not been so much influenced by him. Yet he represents the eighteenth-century classical belief in visual order, and as a portrait painter he is the great psychologist of the male portrait. I agree with Prince Charles that the loss of visual harmony has changed society. It is harder to lead a good life in an ugly house. I also admire the calm success that Joshua Reynolds made of his own life, a great portrait painter, but a classical artist and a man of classical life.

John Locke is the political philosopher from whom I have learned most. I believe that liberty is the chief value of human society, after order itself. I believe that liberty includes the right to own property. I do not believe in the worship of the state, either in the form of a King, a Dictator or a Republic. I believe in the variability of human nature and human motivations. 'The mind has a different relish, as well as the palate; and you will as fruitlessly endeavour to delight all men with riches or glory (which yet some men place their happiness in) as you would satisfy all men's hunger with cheese or lobsters; which though very agreeable and delicious fare to some are to others extremely nauseous and offensive . . . Men may choose different things, and yet all choose right.' This passage from the chapter 'of Power' which Locke added to the second edition of *An Essay Concerning Human Understanding* is a summary of my own political belief. The good society allows liberty and variety to its members. It encourages – another Lockeian phrase – 'the pursuit of happiness'.

Locke is too dry for some people, but not for me. He is also a Somerset man, with whom I have Somerset links. The Strachey family were his close friends; he used to stay at Sutton Court – in the 1930s and 1940s Lord Strachey was Chairman of the local bench on which my father sat. His father was land agent to the Pophams at Hunstrete; my ancestor at the same time, Richard

Mogg, was land agent to the Duchy of Cornwall at Farrington Gurney. He was baptized on 29 August 1632 by Samuel Crook, the Rector of Wrington. Veronica Crook, who has been our nanny for more than twenty-five years, is descended from Samuel Crook and was born in Wrington. Locke's mother was a Keene and the Moggs had also intermarried with the Keenes. I feel the closeness of a neighbour to John Locke.

We have also educated our children on Locke's principles. He writes that 'It will perhaps be wondered that I mention reasoning with children: and yet I cannot but think that the true way of dealing with them. They understand it as early as they do language; and, if I mis-observe not, they love to be treated as rational creatures sooner than is imagined.' I believe, as he did, that the aim of education is to produce rational, self-controlled adults, and that the means must be rational and respectful to children if they are to serve that end.

Finally there is the great Earl of Chatham. He is the most extraordinary Prime Minister we have had. Perhaps not the greatest, for I think his son, Pitt the Younger, was even greater than he, but unique in terms of personal force, immediate achievement and creative intensity. He made the British Empire, India, North America, the year of victories in 1759. He was probably the greatest orator in the history of Parliament – and I have heard Winston Churchill speak in the House of Commons.

His speech in 1775 to the House of Lords, near the end of his life, is the strongest example of his style. 'As to conquest, my Lords, I repeat, it is impossible – you may swell every expense, and every effort, still more extravagantly; pile and accumulate every assistance you can buy or borrow; traffic and barter with every little pitiful German prince, that sells his subjects to the shambles of a foreign prince; your efforts are for ever vain and impotent – doubly so from this mercenary aid on which you rely; for it irritates, to an incurable resentment, the minds of your enemies – to overrun them with the mercenary sons of rapine and plunder; devoting them and their possessions to the rapacity of hireling cruelty! If I were an American, as I am an Englishman, while a foreign troop was landed in my country, I never would lay down my arms – never – never – never.'

Three of the four eighteenth-century heroes illustrate strongly, and the fourth more distantly, a psychological quality that is not usually associated with that century, the concentration of energy. In Pope there is an astonishing concentration of meaning into each line, so that it explodes with meaning as one reads it. Locke, with his range and intensity of ideas, concentrates meaning in his philosophy. Chatham, of all British statesmen, concentrated the power of worldwide action in his period of government, and emotional authority – on the side of liberty – in his speeches. Even Reynolds provides the classical framework in which energy can be concentrated, the firebox for the fire.

History has therefore been for me a resource for psychological development. Just as I believe that prayer, and particularly meditation, can help one to develop the internal life of faith, so I believe that an understanding of historic figures, and particularly those with whom one can sympathize and form friendships, can help to form the energies of the mind. In this process, any personal closeness, the strange links of locality or kinship, can be helpful. I recently discovered that my son-in-law, David Craigie, and therefore my granddaughter, Maud, was descended from Sir Robert Walpole through his favourite daughter Maria, who was also Horace Walpole's favourite sister. That has given me a different and more personal feeling for the Walpoles. Similarly my own descent, on my mother's side, from John Winthrop, the first Governor of Massachusetts, has given me a heightened interest of early American history. But, apart from closeness, we can choose our role models.

It is all very immediate to me. I cannot go back to the eighteenth century, a hundred and fifty years before I was born. But then I cannot go back to the 1980s, fifty years after I was born. I can remember hearing Ronald Reagan speaking in Chicago in 1980 as though it were yesterday, but I cannot recapture the event and make it happen again. History, even ancient history, seems very close and very much alive. And the historic figures who died two hundred or two thousand years before our time can just as much act as our guides and friends as those who are still alive. It is their energy which makes them live.

A PERSONAL VIEW OF THE 1956 SUEZ CRISIS

'My understanding is that the paratroops will go in at dawn tomorrow.' I was sitting in the little room to the right of the front door of the old No 10 Downing Street, a much better house than the refurbished one. The date was 30 October, 1956. My informant, whose office we were in, was Robert Allan, Anthony Eden's PPS.

He had called me in to tell me that the Government had just sent an ultimatum to President Nasser, calling on both sides to stop 'all warlike action' following Israel's invasion of Sinai, an ultimatum certain to be rejected.

I have never been told a more important military secret, or a less accurate one. As everyone knows, the paratroops did not go in; it took British troops longer to reach Egypt from Malta in 1956 than it had taken Nelson before the Battle of the Nile. By the time the invasion started, the diplomatic and political battle of Suez had already been lost.

Robert Allan is long since dead. I cannot therefore ask him whether his understanding about the paratroops had been given him, as I then assumed, by Eden himself, to whom Allan was the most loyal and enthusiastic of supporters. If so, the Suez operation must originally have been planned in an even more dramatic and potentially a far more effective way.

If, in forty-eight hours from the ultimatum, the Suez Canal

could have been seized from the air, I do not believe that the Americans would have seen the matter in at all the same light. Eisenhower might well still have been offended, but his irritation would have been softened by our victory. Suez might still have proved a strategic blunder, but it would have been a tactical success.

As I walked up Downing Street, I remember meeting Ted Heath, then Eden's Chief Whip. With his usual urbanity he asked me 'What are you doing here?' It was a good question. I was there because I had become a junior member of Eden's speech-writing team which Robert Allan organized for him. I had recently fought a by-election at Chester-le-Street, the only by-election between Nasser's nationalization of the Suez Canal and Eden's ultimatum.

I had told the Durham miners through a wailing electrical speaking trumpet, mounted on the roof of an old blue van, that they must not appease Colonel Nasser. They had no more wish than I did to appease Nasser, for whom they seemed to feel little respect, but they had even less wish to vote Conservative; I was defeated by a majority, normal in that seat, of over 22,000.

Robert Allan arranged that I should come back the following morning to join a speech-writing session. So for each of the first three days of Suez I spent a morning hour in the upstairs flat while three or four of us helped Anthony Eden prepare his speeches for the House of Commons.

There have been many stories about Eden's exhaustion and irritability. I saw no sign of it. On the contrary at those meetings he always behaved with complete calm and good humour. He did show a rather boyish spirit, a sort of elated calm in crisis. That seemed natural. It is not every day of the week you invade Egypt, even if your name is Anthony.

Eden liked to do his first work of the day in bed. By the time we arrived at 9 o'clock, he had breakfasted, read the papers, seen his Private Secretary and prepared his mind for the day. I remember that he wore blue pyjamas and that he had two telephones by the bedside, one with a scrambler that he used for diplomatic calls.

On that telephone he spoke about the UN to M. Mollet the

French Prime Minister: 'Ah, *mon cher ami*,' he opened in clear schoolboy French. He told Selwyn Lloyd not to go personally to the UN because he felt that Selwyn and he should stick together while the crisis was at its height. It was a strangely comradely enterprise.

The arguments on which we worked were simple, and I am sure that they represented Eden's real thinking. The first was that Nasser was a dictator determined to expand his power, whose word could not be relied on. He should be stopped as Hitler could have been stopped in 1936, at the time of the Rhineland. Hitler was an analogy never far from the mind of that generation, as vivid to Hugh Gaitskell as to Eden.

The second argument concerned Britain's position in the Middle East. If Nasser got away with seizing the canal, Britain's allies would be doomed. The old kings would be replaced by Nasserite dictators. Britain's one remaining claim to major international status, our influence over Middle East oil, would disappear, and our post-war decline would be taken a radical step further.

The third argument, for which I had to supply a few statistics and a few phrases, was the danger of having our oil supplies pass through a canal under Nasser's unfettered control. The 'free flow of oil' argument was my special area because I was the economic member of the speech-writing team.

Of the three arguments, the Hitler analogy has not stood up well. Nasser was not a Hitler, we learned to live with him, and his successors have given Egypt better leadership than he did. The fall of the kings was not as universal as Eden thought it would be, but in Iraq and Libya they did fall and were replaced by nationalist military dictators, who have proved as bad and hostile as Eden feared. Britain's position in the Middle East was largely destroyed, though it was almost certainly already impossible to maintain. Nasser did not use the canal to interrupt oil supplies – supertankers changed the supply system – but the oil monopoly that Eden feared later occurred in the form of OPEC, with great damage to world trade.

It seems to me that Eden's policy was a serious but impractical attempt to answer the insoluble questions posed by Britain's decline, Arab nationalism and the economics of oil.

He risked too much, and by accepting the advice not to invade from the air, avoided the one risk which might have brought success.

After three days, *The Financial Times*, for whom I worked, rightly decided that there was a conflict between my roles as a politician and as a journalist. Brendan Bracken rang Eden.

At the last of our bedside meetings Eden thanked me with his usual friendliness and courtesy. I never saw him again as Prime Minister. I remember him with affection as a patriotic and honourable man.

28 October 1986

THE MARCH OF HISTORY
THAT HAS LEFT
SOCIALISM BEHIND

In the 1980s a worldwide retreat from socialism has been started. It is one of the greatest political changes of modern history. There is now hardly one major country in which it is not happening.

The great state apparatus, which took more than a century to build, is being reconstructed and reduced in almost all the advanced nations. Not because social idealism has been abandoned, but because people can no longer believe that state bureaucratic power is an effective agency for social ideals, or for economic growth.

The contraction of state power has happened before in human history. In the British revolution of the 1640s, through the bloodless revolution of 1688, the American Declaration of Independence in 1776 and even during the early stages of the French Revolution, men fought to reduce the power of the state.

They chose to give liberty to the individual through constitutional systems of free markets and invested capital. The prophets of that great movement were the English philosopher, John Locke, and the Scottish economist, Adam Smith.

Yet between 1848, the date of the Communist manifesto, and the early 1950s, the tide of history ran the other way. The two world wars imposed war socialism on the participants; primitive industrial development created a mass working movement which made a democratic demand for the extension of state power and brought socialist parties to government in almost every European country. In the United States, Roosevelt's New Deal created an American socialism. The prophet of this movement was Karl Marx. As a result, the world of the early 1950s was divided into three groups of powers: the Communist countries with completely socialized systems; the democratic powers, with systems of state control, taxation and management which dominated their economics; and the developing countries which widely believed that socialism was the natural model for development.

In the mid-1980s most of this socialized world structure does indeed still remain, together with a dangerous degree of socialist consciousness. The work of demolition has been started, but has yet to be carried beyond the first stage. The Communist countries are still Communist, the democracies still allow the state to control nearly half the national income, many of the developing countries still talk socialism and only too often practise tyranny.

Yet the direction of the modern movement is unmistakable and its energy is very powerful. In the two great Communist countries, the economic failure of the socialist system has become apparent even to their rulers. China has moved towards the Japanese model of development, no longer wishing to be condemned to perpetual poverty by state Communism.

The Soviet Union, while repeating the rhetoric of Marxism-Leninism, is reluctantly allowing the economic efficiency of the market a slightly larger place. The great Stalinist dam, which has for so long held back the natural prosperity of a great nation, is beginning to leak.

Mr Gorbachev, simply because he is younger, more intelligent and better educated than the survivors of the Brezhnev hierarchy, has put himself cautiously on the side of reform. No doubt he wants reform to happen slowly, but he is objectively on the side of market capitalism, however much he may subjectively remain faithful to socialism. In the advanced democratic countries the spread of tax reform and privatization has been much more rapid than anyone would have believed possible in 1980.

The old socialist bulwarks have been torn down or are seen simply to be mouldering away, so that even those who favour them in theory recognize the need for anti-bureaucratic reform in practice. The British National Health Service is the largest state employer in Europe after the Red Army; we all devoutly hope that the Red Army enjoys the same standard of efficiency as the NHS.

Why has this process been happening? It owes something to the philosophers of liberty; to those in Britain and the United States who have preached the virtues of market capitalism when such policies were still darkly unfashionable; to Professor Hayek, and politicians such as Mrs Thatcher who were the children of his ideas. It is because she had the courage to align herself with the developing force of her time, that Mrs Thatcher has won exceptional political power. Yet ideas can only conquer where events have prepared the way. The first cause has been the manifest economic success of market capitalism, above all in Japan, compared with the failure of the socialist economies in world competition. As has been said of the Soviet Union, a vastly larger country whose total national product has fallen well behind the Japanese: 'I have seen the future and it does not work.'

The second cause has been the social broadening of prosperity, the worldwide creation of an expanding middle class. Even in Britain the postwar rise in real earnings has been rapid and consistent. When 75 per cent are poor they vote for politicians who promise to use the power of the state to help them. When 75 per cent are affluent, they realize that it is their taxes which pay the costs of state power.

This has accelerated under the impact of the electronic revolution. With computers and robotics, every skilled worker has at his or her fingertips an economic power which belonged, as recently as the 1970s, to a whole regiment of people. With that electronic power there is the capacity for all the skilled to earn a standard of living hitherto reserved for a small and privileged class. Not surprisingly free markets have proved far and away the most efficient medium for advancing the electronic revolution. If the skilled workers of Britain – a relatively poor industrial country – have cars and holidays and houses which were the privilege of their bosses in 1960, they are likely to want the right to enjoy their property. That is what their bosses always voted for. The third cause is that market capitalism has not tended to create greater inequalities, but a more equal opportunity of affluence.

The development of mass affluence has only occurred in capitalist countries. Socialism, where the standard of living depends almost entirely on access to political power, has, in contrast, perpetuated great inequalities.

Of course, this does not solve the problem of those who are the losers by economic change, or who remain poor in a rich society; indeed the very shrinking of that constituency reduces its political power.

But market capitalism has created the wealth to give prosperity to hundreds of millions who would never otherwise have enjoyed it. The thousands of millions who hope to create similar prosperity for themselves make up the irresistible army which is now marching away from Moscow, and away from Marx.

30 December 1986

A MAN BORN BEFORE HIS TIME

Each generation gets the heroes it deserves, but the heroes do not always get their deserts. We may think now that we have silly heroes – from brattish tennis players to ambiguous pop stars. In another age they would certainly have been rewarded differently, but society might have shown equal skill in raising them up as idols, exploiting their weaknesses, and then destroying them.

On Wednesday 27 March, 1754, between seven and eight o'clock at night, Ambrose Dawson, a successful society physician, was halted in his chariot in a traffic jam outside Lord Bath's house in Piccadilly. A cloaked figure on horseback rapped on his carriage door and called to him, 'Let down your glass'. When he did so, he saw a man with a pistol in his hand, who asked him courteously for his money and his watch, addressing him in the Johnsonian style as 'Sir'. Dr Dawson handed over two guineas and a gold watch with a gold seal. The man then rode off.

On Wednesday 5 June, of the same year, John Parry, having been convicted at the Old Bailey of this highway robbery, was hanged at Tyburn. Thus ended the brief career of one of the few eighteenth-century highwaymen to approximate to the romantic legend of the gentleman of the road. Though he had committed other crimes, he seems to have been a highwayman for only a week.

304

I spent last weekend cataloguing the account of his life that Parry gave to the Ordinary of Newgate who, as prison chaplain, prepared him for his death. Parry was born at Pontypool in 1726, the son of a prosperous Welsh innkeeper. He was given a good education, rather above that expected in his chosen occupation as a footman. He was an attractive boy, and his parents perhaps spoiled him.

He became a fine looking young man, and was in service with the best families. His first master lived in Berkeley Square. Parry learned to play fives at Higgins's Fives Court, near Leicester Square. He next won promotion to the office of Captain's Clerk on board the Man of War, *Eagle*, a post which often led to a good professional career in the Royal Navy. He walked the quarter deck and himself believed 'he might have been preferred in time'.

Unfortunately he did not enjoy life at sea, and returned to London. After moving from job to job, he became servant to a noble lady in 1750. He did the job well, 'being looked on as a handy fellow, and of good appearance, he was frequently borrowed to wait at table by nobles of the Lady's acquaintance'.

Parry carried out financial business for his mistress, who trusted him to pay her bills and to handle large sums. He was indeed a valued confidential servant. In July 1753 he decamped to France with £1,100, perhaps the modern equivalent of £50,000 or so. In Paris he passed for a Welsh gentleman, under the name of Lewis. 'He cut a great figure at the tennis court there, and beat the best players in Paris; and 'tis thought he was the best player at fives and tennis in Europe. He made the most of himself, and appeared the great man at all public places throughout the whole City of Paris.'

He spent much of the money buying fashionable clothes from an Irish tailor, who then betrayed him to the authorities. He still had £400 left, which was taken off him, but the French would not extradite him; after nineteen weeks in jail, they gave him twenty-four hours to leave Paris. He went to Italy, perhaps ran into some trouble over a woman in Leghorn, and decided to return to England. While in Italy he pretended that he had fled from England on account of a duel.

Parry arrived back in England on Sunday 24 March, 1754, and

took rooms at the Vine in Vauxhall; he slept all day Monday; he robbed a young lady of her watch on Tuesday night, in Mayfair, just by the garden wall of Lord Chesterfield, of the letters; he bought a brace of pistols in the Strand on Wednesday, and that evening he robbed Mr Nisbet of his watch and seven guineas in Berkeley Square, following which, without leaving the square, he stopped Lord Carisforth's coach and robbed him and Captain Proby of about nine pounds. He then rode down to Piccadilly and had what was to prove his fatal encounter with Dr Dawson. Three highway robberies in Mayfair within a couple of hours.

He pawned the watches in St James's and spent the night with a woman at Leicester Square bagnio. On Thursday he committed no robbery. On Friday he robbed a young lady of her watch in Brook Street, which he pawned in Jermyn Street; he spent that night with 'a favourite woman of his' whom he met at the Bedford Arms Tavern in Covent Garden. Again they went to Leicester Square bagnio. On Saturday he committed a more suburban robbery near Putney Bridge, returned to Mayfair and was challenged by four thief takers, again in Brook Street. He tried to ride off, but they had a bitch with them who seized Parry's horse by the nose. The thief takers brought him 'before Henry Fielding Esq; he confessed the whole affair'. The end had come, and not a bad climax, to confess to the author of Tom Jones, who was also a picaresque hero with a Welsh name.

What an eighteenth-century tale it is, yet what a twentieth-century character John Parry seems to have been. Sexually attractive, probably to men as well as women, a role player, a very gifted athlete, ambitious but idle, the somewhat petted young Welshman keen to make his way in the world, reckless with money, yet able to earn trust, fashionable in dress and manner, Parry had a character we are all familiar with.

In the twentieth century such a career would lead perhaps to fame in sport, possibly even to a Wimbledon championship, more likely to fame in films and television; the gentleman highwayman had all the qualities needed for the celebrity of an electronic age. He would have had several favourite wives, a nose blistered by cocaine, a Swiss bank account and an agent who lived in Beverly Hills. In the eighteenth century they hanged him on Tyburn tree. What a tragedy it is for a great man to be born out of his time.

28 April 1987

LANDMARKS IN A LIFE
WHICH HAS SEEN THE
SHADOW OF WAR LIFTED

On my tenth birthday, 14 July 1938, I was given an ice-cream cake with a cricket bat and ball on top; it was big enough to be shared with the thirty boys in my house at school. Four months before, Hitler had invaded Austria, with the enthusiastic consent of most of the Austrian people. Two months after my birthday, Neville Chamberlain flew to Munich.

I remember going to Mass at Midsomer Norton in Somerset the Sunday after Munich. The church, then as now, was served by monks from Downside. At that time, the parish priest was Father Turnbull, a member of the Glamorgan cricketing family, who bore a striking resemblance to God the Father as perceived by William Blake. We said a prayer of thanksgiving for the preservation of peace. As a ten-year-old, I felt a certain let-down; the idea of going to war was exciting, if alarming. Peace seemed by contrast both an anti-climax and insecure.

By my twentieth birthday in 1948, the Second World War had been fought and won, the first atom bombs had been dropped on Japan, the Jewish population of Europe had been destroyed, and the Cold War had begun. I was about to be demobilized from the Royal Air Force after two years of national service. We had an early television set in the sergeant's mess, and I remember watching Lindsay Hassett, the Australian Test cricketer, score a century through a hailstorm of electronic flickering. My demobilization was nearly delayed by the emergency caused by the Berlin airlift. Czechoslovakia had already been seized by Stalin. In Britain, after the devaluation and fuel crisis of 1947, the long post-war economic decline had begun. The British Empire was already being dismantled, but the communist empire was growing, with Mao victorious in China.

By my thirtieth birthday in 1958, I was writing a leader a day for *The Financial Times*. The Korean War had come and gone. The Suez crisis had come and gone. I had fought a by-election in Chester-le-Street in 1956 and been defeated by the routine 20,000 votes. I was still trying to find a good Conservative seat and had in the past year been the runner-up for the Conservative nomination in Chichester, the Isle of Wight and the Hallam division of Sheffield, which I missed by a single, perhaps providential, vote on the executive committee. It was the year I met my wife – though we did not marry for another four years – at a Conservative rally at the Alexandra Palace.

Certainly in 1958 the world looked a better place than it had ten, let alone twenty years before. In 1948 we had to assume that the Third World War was a probability, not just in our lifetime, but inside a few years. When I was twenty, I thought it was an even-money bet that none of my generation would live to see thirty, so I decided to conduct my life on the basis that I would live to be eighty. By 1958, the world seemed to be returning to sanity. But Britain's decline went on. Investment was low; productivity was low; Suez had demonstrated our loss of international power; the first European opportunity had been missed; other nations were overtaking us.

I was forty in July 1968. My own life had many joys in it. I had married in 1962 and we had three children. We lived in one of the most beautiful large houses in Somerset. I had been editor of *The Times* for eighteen months, and the circulation had increased by about 50 per cent. Of course, it was widely said that *The Times* was not what it had been. At the weekends, we travelled down to Bath on the Pullman, often with Arnold Weinstock who taught our second daughter arithmetic over the tea cakes by pretending to get elementary sums wrong so that she could triumphantly correct him.

The world of 1968 was one of riots: riots in Paris; student riots at Berkeley; riots at Chicago during the Democratic convention. Young Winston Churchill, who did some very courageous work for *The Times* covering the war in Biafra, was reporting the Chicago convention. 'Who are you?' said one of Mayor Richard Daley's cops. 'Winston Churchill.' Wham! Down came the truncheon as a rebuke for insolence. The Vietnam War was at its height, unsolved, insoluble, with a manic momentum. That was also the year Robert Kennedy was killed. I remember hearing the news of the shooting and walking along Blackfriars embankment praying for his survival.

In Britain there had been another devaluation. The hopes originally raised by Harold Wilson had all turned to disillusionment. *The Times* leaders were angry and scornful at what we saw as the cowardly and foolish failures of government.

In 1978, at my fiftieth birthday, my own life had more difficulty in it. The happiness was that we had a further child, and another child due to be born in 1979. But 1978 was the year my mother died; it was also the year we had to sell Ston Easton, our home, the victim of high interest rates and inflation. *The Times* was more of a responsibility than a joy. We had lost Roy Thomson, a proprietor of unending courage, supportiveness and truth. The trade unions would neither let us introduce computers nor even produce the paper regularly. By the end of the year, *The Times* was shut; a bitter struggle, with an inadequate strategy, which led to the sale of the paper. Britain's own decline was accelerated by the world inflation of the 1970s.

My sixtieth birthday I celebrated last week. My own life at present is extraordinarily fortunate, and I enjoy what I do – including writing for *The Independent* – more than I can remember at any earlier time. In the early 1980s, I bought – with my redundancy money from Thomsons – an antiquarian bookshop, Pickering & Chatto, which is now third only to Quaritch and Maggs in the London market. The pleasures of trade are very intense. My children are grown up, save for the youngest, and have educated me, as she continues to do.

It would therefore be natural for me to feel optimistic about the world, since we all see its business in unduly personal terms.

But the world is a much better place than it was on any of my previous decadal birthdays. There is little threat of world war. Since 1979, Britain has recovered confidence both politically and economically – that long night which darkened most of my adult life is over.

There are still great evils and dangers in the world, but also great blessings – huge nations, such as China and India, are raising the living standards not just of millions, but of billions of people, to a new and more tolerable level. My childhood and youth were lived in a period of war, threat of war and mass murder; my middle age in a period when my own country was in steep decline. We have passed out of the generation of war; we have passed out of the generation of decline; Britain has survived both; 1988 is a great year to reach sixty.

19 July 1988

A DIFFERENT DYNAMIC IN
FEMALE LEADERSHIP

In the mid-1970s I went to Oxford University to speak to the Labour Club. Among my hosts at dinner was Miss Benazir Bhutto, then aspiring to become president of the Oxford Union. Her father – one of the dozen or more people I have met who were later murdered for political reasons – was still prime minister of Pakistan. I was extremely impressed by Miss Bhutto's intelligence, self-possession and sense of destiny. Not to mention her beauty.

She has now joined the group of women political leaders who have succeeded the old men as the statesmen of authority in the world. The post-1945 generation – Churchill, Adenauer, de Gaulle, Eisenhower, Ben-Gurion, Nehru – were leaders who had created their authority by their conduct in the Second World War or in the struggle for national independence. They dominated the generation of the post-war settlement, down almost to the end of the 1960s.

In the 1970s and 1980s, nations facing great challenges have tended to turn to women leaders – Golda Meir, Margaret Thatcher, Indira Gandhi, Corazon Aquino – and now Benazir Bhutto. These women have been outstanding among the world leaders of their time: indeed, if Mr Gorbachev had not been a man, one might think women alone were capable of radical leadership. They are a formidable group; they are a radical group; and their leadership has revived the confidence of old nations.

Even Mr Gorbachev is not as authoritarian a figure as women leaders. The small nations of the Soviet Union are making demands on him they would not have dared to make to his predecessors; when similar demands have been made by Scotsmen, Arabs or Sikhs, they have found little sympathy from Mrs Thatcher, Mrs Meir or Mrs Gandhi. Of course, the Soviet Union is in an entirely illegal occupation of Latvia, Lithuania and Estonia – an occupation which was the first fruit of the unspeakable Nazi/ Soviet pact of 1939.

In the 1980s the shadow has fallen on the male statesmen. The modern man in office is a remarkably dull person; they might most of them have been recruited at random by the postal service. Compare and contrast Benazir Bhutto with Chancellor Kohl. Why have women become so much more exciting and so much more effective as world leaders?

The record of the few women in past history who achieved political power was already impressive. There were two Russian tsars called 'The Great', they were Catherine and Peter. No English king since the death of Edward III should be put quite in the first class – the average is mediocre. The queens are another matter. Elizabeth I was the greatest of our monarchs since the Conqueror himself, and Victoria was the greatest monarch of her line. Our present queen is the best monarch of our century. The historic record is that fewer women than men have attained political power, but their performance averages out higher.

One explanation is that women find it harder to obtain power and therefore the few who do attain power are more exceptional than men. Yet that hardly applies in hereditary monarchies, where women succeed to the throne merely because of the absence of male heirs.

In British politics the timing of political careers differs between the sexes. A woman finds it harder to obtain a seat in Parliament. Having done so, it is easier for her to obtain office, simply because many of her women competitors have been eliminated at an earlier stage. In Margaret Thatcher's career, winning the

Conservative nomination at Finchley was really difficult – and crucial.

She did not have as much difficulty in getting into the Cabinet as her male contemporaries. The Prime Minister, Edward Heath, neither liked nor admired her. If she had been a man, he would probably have left her on the back benches, but he felt that his Cabinet ought to have a woman in it; he paid dearly for his liberal instincts.

Indeed, it could be argued that competition between male politicians is one of the causes of their comparative dullness, that it is the bird's bright plumage which attracts the gunman's fire. Certainly a modern British politician has to crawl across twenty years of no man's land while he progresses from being a humble candidate to being a Cabinet minister with at least a theoretical right to his own opinion. He learns to keep his head down, and to crawl stealthily from mudhole to mudhole. The woman politician has more freedom in this stage of her career.

The psychological argument seems, however, to be the stronger. Women make better political leaders than men because they have a more profound confidence in their convictions. Indeed, there is a whole masculine folklore about this aspect of feminine psychology, ranging from Kipling's view that 'the female of the species is more deadly than the male' to the widespread male belief that once a strong-minded woman gets an idea into her head, nothing on earth will ever get it out again.

Obviously this is not an exclusively feminine attribute, and some deny that it is a feminine attribute at all. Yet I have tried at one time or another to persuade Golda Meir or Margaret Thatcher of propositions they did not accept. It was not like battering against a brick wall, for brick walls can be knocked down. It was like pushing against a rock face, with solid granite behind it to the glowing centre of the earth. Feminine conviction has the power of a natural force. With the exception of Indira Gandhi – who was corrupted by a hereditary caste arrogance – this unalterable feminine conviction may be benign, but it is obviously capable of being mistaken.

The authority of women rulers is derived psychologically from the authority of motherhood. Strong women make and maintain strong families. The women leaders see their nations as their families, and their innermost belief – particularly clear in Golda Meir – is that mother knows best. Male statesmen do not imagine that father knows best, indeed, the wise ones have learnt a certain humility from life.

This maternal confidence has the benignity but also the ruthlessness of the maternal role. You have to be ruthless to protect children. It seems often to be formed around a childhood relationship with a heroic father – Margaret Thatcher, Indira Gandhi and Benazir Bhutto were very close to fathers they admired and loved.

The danger comes when mother gets it wrong, as, in my view, Golda Meir missed the best opportunity for peace in the Middle East because she did not doubt herself enough. Yet this feminine conviction is a dynamic force for good. It changed Israel; it changed India; it changed the Philippines; it has certainly changed Britain; it will very probably change Pakistan.

22 November 1988

A DIRECT LINE FROM 1789
TO THE RISE OF HITLER

B y an accident of birth, I have been thinking about the French Revolution for as long as I can remember. I was due to arrive in the world on 13 July 1928. My mother, who was not normally superstitious, resolved that I should not be born on Friday the thirteenth, so she struggled through an exceptionally hot night, and I finally came into the world at about 4 a.m. on the fourteenth.

Like all children, I took into my nest of self-conceit any bright materials which came to hand; to share a birthday with France was an attractively gaudy feather to weave into the fabric of nursery egotism. It had one drawback: I much preferred the France that had existed before the Revolution to the one that had been created after it.

When I first read the history, I was wholly on the side of Louis XVI, and took the same lively satisfaction in the fate of Robespierre, shot in the jaw and then guillotined, as I did in the execution of Thomas Cromwell. I liked to see the bad people get their deserts. My one regret was that Oliver Cromwell did not get his, and had to be dug up in order to be beheaded. The motto of my childhood was: 'Death to regicides.'

I therefore enjoyed spending my sixty-first birthday in Paris discussing the consequences of the French Revolution on a day-long broadcast for Channel 4. Melvyn Bragg was in the chair and the impromptu studio at Les Invalides was full of interesting people: Régis Debray, George Steiner, Peter Ustinov, Michael Foot, Roy Jenkins, Gore Vidal and Olivier Todd. For much of the day I was the anchorman for those who found the French Revolution a matter for regret. Indeed I found myself defending Mrs Thatcher's somewhat similar views, with Michael Foot playing the role of an incredibly amiable Jacobin.

It was George Steiner who raised the question which I found most interesting: the impact of the French Revolution on Germany. He quoted Goethe as saying that the French Revolution was so important an event he would have to spend the rest of his life working out what it meant. It was not an issue we followed up.

In its impact on Germany, the Revolution has to be taken as a whole, that is from 1789 to 1815: National Assembly, Robespierre, Napoleon, the story of a European generation. Unquestionably this historic process, including Napoleon's military victories, destroyed the old Germany, the provincial Germany of small states, ghettos and petty princes. It prepared the way for the nineteenth-century unification of Germany under Prussia. Bismarck was the direct heir of the German reaction to Napoleon, and Bismarck's state was based on the centralizing and reforming principles adopted by Napoleon.

The ideology of the new German state was founded on the patriotism of defeat. Johann Gottlieb Fichte, the great German philosopher, spent the closing years of his life in Berlin, where he was rector of the new university from 1810 to 1813. He was the philosophical parent of the new Prussian nationalism. His Berlin lectures of 1807, a response to the impotence of a divided and unmodernized Germany in the face of Napoleonic aggression, were the first learned call for Prussian nationalism, by a philosopher who ranks between Kant and Hegel in the development of the German school.

One can see the stone tumbling down the mountain, falling further each time it strikes. The Fall of the Bastille is the symbolic destruction of the old order in France; that leads not to a philosopher's state, but to the totalitarianism of the period of Jacobin dictatorship, to the Terror. That in turn leads to anarchy and to the coming to power of Napoleon.

French nationalism and the Bonapartist ambition of Empire then destroys most of the old Europe, and even invades Russia. After its defeat, a new Europe, and particularly the new Germany, is born in a spirit of reaction to French aggression, but in a spirit of sympathy to the French organization of state power. Both modern nationalism and the totalitarian state have been born.

Germany is united under Prussia, whose history and philosophy is both nationalist and militarist. Bismarck wins Prussia's historic revenge for the disasters of 1806 in the war of 1870 which, by a paradox, destroys Bonapartism in France and fulfils the democratic purpose of 1789. Bismarck is indeed the father of the Third Republic. But this process in its turn prepares the way for the great European wars of the twentieth century, in which German nationalism becomes completely poisonous. This is the chain of causation from the Fall of the Bastille to Hitler, a chain broken only when the Allies occupy Berlin in 1945.

Of course most of these are unintended consequences. At each step men intended far better, far more favourable outcomes than they actually achieved. Yet there is a real link between the phenomenon of the French Revolution and the phenomenon of Hitler. Both are true revolutions, highly destructive of old systems of order, totally prepared to replace what actually exists by an ideal of what might exist.

Both involve terror, and mass murder. The repression of the Vendée is Nazi in scale. Both rely on nationalism as their main emotional force. Both end in an attempt to conquer Europe. Both are defeated by Britain and by the Russian people; both freeze in the hell of a Russian winter. Both use enemy groups, aristos or the Jews, as a focus for popular hatred. Both win power partly by mobilizing mobs on the streets.

Of course the French Revolution has a more positive side as well. *Liberté, Egalité, Fraternité* is a much nobler slogan than *Ein Völk, Ein Reich, Ein Führer*. It is possible, with however many reservations, to celebrate the positive consequences of the French

Revolution 200 years later, while the celebrations in 2133 in Germany are likely to be on a small and private scale. The French Revolution, like Prohibition, was a noble experiment. Unfortunately, also like Prohibition, it gave the gangsters, both in France and in Germany, their chance.

What are the political lessons that one should draw? The first is that nothing which is done without patience is done well. The Nazi Revolution was indeed a crime because its purposes were evil; the French Revolution was a tragedy because its purposes were good, but many of its consequences were evil. It failed, where the American Revolution succeeded, because it did not recognize the overriding need to limit human power. Almost from the start, it opened France to unlimited power: the power of the Jacobins, the power of Napoleon, which let loose monsters upon the French people and upon Europe. The people of France, but most tragically of all the Jewish people, have paid the price for this fatal European mixture of revolution, nationalism and unlimited state power.

18 July 1989

THE GENETIC MYSTERY OF SCIENTIFIC GENIUS

W hat is the electrical unit which measures how much current one volt can send through one ohm? The scientifically literate will immediately respond: an ampere or an amp; while the rest of us, who cannot tell the difference between a watt and a joule, will feel uncomfortable in our ignorance. What is the unit of intensity of a magnetic field, whose measurement is the product of a Weber at the distance of one centimetre? Even the quasi-scientific may pause for a moment. The answer is a Gauss.

How many know who André Marie Ampère and Carl Friedrich Gauss were? Most readers of *The Independent*, whether or not they have read any of the works of Voltaire or Goethe, know of their existence, and many readers of *The Independent* will at some stage in life have read *Candide* or *Faust*, at least in translation.

Ampère may not be quite as great a figure in science as Voltaire in literature, but Gauss is fully comparable in intellectual stature to Goethe. It is one of the deficiencies of our culture that even those who have a good smattering of literature are all too often scientifically ignorant and innumerate.

There are extraordinary parallels between their two lives, and they still hold great interest for us. Ampère was born in Lyons in 1775 and died in Marseilles in 1836. Gauss was born in Brunswick in 1777 and died in Göttingen in 1855. Both were members of that very small group who start as infant prodigies and continue to enjoy eminent intellectual gifts in adult life. Mozart, born a few years earlier, is another example, as is Pascal in the seventeeth century.

Gauss taught himself to calculate before he could talk. When he had learned to talk, he corrected an error in his father's wage calculations at the age of three. At the age of eight he astonished his teacher by an instantaneous solution of a 'busy-work problem'; he found the sum of the first hundred integers.

When he entered Brunswick Collegium Carolinum, at the age of fifteen, he had already independently discovered Bode's law of planetary distances, the binomial theorem and the arithmetic-geometric mean. His mind in childhood was not only capable of astonishing calculation, but of the most advanced mathematical insight.

Ampère's father was a French merchant much influenced by reading Rousseau's *Émile*. Gauss was left to himself, because his parents were unintellectual and relatively poor; Ampère was put into a library of the French enlightenment and encouraged to read what he chose. But Ampère also had a fascination for numbers, and taught himself number theory.

His prodigious numerical powers were first noticed at the age of four. Like the young Pascal, he was discouraged from geometry because it was thought he was too young for it, but he defied his parents and worked out the earlier books of Euclid by himself. When the librarian in Lyons told him that the works of Euler and Bernoulli were written in Latin, he went home and taught himself Latin, so his precocious powers were not simply mathematical.

Nor were those of Gauss. He too made a rapid early progress in the classics, and in his years at Brunswick contemplated becoming a philologist rather than a mathematician. Both were remarkable as children for their verbal as well as for their mathematical powers. We are not therefore dealing simply with the unusual development of a single intellectual faculty.

Both undoubtedly suffered from a certain isolation from their fellows. Ampère's life was tragic, and Gauss's life, if not fully tragic, was unhappy. In the French Revolution Ampère lost his loving and protective father – guillotined when Lyons fell to the Republicans. His first marriage was extremely happy, but his wife died; his second marriage was disastrous. His later life was one of relative poverty and ill health.

Gauss also lost a happy first marriage, also made a second marriage which, though not in his case disastrous, was no marriage of true minds. He lived the life of the lonely professor, writing that 'death would be preferable to such a life', and that he felt like a stranger in the world.

It is hard to imagine the intellectual processes which led to their scientific discoveries. Ampère's central discovery was that magnetism is electricity in motion, a discovery which unified the fields of electricity and magnetism. His most important work was done in a surprisingly brief period and at a relatively advanced age.

Hans Christian Oersted's discovery of electromagnetism was first reported on 4 September 1820. Ampère read his first paper on the subject on 18 September, and continued his account of his discoveries on 25 September and 9 October. Thus the main scheme of his life work appeared to his mind in a period of about five weeks in his forty-sixth year.

Ampère stated that his mind leapt immediately from the existence of electromagnetism to the idea that currents travelling in circles through helices would act like magnets. There is a rather similar statement by Gauss, writing in 1817 about one of his seven proofs of law of quadratic reciprocity:

'It is characteristic of higher arithmetic that many of its most beautiful theorems can be discovered by induction with the greatest of ease, but have proofs that lie anywhere but near at hand . . . Sometimes one does not come upon the most beautiful and simplest proof, and then it is just the insight into the wonderful concatenation of truth in higher arithmetic that is the chief attraction for study and often leads to the discovery of new truths.'

Not all the great scientists exhibit this phenomenal calculating ability in infancy, nor do all children who have the gift retain it in adult life. Yet it does seem to be part of a syndrome of genius.

322

In other respects scientific genius looks more like poetic genius than like a powerful computer.

Certainly there seems to be a subliminal or subconscious process at work. The uprush of ideas in Ampère's great period, or throughout Gauss's career, is characteristic equally of poetic composition and of scientific discovery. Gauss sees mathematical theorems and their proofs as beautiful rather than simply as true or accurate. In the formation of their minds the computational faculty, even when present, is matched by a faculty for visualization, and often with remarkable powers of verbal communication. Charles Darwin, for instance, was one of the best writers of English in the nineteenth century; his prose style is the equal of that of the great novelists and is free of their redundancies.

The loneliness of these lives is matched only by our inability to understand what the mathematical scientists are thinking. Gauss is as remarkable a genius as Goethe, but we can follow Goethe and we cannot understand Gauss. Yet Gauss is one of the makers of the modern scientific world.

There is also an interesting genetic question. There are enough examples of this syndrome of scientific genius, which often appears in otherwise unremarkable families, for it to be certain that there is some unusual genetic mutation which triggers these self-taught prodigies. If this were a stable gene it would spread through families, as a certain scientific ability spread through the Darwins. But neither Gauss nor Ampère had children of exceptional ability. The human race has been changed by scientific genius, but can neither understand it, nor be sure of reproducing it.

18 December 1989

LENIN'S LITTLE
BOARDROOM REVOLUTION

Vera Zasulitch told Leon Trotsky that she had once said to Lenin, 'George Plekhanov is a hound – he will shake a thing for a while and then drop it; whereas you are a bulldog, yours is the death grip.' When she recalled this conversation, she added: 'This appealed to Lenin very much – "A death grip," he repeated, with obvious delight.' As she said this, she mimicked Lenin's intonation and accent. He could not pronounce the sound of 'r' clearly. So it was Lenin's 'death gwip' which Mikhail Gorbachev finally unclenched last Wednesday, after eighty-six and a half years.

In chaos theory, which is itself a formidable refutation of the principle of bureaucratic planning, the future of large and complex systems is unpredictable because it can be altered by the influence of small events. A butterfly in China can change the whole pattern of world weather by the flapping of its wings. In the case of Bolshevism the trivial birth event, the butterfly in China, was a dispute over the membership of the editorial board of the revolutionary paper, *Iskra*.

The dispute took place in London in 1903. Small as it was, it changed the whole of world history. From that struggle flowed the form if not the fact of the Russian Revolution, Leninism and Stalinism, the Russian famine, the character of Communism round the world, the character of Nazism as Communism's mirror image, the Nazi–Soviet pact, the Second World War, the Holocaust, the Gulag Archipelago, the development of nuclear weapons, the revolution in China, the Vietnam War, and every event of the revolution of liberty in Eastern Europe in the past twelve months. None of these things would have happened as they did, and some of them would not have happened at all, if the *Iskra* board dispute had not split the Communist Party.

In her charming memoirs, we have Nadezhda Krupskaya's description of first coming to London, in April 1902, as Lenin's young wife. In London the young Lenins 'loved going for long rides about the town on top of an omnibus . . . it was also our custom to ride out to the suburbs. Most often we went to Primrose Hill, as the whole trip only cost us sixpence . . . From the conspiratorial point of view things could not have been better.'

The Lenins left London in April 1903, but came back again that summer when the Second Congress had to move hastily from the attentions of the Brussels police. The Congress was to approve a policy statement drawn up by the editorial board of *Iskra*, but also had to elect the board itself.

Lenin was determined to secure his own power on the board. He wanted to exclude most of those he regarded as 'soft'. He proposed a triumvirate of himself, George Plekhanov, the father of Russian Marxism, and Julius Martov, who was a moderate and became the leader of the Mensheviks. The words 'Bolshevik' and 'Menshevik' mean those who were in the majority and the minority at this Second Congress, which was attended by only forty-three delegates.

Trotsky describes the relationship between the two men. Lenin was the political leader of the *Iskra* board, Martov the literary power. When the Congress opened, Martov was still regarded as Lenin's closest comrade. 'They were still addressing each other as *'ty'* (thou), but a certain coldness was beginning to creep in . . . one can say of Lenin and Martov that even before the split, even before the Congress, Lenin was "hard" and Martov was "soft" . . . Lenin would look beyond Martov as he talked, while Martov's eyes would grow glassy under his drooping and never quite clean pince-nez.'

At the Congress Lenin won Plekhanov over, which secured his majority, but he lost Martov, which he had not intended to do. Plekhanov he was not able to hold, and the loss of Martov was permanent. In personal terms Plekhanov saw the danger of Lenin's temperament; he said of him, 'of such stuff Robespierres are made'. But the division with Martov involved both personalities and a historic issue of policy, the issue of party and personal dictatorship.

With Plekhanov's help, Lenin was able not only to secure the nomination of the board he wanted for *Iskra*, but also to put through a formal Congress commitment to 'the revolutionary dictatorship of the proletariat'. The Mensheviks wanted a more democratic party, with openness towards liberal and middle-class groups of the left-centre of Russian politics.

At the 1903 Congress Trotsky was close to Martov and supported the Menshevik position, a decision he came to regret. He then regarded Lenin as 'a despot and a terrorist'; in his memoirs he deals with the issues more cautiously, but puts the real question clearly enough. 'Revolutionary centralism is a harsh, imperative and exacting principle. It is not without significance that the words "irreconcilable" and "relentless" are among Lenin's favourites. In 1903, the whole point at issue was nothing more than Lenin's desire to get Axelrod and Zasulitch off the editorial board . . . I thought of myself as a centralist. I did not fully realize what an intense and imperious centralism the revolutionary party would need to lead millions of people in a war against the old order . . . In the midst of the still vague moods that were common in the *Iskra* group, Lenin alone and with finality, envisaged "tomorrow" with all its stern tasks, its cruel conflicts and its countless victims.'

It is uncanny, as one reads the accounts of the 1903 Congress, how the petty personal issues and enormous and terrible historical consequences relate to each other. Lenin wanted to remove Vera Zasulitch from the editorial board of *Iskra*. She was then sharing a house in London with Martov and with Blumenfeld, the printing-press manager of *Iskra*. They found a room for Trotsky, whom Lenin was trying to detach from the Martov influence.

Zasulitch herself had a heroic revolutionary past, but she was also very clever, with a broad historical knowledge and 'rare psychological insights'. Lenin disliked her links to Martov, disliked her soft views, and was bored by repetitive intellectualism. He was determined to dominate.

His aim was to control the *Iskra* board absolutely. The historic consequences of revolutionary centralism were revolution, dictatorship, famine, war and death. Trotsky himself became one of the 'countless victims' of this imperious dictatorship when Stalin's agent put an ice pick in his head. He could remember when it all began. In 1903 he said to Lenin: 'This will mean a complete dictatorship of the editorial board.' Lenin replied: 'Well, what's wrong with that?' We know now what was wrong with that.

12 February 1990

A WRONG THEORY WITH
THE WRONG RESULTS

'Today our country is sick. We have no quarrel with those who are gloating over our situation and our problems. We are even ready to sympathize with them. For instead of truth, they prefer self-deception and self-adulation.' Eduard Shevardnadze, the Soviet Foreign Minister, was remarkably frank in Ottawa, but he is wrong to think we are gloating and that we prefer self-deception, let alone self-adulation.

The last year has indeed seen a historic victory for one of the two great revolutionary theories which have dominated this century. The older is the theory which makes the individual the master of society. It demands for him the equal right to choose his own government, the principle of political democracy. It also demands for him the right to make his own economic decisions, choosing his own job, planning his own finances, buying and selling for his own advantage in a free market. That is the principle of economic liberty. Liberty also makes the individual responsible for his own fate.

This theory was formulated in the seventeenth century. The greatest names associated with it are John Locke and Adam Smith. Its fruits include the industrial revolution, and the revolutions of democracy in England, America and France. Modern results are the revolutions taking place in South Africa, Eastern Europe and the Soviet Union.

The alternative theory, developed in the nineteenth century, is that human societies ought to be organized from a single command centre to ensure the equal distribution of benefits. This theory makes the bureaucratic masters of the state the sovereign power, but these controllers of the state are representatives, at least in name, of the industrial workers, of the proletariat.

This theory is also associated with great names, particularly Marx and Lenin. In the mid-twentieth century, the industrialized world was divided between the two theories, which formed separate political and military camps. The Lockeian world centred on the United States, the Marxist world on Moscow. In Britain there were those who compromised. They were Lockeians in politics but Marxists in economics. They advocated a doctrine of democratic socialism, which would retain the sovereignty of the individual in terms of political elections but create the sovereignty of the state over what was termed 'the commanding heights of the economy', and therefore make the individual the servant of the state.

The Labour Party won the election of 1945 on these principles, and took economic power for the state through nationalization acts, punitive taxation and controls over trade and finance. By 1950, Britain was still a democratic society in terms of politics, but a socialist society in terms of economics. There is always an instability in a society which is half-slave and half-free.

The Soviet union after 1917 became a slave society in that the power of the state was subject to no political control by the citizen and that the state controlled all economic decisions through a centralized bureaucracy.

Both types of socialist systems have failed. Democratic socialism could never be completed. The Labour Party was removed from office in 1951, and though it regained power in 1964 and again in 1974, it never again had the confidence to do more than try to patch up a part of its system. In the 1980s the Conservatives, with successive election victories, were able to restore free markets in more than half the areas in which socialism had taken state power.

Leninist socialism went on longer and failed more completely. Socialist governments lost the will to oppress their own people.

Once it became clear the the communist governments would not shoot, they were doomed, because, as Mao had observed, their power had grown out of the barrel of a gun. In China, where they still were prepared to shoot, socialist power has, at least for the present, been maintained.

The political tyranny of the Soviet Union was more inhuman than the economic, but the economic failure was equally disastrous. The communist economies have simply collapsed. They cannot go on. The shortages are too acute, there is too much pollution, the goods are low in quality, distribution has failed, food production has failed. The Eastern European economies, after forty-five years of peace, look as though they have just emerged from the devastation of a world war. It is only devastation of socialism.

The reason for this failure is that Locke and Adam Smith were right, and that Marx and Lenin were wrong. It is not gloating to tell Mr Shevardnadze that, any more than it would be gloating to offer antibiotics to a patient with pneumonia when he was being treated with cupping, bleeding and leeches.

The theory of socialism has proved to be a lethal blunder which is virtually the sole cause of the present collapsed state of the Eastern Europe economies. There are reasons in politics, psychology, sociology, philosophy and information theory why economic socialism is a mistaken theory. Most of the important work which establishes the counter-arguments has been done by those trained in the Viennese academic tradition, including Karl Popper, Friedrich Hayek and Ludwig von Mises. People prefer to live in an open society, but it is also far more efficient. Why?

The primary arguments are those of motivation. Locke argued that people need economic liberty because they want different things. That is where the phrase 'the pursuit of happiness' comes from. Adam Smith argued that people would supply goods and services for the sake of profit which they would not supply for charity. Ludwig von Mises argued that it is not a question of plan or not plan, but of whether the individual should plan for himself or someone else should plan for him.

One can reinforce these arguments by studies of information theory developed in the computer age. These show that a successful communication system requires a strong flow of information, a capacity for rapid response and feedback of the action taken. A tennis champion will have an accurate perception of what is happening on court, a rapid ability to play the ball, and rapid recognition of the impact of his shot – information, action and feedback.

The market system has all these qualities. The information flow and the feedback are maximized because all the potential buyers and sellers operate through the market. The market knows what bureaucrats cannot possibly know, and eliminates those traders or producers who are not able to respond quickly. Competitive pressure means that the best qualified survive.

The socialist command system is not at all like this; it knows little and responds bureaucratically. It does not know what demand is, except through the length of queues. It has no automatic feedback. It is like a blind, one-legged centenarian on the Centre Court at Wimbledon.

The failure of the command economy is as natural a consequence of democratic socialism as it is of socialist dictatorship. The basic economic arguments against socialism apply equally to both forms.

Russia is a poor country because it was seized by a socialist dictatorship in 1917. But Britain is a moderately poor country because we elected a democratic socialist government in 1945. If you choose the wrong theory, you get the wrong results.

19 February 1990

STICKS AND STONES AND DONNISH SNEERS

Socialism has been a profound century-long misjudgement for which the intellectual left is responsible. At its worst it involved the support and admiration which Fabians such as the Webbs and Shaw gave to Stalin. Throughout – even in the Brezhnev era – it has involved a sympathetic acquiescence in communist dictatorships. At home it has provided a continuous and complacent intellectual propaganda for state regulation of the economy.

The intellectual left remains strong in the universities and the media; they continue to teach in accordance with their own prejudices. They have never apologized for supporting Stalin; they have never apologized for conniving at Brezhnev; they are now trying to shift the blame for the ruined economies of Eastern Europe away from the socialism which caused that ruin.

A central claim, often made seldom justified, is that these 'progressive' intellectuals have superior information and under-standing. This arrogant assumption is one of the commonest faults of British academic life. Let me take a case from last week's *Independent*. A Cambridge don decided that I was too ignorant to be answered coherently. We are indeed all ignorant of more than 99 per cent of the information we might reasonably wish to possess; that is the fate of the human mind confronted with a complex universe.

Last Thursday *The Independent* published a letter from Mr Peter Clarke, who is a reader in modern history at St John's College Cambridge. The letter sought to answer the article I had written last week on the advantages of economic and political liberty over socialism. It notably failed to address the central issues to which I had referred. In particular Mr Clarke made no reference to the collapse of the communist economies in Eastern Europe and the Soviet Union, nor tried to offer an alternative explanation for the failure of these socialist societies.

The tone is set in Mr Clarke's first paragraph. He writes that he is 'often amused' by my column – suggesting, pleasantly enough, that even superior intellects can derive occasional entertainment from such trivial material – but goes on to say 'I would advise him to stick to topics he knows something about.'

In the lifetime of *The Independent* I cannot recall a letter which made a crude and unsubstantiated allegation of ignorance that did not come from a university teacher. Yet it is an obviously unscholarly argument. Mr Clarke has no knowledge of my studies, broad or narrow, into the subjects I was discussing, any more than I have of his. He is therefore at best making an assertion for which he has no evidence.

The fact that Mr Clarke and I have come to different conclusions about the place of ideas does not mean that either of us is ignorant of the writings of John Locke or of the seventeenth-century historical influences on his thought. I believe Locke was a major influence on the development of the philosophy of liberty; I do not know what Mr Clarke thinks Locke achieved, but not that.

The assumption that those who disagree with one must be ignorant is, I suppose, a common temptation for a tutor of undergraduates. All undergraduates come to their tutors to learn. It is natural that the tutor should, at that stage, have an advantage of knowledge, though with the best of his students he will have no advantage in intellectual powers. Yet even with students the assumption of superiority is a poor teaching method, because it implies a lack of respect.

Mr Clarke continues: 'Lord Rees-Mogg shows a lamentable ignorance of a whole generation of historical scholarship with his misleading stereotypes.' The word 'lamentable' means such as to cause weeping. I find it hard to believe that the Fellows of St John's College have every Monday been sniffling into their handkerchiefs as they lamented my ignorance of 'a whole generation of historical scholarship'.

Mr Clarke does not specify who these historical scholars are, nor what they have written, nor where – on his assumption that I have not read them – I might look them up. In the London Library there is no shelf labelled 'generation of historical scholars which William Rees-Mogg has not read'.

It is of course true that there must be many books that Mr Clarke has read which I have not. No doubt the converse is also true. Those books may well contain valuable truths, as well as controversial matters and plain absurdities. If Mr Clarke will tell me precisely which books prove what points relative to the argument he is attempting to make I will try to obtain them, and will judge for myself whether they establish what he thinks they establish. But 'a whole generation of historical scholarship' is not a meaningful phrase. It is merely the 'fee, fi, fo, fum' of pedantic authority.

What Mr Clarke is mainly seeking to establish is in his next paragraph. 'His Manichean view of the clash between coherent systems of liberty and tyranny is likewise another fantasy.' It would be pleasant for socialist dons if that were so. But is it? Is there no difference between forming one's mind on the views of Locke, Smith, Mill, Popper and Hayek and forming it on Marx, Engels, Lenin and the Webbs? Is there no school of liberty? Did Locke make no contribution to it? Is Locke to be reduced from his own clear and vigorous language to a mere welter of cross-references?

Mr Clarke can of course retreat into the argument that neither the system of liberty nor the system of socialism is completely coherent, that both have inconsistencies between what different philosophers have taught at different times. But this is a reductionist argument which would prove far too much. If one requires complete coherence, no school of thought and no religion can show it, but that does not mean that there are no schools of thought and no religions. It may be difficult to know exactly what

Christ taught or exactly what Mohamed taught, but that does not mean there is no Christianity and no Islam.

The issue is an important one. The arguments between tyranny and liberty have been discussed for over 2,500 years by the greatest philosophers. The argument between market individualism and socialism has dominated the political life of our century. To such an argument neither my article nor Mr Clarke's letter can make more than a trifling contribution. Yet the young whom Mr Clarke teaches have to form their own view and they should do so by reading the authors of liberty and those of socialism and deciding whose arguments they prefer. They should not accept donnish authority or admire donnish sneers.

I believe that the idea of liberty exists and that it has inspired both a philosophy and a state of political society. Liberty puts the individual in command of his own decisions; his vote is the ultimate political sovereign in a democracy; his purchase is the ultimate economic sovereign in a free market. Socialism always denies this economic liberty; communism always denies political liberty as well. Socialism is also economically disastrous, apart from its authoritarianism.

Mr Clarke may believe none of these things. But he should not pretend that these beliefs are other than diametrically opposed to the beliefs of socialism. That would merely be a smokescreen to cover the disasters, 'the uncounted victims', to use Trotsky's phrase, which are socialism's legacy to the modern world.

26 February 1990

THE WHIGS IN THE WINGS

Yesterday I was asked to become Chief Whip of the Whig Party in the House of Lords. My sense of the profound honour of the offer, and the secrecy which has for many years enveloped the operations of our party, forbid me to say whether or not I shall accept. However, a recent attack on my party's reputation has been made by a Conservative MP in the letters column of *The Times*. I feel that some explanation of Whig principles and the Whig role is necessary.

Mr Cyril Townsend, who sits for Bexleyheath, writes that 'time is short, but not too short for the Cabinet to stop behaving like nineteenth-century Whigs (the Harrods affair was the latest example) and to bring back the virtues and traditions of our party, under leaders of the calibre of Churchill and Macmillan.'

Though obviously intended to be offensive to the Whig party, it is almost impossible to make sense of this sentence. Who were these nineteenth-century Whigs, and what do they have to do with Harrods? Is he thinking of Charles, Earl Grey, the Prime Minister who introduced the Great Reform Bill? Does Mr Townsend want to return to the old system of family-controlled seats and rotten boroughs?

I do see that there is a strong historic argument that the unreformed Parliament of 1688 to 1832 did better for Britain than the reformed Parliament from 1832 to the present day. The Great

Reform Bill coincided with the start of our national decline. But I do not imagine that Mr Townsend would urge the electors of Bexleyheath to disenfranchise themselves, or even to sell the seat to the highest bidder.

Even stranger is the reference to Churchill and Macmillan, the last two great Whig prime ministers. Perhaps Mr Townsend objects to nineteenth-century Whigs, but admires twentieth-century ones, and, I would hope, eighteenth-century ones as well. Perhaps he approves of Walpole and Chatham, but dislikes Grey, Lord John Russell and the Duke of Devonshire, to return in a blaze of admiration for Churchill and Macmillan (who did after all marry a Cavendish). I would rather sympathize with that – the nineteenth-century was the period in which my party suffered a grievous decline in its political fortunes – but what about Lord Melbourne? Surely Harrods cannot be blamed on him?

The nineteenth-century Whigs did in any case make the discovery that it was possible to serve Whig principles and Whig personalities without the troublesome business of electing the Whig party. The principles of my party are liberty and the people; our tactics are those of the cuckoo. We invented entryism.

Not that we are bad at elections. Our great founder, Lord Shaftesbury, with the aid of Titus Oates, inspired the Popish Plot, the first and greatest of political scares, one which nearly overthrew not just a government, but the Stuart monarchy. This was not the Lord Shaftesbury who was a philanthropist, nor the philosopher, but the one whom Dryden described as 'the false Achitophel'; he was 'Sagacious, bold, and turbulent of wit . . . A daring pilot in extremity; Pleased with the danger when the waves went high, He sought the storms, but, for a calm unfit, Would steer too nigh the sands to boast his wit.' All the best Whigs have a tincture of Achitophel.

We also invented party trees – the lime is a Whig tree – and party colours – 'hurrah for the old buff and blue'. If you see a man wearing a light-blue tail coat with buff trousers and with gilt buttons on a buff waistcoat, you may be sure he is a Whig. For reasons of discretion we do not always wear our uniform. We also use sex appeal to win elections. What red- – or blue- –

blooded man would not have voted for Charles James Fox in the Westminster election of 1784, in return for a kiss from Georgiana, Duchess of Devonshire?

But, above all, the Whigs invented the modern British political system, with its balance between institutional and popular elements. We were responsible for the Revolution of 1688 and still take a friendly interest in the well-being of the Royal Family, because we put them on the throne and passed the Act of Settlement to keep them there. Whig ideas were responsible for the American Revolution. The central Whig doctrines are those of liberty, property and popular sovereignty, and do they not still reverberate in the modern world?

In this century there have been Whigs in all parties and indeed there have been Whig leaders of all parties. Arthur Balfour was a Whig. Asquith was a Whig Liberal. Churchill was a Whig who never fitted easily into the twentieth-century party system, and as he said, not only 'ratted' from Conservative to Liberal, but 'reratted' from Liberal to Conservative. Macmillan, who gave up the Conservative Whip before the war, was certainly a Whig, even in his manners.

We nearly had a fully paid-up Whig leader of the Labour Party in Roy Jenkins, but there were strong Whig elements in the characters of Hugh Gaitskell and Michael Foot. Michael Foot is a Foxite Whig: one can imagine him supporting Charles James Fox in 1798 when Fox's name was erased from the Privy Council for giving the toast, 'Our sovereign, the people'. No one can be called a true Whig who would not drink to that toast.

Why have we had to exercise our influence in this century through other and lesser parties – the Conservatives, the Liberals, the Labour Party? It is, I think, because the central political ideas of personal liberty and popular sovereignty have appeared to be in conflict with each other. By and large, most Conservatives believe in liberty. They believe in freedom of markets, which was already part of the Whig system in the days of our great philosopher, John Locke, and was reinforced by our adoption of Adam Smith. They believe in personal liberty rather than bureaucratic control.

Yet conservatism has in it an inherited tendency to authoritarianism. We have never had a Whig party conference, partly because we do not wish to embarrass other parties with a public display of our obvious superiority, but if we did there would be no calls to bring back the rope or to keep out our Whig brethren from Hong Kong. Nor would there be any standing ovations. Perhaps the occasional toast to our leader in Château Mouton Rothschild, but nothing more enthusiastic than that.

Similarly the Labour Party, while as attached as we are to the sovereignty of the people, holds views about the power of the state similar to those of King Charles I, a monarch of whom we did not approve. A firm principle of Whiggery is to keep our rulers in a subordinate position; Labour does not share that objective.

If I decide to become the Whig Chief Whip, I shall have to canvass our members' views on the next leader of the Conservative Party, a party to which many of them belong. I know that most Whigs think quite well of the present Prime Minister; they are not sure what Thatcherism is, but feel that on the whole it acts on the side of liberty and property.

The real Whig hero among Conservative ministers of the 1980s was a rather stout gentleman with black ringlets, of a distinctly seventeenth-century cast of mind. He had a fine intellect, believed in liberty, regarded the people as sovereign without taking them too seriously, and cut taxes. These are the true Whig characteristics, particularly cutting taxes. If the next Conservative leader has the initials NL, you will know that another Whig coup has taken place.

2 April 1990

THE DAY CIVIL SERVANTS PLANNED THE HOLOCAUST

One of the most important events in the history of the twentieth century occurred on 20 January 1942. A high proportion of one section of the readers of *The Independent* may recognize that date. For most of the rest – and not only the younger readers – it may mean nothing. The event, which ought not to go unremarked as we approach its fiftieth anniversary, was the Wannsee Conference. For many of us, that is a strange and unfamiliar name. Where was it?

The Wannsee is a large lake near Berlin, and the conference was held in a villa on its banks. In the chair was Reinhard Heydrich, who for eleven years had been head of the intelligence service of the SS. He had only a few months to live. On 27 May 1942 he was wounded in Prague by two Czechs who had been parachuted in from Britain; he died eight days later. His death was revenged by the massacre at Lidice.

Who were present at the Wannsee Conference? The SS was in the chair, but it was an inter-departmental conference, intended for the execution of policy, not for its creation. Senior civil servants represented the Ministry for the Occupied Eastern Territories, the Ministry of the Interior, the Justice Ministry, the Foreign Office, the General Government of Poland, the Race and Resettlement Office and the Plenipotentiary for the Four Year

Plan. It was a conference such as occurs in every civil service to deal with outstanding administrative problems.

As chairman of the conference, Heydrich made the opening address. He told the assembled civil servants that he had been appointed as 'Plenipotentiary for the Preparations of the Final Solution of the European Jewish Question'. A full account is given in Martin Gilbert's *The Holocaust,* one of the few books of this century which everyone has a duty to read, though it is almost unbearably painful. Heydrich explained that Goering had asked for 'a draft project' involving all the ministries.

In his opening address, Heydrich ran through the statistics. He said there were about eleven million Jews in the whole of Europe, of whom almost three million were in Ukraine and more than two million in Poland. He included in the count 330,000 Jews living in Britain, not yet conquered, and even 4,000 Jews living in neutral Ireland. It was intended that all the eleven million Jews of Europe should 'fall away': in the event about six million were killed.

One of the officials at the Wannsee Conference was the young SS officer, Adolf Eichmann. In 1938 he had been appointed head of the Central Office for Jewish Emigration, in Vienna. He was eventually tried, convicted and hanged in Israel. He could remember 'that at the end of the Wannsee Conference, Heydrich, Müller [the chief of the Gestapo], and myself sat very cosily near the stove . . .We all sat together like comrades. Not to talk shop, but to rest after long hours of effort.'

The original decision to destroy the European Jews had come earlier. The first official reference to 'the doubtless imminent final solution' comes in a circular letter of 20 May 1941 which states that Goering had banned all emigration of Jews from the occupied territories, including France. The decision itself must have been taken before that. When Germany invaded Russia on 22 June 1941 the advance troops were accompanied by SS Einsatzgruppen, whose job it was to destroy Jewish communities.

Their first action occurred in the days after 22 June along the Soviet frontier. For instance, at the village of Virbalis, the Einsatzgruppen made Jews lie down along two miles of an anti-tank trench and killed them with machine-gun fire. This process was repeated seven times. 'Only children were not shot. They were caught by the legs, their heads hit against stones and they were thereupon buried alive.'

There does not seem to have been a written order to establish this policy. In evidence at his trial, Eichmann, who was the main organizer at the senior staff level, said he had never seen one. However, he had no doubt that he was acting on Hitler's personal authority. 'All I know is that Heydrich told me, "The Führer ordered the physical extermination of the Jews".' Goering, Goebbels, Bormann, Heydrich, Frank, the governor of Poland, Himmler and Müller were certainly among those involved in the passage of the decision from Hitler to the state machine. At every stage close security was observed.

The Final Solution began, therefore, with the invasion of Russia in June 1941, at the high tide of German victory. It was not a reaction to defeat. It started by using the Einsatzgruppen trench-and-machine-gun technique of massacre, an essentially local and therefore public method. The Nazis had already developed an euthanasia programme for the mentally ill, which used the technique of gassing in bath houses. After the Wannsee Conference, the death camps were built on this model: Chelmno, Belzec, Sobibor, Treblinka and Auschwitz-Birkenau.

The programme was extended to include the killing of gypsies, homosexuals, people of various religions, and Russian prisoners of war, two and a half million of whom were murdered. It continued right down to the last days of the war. Transport to the death camps put a great strain on the German railway system. Starvation was used as a reinforcement to more direct means of killing, but the death camps were the main assembly line; at Chelmno alone the throughput was 'ein Tag, ein Tausend' – a thousand a day. There are twentieth-century parallels. Stalin killed larger numbers than Hitler; he was also anti-Semitic, but never exclusively so. Mao probably killed larger numbers than Stalin, and his successors are still in power. Pol Pot is still alive. Yet the Holocaust remains the crime we have the greatest difficulty in understanding, because it occurred in our own culture, the culture of Europe. Most of the Jews who were killed were poor people from Eastern Europe.

The Final Solution was certainly not carried out by Christians, whatever part Christianity may have played in the history of anti-Semitism. When one of the Polish trenches was opened up, they found hundreds of Polish Roman Catholic priests and seminarians alongside the Jews and the Russian prisoners. It was perhaps motivated by what Jung called 'the Nazi psychosis'. But it was carried out by people not so different in their way of life from us. As Himmler commented to a group of senior SS officers in 1943: 'Most of you know what it means when 100 corpses are lying side by side, or 500, or 1,000. To have stuck it out and at the same time to have remained decent fellows, that is what has made us hard.'

There is no adequate way of dealing, intellectually, emotionally or morally, with such a crime. It can threaten the faith of the humanist in man or of the religious in God. To the Christian, and perhaps to many Jews, the words that seem most appropriate are those of the 22nd Psalm, perhaps the last words of Jesus on the cross: 'Eloi, Eloi, Lama Sabachthami' – 'My God, my God, why has Thou forsaken me?'

Four of Sigmund Freud's sisters, all then in their eighties, were killed in the camps, two at Treblinka, one at Auschwitz and one at Theresienstadt. Their brother's work showed the danger of repressing into the subconscious mind what is too painful for the conscious. At least in this anniversary year the suffering of the Holocaust should be remembered by all the Christian churches, as it will be in every synagogue. In facing such an evil, thought may be less valued than prayer.

30 December 1991

PART SEVEN

CRICKET AND OTHER AFTERTHOUGHTS

'Personality is everywhere spreading out its fingers in vain, or grasping with an always more convulsive grasp a world where the predominance of physical science, of finance and economics in all their forms, of democratic politics, of vast populations, of architecture where styles jostle one another, of newspapers where all is heterogeneous, show that mechanical force will in a moment become supreme.' W. B. Yeats, *A Vision.* 1937. p. 296

Anyone reading this book will at once see how direct a reproach this passage from Yeats must be to my work; I see it in this way myself. The journalist has a convulsive grasp on a world of mechanical force; I have been interested in finance and economics in all their forms, and in democratic politics; I have written for and edited newspapers 'where all is heterogeneous'. Yet at the same time this is a passage with which I can fully identify. The protest is against developments against which, in one way or another, most of my articles protest. I reject the monopoly claim of physical science; I detest the clutter of opposing styles, in literature as much as in architecture. Above all I wish to assert the validity of the spiritual as against the complexity of the machinery in which I work, have worked and have made my living.

Some of the themes emerge straightforwardly enough, but there are others which have been spat out like the pips of an apple, individual responses to particular interlockings of events. The first piece I wrote for *The Independent* which really pleased me was such an article of protest against what seemed to me in 1986 to be the wanton, and dishonourable, destruction of Somerset cricket. My foreboding proved to be correct. In 1992 Somerset were bottom of the county table and, worse than that, were a side of no consequence.

The protest was not however simply concerned with placing on a table of cricketing success. I felt about the Somerset side of the early 1980s with Botham, Richards and Garner rather as Carlyle felt about Frederick the Great. Cricket is only a game, but then opera is only dramatic song. Great cricketers, like great operatic singers, show a particular side of human nature. In a lifetime we see very little greatness but when we see it we find it easy to recognize. Unfortunately greatness always provokes jealousy as well as admiration. Nothing is so much hated as greatness by the respectable mediocrities.

Two of the three cricketers involved were black: Viv Richards – the greatest batsman of his generation – and Joel Garner, the amiable but unforgettable West Indian fast bowler. I do not like to think that racial prejudice determined the decision not to renew their contracts. At least I am sure that the committee did not realize that it was prejudiced. What I have seen of such prejudice is that it more often appears in assumptions than in direct hostility. It is not that provincial committee people – or metropolitan people for that matter – say to themselves, 'I cannot stand black people.' More often they say, 'I like and admire black people, but I do not regard them as quite the equals of white people.' Richards, a proud man, was not treated like a slave, but he was treated without respect, not quite as a white cricketer of his standing in the game would have been treated.

Ian Botham, of course, was not dismissed. He dismissed himself as a protest against the way in which his colleagues and friends were being treated. That was an angry and loyal decision, and for Somerset a sad one. The argument against Botham and Richards was that they were difficult – even that was not suggested against Garner, the friendliest and least difficult of men. When I was an editor, which is now beginning to seem rather a long time ago, I thought it was part of the job to maintain a good relationship with talented but difficult colleagues. People of exceptional personal force tend to create problems which do not arise with people of easier temperaments and less energy.

There is some similarity of theme in the article I wrote in

December 1987 about the decline of the intellectual in politics. I am glad that Malcolm Rifkind, whom I referred to as 'the only natural intellectual' left in that Cabinet has prospered in the subsequent years and is now Secretary of State for Defence. I was glad too that Nigel Lawson, for whom I retain a high respect, accepted that he was not an intellectual, and agreed with what might have been thought an unsympathetic judgement.

Yet politics require people of outstanding intellectual qualities just as cricket requires players of genius as well as players of talent. Without them there is a fatal loss of creative power, and a loss of public interest. From Gladstone to Balfour, a period of forty years, all the successive prime ministers were men of exceptional intellectual power. Now intellect might be regarded as a positive disqualification for the highest office, and some disqualification for any office at all. During the 1992 election campaign William Waldegrave, who is an intellectual but was not in the Cabinet in 1987, was picked on in debate as though he were a white crow, offensive to the normal black crows of the parliamentary woodland.

Powers of mind are not always essential to the successful government of human affairs, but they are important to good government. Policies need to be thought through, not merely thought about; they need to be co-ordinated and not merely arranged. The modern world is certainly less enthusiastic about intellectual politicians than was the world of Queen Victoria. So much the worse for the modern world.

Just as I admire bold cricketers and intellectual statesmen, so I admire Princes of the Church. I never think of Pope John Paul II without a feeling of gratitude – a church of 950 million people could not be held together by a man who doubted his own authority. I was thought to be ironic when I deplored the decline in the pay of Anglican Bishops and Archbishops, and pointed out that Cosmo Gordon Lang was paid the gold equivalent of £750,000 in 1931 when he was Archbishop of Canterbury. I am not sure that Archbishops need to be paid quite that much, but in the periods when the Christian churches have been most important in people's lives, Christian Bishops have been given a very high status.

'Democratic politics' and 'vast populations' which Yeats listed among the drawbacks of the modern world, and 'heterogeneous newspapers' all make for equalization. Committees dismiss great cricketers because they stand out from the team, and this is thought unfair. Intellectuals are ridiculed by the know-nothing sections of the press, which regard high intellectual ability as an alienation from popular culture; it usually is. Bishops are paid on a scale which would have been thought ungenerous for their chaplains only a generation or so ago.

Surprisingly, and largely thanks to Margaret Thatcher, the 1980s saw a counter-attack on this social egalitarianism in terms of earnings and taxation. But there was no such counter-attack on cultural egalitarianism. There is still a confusion between unjustified privilege – unjustified because unearned – and the privilege which arises from the possession of superior talents or the performance of a superior function. I have written on the side of the exceptional talents, and my heart is with them even when they fail.

THE LAST GREAT CRICKETERS AT THE SOMERSET CREASE

Vivian Richards, Joel Garner and Ian Botham will never play for Somerset again. They have given me great pleasure, as great pleasure as I have ever had from watching cricket. Their coming together in one English county side, and my own county, was astonishing good fortune.

For a few years Somerset, of all cricketing counties, has been the most exciting team to watch in the world. Last Saturday it all ended in a drafty barn near Shepton Mallet where, by more than two to one, the Somerset members voted to sack Viv Richards and Joel Garner, well knowing that Botham would also leave the side as a consequence.

Such a verdict cannot be overturned. I would like however to express the gratitude which those who voted to turn out the committee feel that the club itself ought to have shown. I believe in gratitude; I believe in loyalty; I am ashamed that the Someset Club does not.

I have never met any of the three; my own gratitude to them arises simply because their cricket has been so delightful to watch.

I feel grateful to Joel Garner because he combined such ability as a bowler with an obvious sweetness and simplicity of nature.

That made him the favourite of the Somerset crowds, particularly the children, who used to hang out banners at Lords with 'Big Bird' written on them. They have fired the big bird now.

His bowling seemed even from the pavilion to be unplayable, rising up from the pitch at an acute angle corresponding to his great height, presenting the batsman with a problem in three dimensional geometry at more than motorway pace.

Viv Richards is the best batsman I have ever seen, save only for Bradman. In both men the speed of their reactions set them apart, making the fastest bowlers appear to be of medium pace, and medium pace bowlers appear to be slow. Richards never wears a helmet because he can trust himself; at Taunton he would have done well to wear a backplate.

He has a commanding personality; his visage is ancient and dignified, almost semitic, as though Haile Selassie, the Lion of Judah, had taken to cricket when he was in temporary exile in Bath. Even more than Bradman his batting is power in action – he is a stronger man than Bradman was; that combination of power, agility, intent and speed of reaction is now for Somerset only a memory.

Ian Botham is Ian Botham. I suppose he is impossible – though no more impossible than great tenors in the world of opera. I doubt whether anyone can have these surges of energy when performing without them coming from some deep and perhaps uncontrollable source in the personality. Yet on the cricket field for Somerset and even more for England he has repeatedly performed the impossible.

I did not speak at Shepton Mallet, but another member, Mr Blanchard, put what I felt, in referring to 'an extraordinary ingratitude, not only in the deed but in the way the deed was done.'

What makes a good friendly Somerset crowd support an obviously inadequate committee, who have so mishandled things that the one spell of glory in Somerset's cricket history has ended in such disunity and dark ingratitude? Why do we support people who have shamed us?

Not, I think on any cricket argument. 'Dasher' Denning, from Chewton Mendip, perhaps the one man whose cricket record could have persuaded me to support so feeble a committee, put a point which went entirely unanswered. 'Bowlers win matches – why get rid of your only strike bowler?' Crowe, the white knight from New Zealand, who describes himself as 'very ambitious', has a bad back and can no longer bowl much. Next season Somerset may well get some runs, but they are going to be hard put to bowl any other county out.

The roots of the desire to humiliate genius go very deep in human nature. Most of us have a very English preference for mediocrity. Ian Botham is, in particular, a disturbing character. He represents, in an open form, energy which is chained in every man's subconscious mind. There is in his cricket none of the repression which helps the rest of us to function as civilized beings. Yet the result of his unrepressed libido is an explosion of energy which none of the rest of us could ever have achieved.

Garner, I think, is a threat to none. He has merely been trapped by being a third in what Nigel Popplewell, a retired player, son of the Judge, called the 'Superstars'. I thought it unjust and ungenerous of Popplewell to include Garner in what was properly a criticism of Botham and Richards.

Viv Richards is a threat, which is why he is so formidable at the wicket. Botham and Richards are extraordinary men as well as extraordinary players; they have a Jungian archetypal force about them, reinforced in Richards' case by the blackness of an Othello. People project onto such figures psychic material from the sub-conscious mind, often material they cannot face in themselves. That makes such heroes exciting to watch, but also deeply threatening to men of infirm psychic confidence. The committee were also much influenced by Roebuck, the county captain, an edgy young man who was put in a position that was perhaps too difficult for him. It is never easy to lead one's betters. Roebuck is a batsman of almost painful talent who owes his success more to determination than nature. It seems likely that he thought that he was meaning well, though he does not seem to have been able to behave with complete frankness.

The gap between talent and genius is always a tormenting one, however good one's intentions. It is tempting to feel that God plays an unfair trick in giving only talent to the men of good character, but bestows genius on those apparently less worthy of it.

With such less gifted cricketers I have some sympathy; I have never found men of genius easy, and I do not suppose they did. With the committee I have no sympathy at all; they have lost the Somerset Club's honour and fouled the memory of its greatest period. No good will come to any of them, nor to Mr Crowe, from this affair. But then no good came to Salieri when he stood, grinning with grief and envy, by Mozart's open grave.

11 November 1986

MOURNING THE DECLINE
OF THE INTELLECTUAL IN
POLITICS

One of the most remarkable changes in British and American political life has been the decline and virtual disappearance of the political intellectual, that is, of people for whom the process of thinking is the centre of life.

Mrs Thatcher's Cabinet has some highly intelligent men – including notably Nigel Lawson, whose mental power is not to be understated – but the only natural intellectual left is Malcolm Rifkind, the Secretary of State for Scotland. In earlier Cabinets, Mrs Thatcher had a fair number, including Ian Gilmour, Lord Hailsham, Lord Joseph, John Biffen, Lord Gowrie and that Bolingbrokian figure we must now learn to call Lord St John.

The Labour Party used to be the intellectuals' party with leading ministers such as Richard Crossman, Hugh Gaitskell, Hugh Dalton, Stafford Cripps, Tony Crosland, Roy Jenkins, Denis Healey and numerous others. There are even today one or two good writers left on the front bench, but hardly a soul who would have qualified as an intellectual by, say, Tony Crosland's standards.

Even more astonishing is their total absence from the Alliance, which was almost created to attract their support. Roy Jenkins is a bona fide intellectual, but he is now Chancellor of Oxford University. David Steel is not an intellectual nor, though he has a more cogent mind, is David Owen.

The same thing happened in America. No President has chosen to welcome intellectuals to the White House since President Kennedy. George Will does get invited to the White House, but that is because he is a powerful journalist. Lyndon Johnson disliked intellectuals because he knew they preferred Kennedy and because they lived in Georgetown. Nixon disliked them because he found it hard to trust anyone he could not control. Carter did not like them unless they had been born in Georgia – though he rather liked being praised by Peter Jay. President Reagan does not live in a world of rigorous mental endeavour.

Again, the comparison with past times is depressing. From Roosevelt to Kennedy, the Democratic Party, if not the Republicans, saw the intellectual formulation of policy as an essential part of government. It was not that Roosevelt was an intellectual himself; in essence his temperament was that of an aristocrat. Yet he wanted the instruments of his policy, and his advisers on policy, to be men of the highest mental power.

Policy itself he decided on political grounds and by largely intuitive means. But he wanted to be sure that he had heard the best advice and that the analysis was done by people who were comfortable in thinking about complex problems. Above all he recognized the essential contribution that intellectuals bring to the creation of political ideas.

The decline of the intellectuals is in one sense not suprising. There developed, particularly in the 1930s, a leftist doctrine of the progressive intelligentsia, which was both authoritarian and sentimental. The echo of those beliefs is still found in the dogmatic assumptions of many of the articles in *The Guardian* or *The Observer*; these are assumptions the general public has never accepted without reservation. We can, I suppose, all think of academic or professional figures whose consistent and high-minded progressivism serves as a cover for shallowness of thought and depth of self-interest.

Yet it is surprising that the role of intellectuals in Mrs Thatcher's third term should be as unobtrusive as it is. After all, Thatcherism is itself a revolution of ideas, and she is the most ideological prime minister of modern times. Her concern to discover a philosophically valid base for what is, in economic terms, the new individualism, has been entirely sincere. Her acceptance of certain American monetarist ideas (Milton Friedman) and her rejection of others (Art Laffer) has probably determined the success of her administration. The opposite choice by President Reagan has probably determined the failure of his.

Mrs Thatcher may have been unlucky. Of the intellectuals who have left her Cabinet, two, Ian Gilmour and Norman St John Stevas, held views well to the left of hers; Ian Gilmour became perhaps her most distinguished Conservative critic. Lord Hailsham retired from age. Grey Gowrie left to better himself in commerce.

The loss of John Biffen might with a little more flexibility have been avoided, though as John Biffen described himself as a philistine he is perhaps only demi-cerebral. An intellectual who does not truly love at least one of the arts may be thought to be a poor fish. Yet it is surprising that the ideas of the new right, which are much more exciting than those of the old left, have not thrown up some equally interesting young politicians to develop the actual policies which the Prime Minister has wished to introduce.

The English still have a fear, as do most American Republicans, that those who can think cannot act. It is, of course, in some cases true. Even Lord Joseph, who provided the main original ideological impetus for Thatcherism, was far more effective as a thinker than as a doer; he is a very good man, but he was never a very good minister. Yet the post-1958 example of France shows how much policy can benefit from the virtues of sharpness of analysis and reference to principles in decision, qualities which the Prime Minister values in herself.

The Presidents of France since de Gaulle have all been intellectuals. Admittedly, de Gaulle was that unusual and stiff-necked thing, a military intellectual, but his whole process of thought was both radical and highly rationalized. The successive Presidents, Pompidou, Giscard d'Estaing and Mitterrand, have all been natural intellectuals, men for whom the qualities of mind were the prime qualities. President de Gaulle had to achieve – and did achieve – a reversal of the French decline at least as remarkable as Mrs Thatcher's reversal of the English decline. Any serious historical perspective seems now to show him as the greatest French leader since Napoleon. But France has had mentally stringent government for thirty years, and the French, without North Sea oil, are as a result considerably richer than we are with it.

Intellect is not the only quality needed for good government; it stands beside honesty, courage, judgement, will-power and, above all, sound principles. Yet the prolonged delays in the history of trade union, educational and health services reform show how greatly Mrs Thatcher's administration would have benefited from having a better supply of effective ministers of real intellectual character. Of course, the lack in the major opposition parties is an almost fatal gap in their equipment. They indeed are the 'bare ruin'd choirs, where late the sweet birds sang'.

1 December 1987

AN UNSCIENTIFIC GUIDE
TO A LONGER LIFE

A great division between the sciences and the arts is that the sciences advance and the arts do not. Every first year student of physics at university has information and powerful theories which were not available to Sir Isaac Newton. No such advantage exists for the artist; our poets do not have an advantage over Milton, or over Homer for that matter; our composers have no advantage over Mozart.

Medicine is partly a science and partly an art. The science has advanced enormously. For the cure of diseases by specific drugs the latest medical school graduate is immensely superior to the most eminent doctors of the seventeenth or eighteenth century. Yet the art of medicine, which is much concerned with the support of health rather than the cure of diseases, advances very slowly, if at all.

This is apparent in the advice that modern doctors give on how best to enjoy a long and healthy life. They say that one should take exercise, eat sparingly, drink sparingly, avoid tobacco, remain cheerful, cultivate relationships and avoid stress, particularly in one's later years. That is the essence of the doctrine. It was, almost word for word, the doctrine of the best English doctors of the eighteenth century, and indeed of the best doctors of ancient Greece. Very similar advice can be found in the Book of Proverbs.

At the end of the eighteenth century, James Easton, a Salisbury bookseller – he was not even a doctor – tried to set this advice on a more scientific footing, in his book: *Human Longevity, recording the name, age, place of residence and year of the decease of 1,712 persons who attained a century, and upwards, from AD 66 to 1799*. In fact his cases are mainly drawn from Britain in the period between 1650 and 1799, and he has more information on men than women. Some of his earlier cases and some of his foreign cases are probably unreliable, but seventeenth- and eighteenth-century Britain had a sound system of parish records.

The early cases include a number of great men. St Anthony, the founder of Christian monasticism, is said to have died at the age of 105 in the year 356. St Patrick, the patron Saint of Ireland, is said to have been 122 years old when he died in the year 491. Attila, king of the Huns, was even older. He died in the year 500, at the age of 124. 'Hearty and strong at such a great age, he led to the altar of Hymen, as a second wife, one of the most beautiful princesses of the age, and the next day died of excess.'

Attila was not alone in retaining strong sexual appetites after the age of 100. Thomas Parr, of Winnington, Shropshire, seems to have been slow to get started: 'At the age of 88, he married his first wife, by whom he had two children . . . At the age of 102, he fell in love with Catherine Milton, whom he got with child, and for which he did penance in the Church. At the age of 120, he married a widow woman.' He is said to have lived to the enormous age of 152 and died in 1635.

William Iven, who died at the age of 115 in 1778 'married his fourth and last wife at the age of 105, because, as he said, he was resolved to die virtuous'. One of the best cases is unfortunately anonymous. In 1776, there died at the age of 105, 'a farmer in the neighbourhood of Festiniog. By his first wife he had thirty children; by his second, ten; by his third, four; and by two concubines, seven; his eldest son was 81 years older than the youngest and 800 of his descendants attended him to his grave.'

Jonas Surington of Bergen in Norway had an even larger gap between his eldest and youngest son. When he died at the age of 159, 'he had been several times married, and left behind him a young widow and several children, his eldest son being 103, and his youngest nine years of age'.

The impression is that extreme longevity is normally the prerogative, as one might expect, of those, both men and women, who have strong animal instincts in general. Old Mr Hastings only lived to be 100; he was a member of the Earl of Huntingdon's family and therefore had quite recent Plantagenet blood. He died in 1650 at his mansion-house at Woodland in Dorset.

'His great old green hats were full of pheasants' eggs, and litters of young cats. Tables, dice, cards and books were not wanting. The pulpit in the chapel was well stored with gammons of bacon, roast beef, venison-pasties and large apple pies. His cellar, in which was plenty of excellent strong beer, was always open to his neighbours. He dived into the secrets of a great majority of the maids, wives and widows in his neighbourhood. He was very temperate at meals, when he only drank one pint of small beer stirred with rosemary, and one or two glasses of wine with syrup of gilliflowers.'

People who reached the age of 100 were of no single type. One woman was only two feet, eight inches high, whereas the tallest man was seven feet, six inches. Some were corpulent, or very stout. A number grew a third or even a fourth set of teeth at an advanced age. Many kept dark hair to the end of their lives. Several of the soldiers had lost limbs in battle, and survived their gruesome amputations, without anaesthetic, for eighty or more years afterwards.

There seems to be no doubt that marriage is a preservative. Some indeed of the centenarians married several times, but an interesting number had spouses who also lived to a great age, sometimes becoming centenarians together, and sometimes dying within a few days of each other. Easton does not record a marriage lasting a hundred years, but he does record marriages lasting for more than eighty.

Most of the centenarians were sparing in their diet, at least in their later years. One ate nothing but potatoes for her last twenty years; James Macklin, the actor, lost his teeth in his late sixties and thereafter lived on fish, eggs, puddings, custards and jellies.

'Finding that tea did not agree with him, he used, as a substitute, milk, with a little bread boiled in it, sweetened with brown sugar.' Macklin, like Maynard Keynes and Queen Elizabeth I, distrusted baths, and 'for the last twenty years, never took off his clothes, unless to change them, or to be rubbed all over with warm brandy or gin; a custom he often repeated, and occasionally steeped his feet in warm water.'

On the other hand, an American centenarian, John Weeks of Connecticut, who lived to be 114, 'a few hours previous to his decease ate three pounds of pork, two or three pounds of bread and drank nearly a pint of wine.' Cardinal de Salis, who lived to be 110, recorded of himself, 'my diet was sparing, though delicate; my liquors, the best wines of Xerez and La Mancha, of which I never exceeded a pint at any meal, except in cold weather, when I allowed myself a third more.'

A good marriage, or several marriages, a habit of walking long distances, the ability to grow a new set of teeth after eighty, avoiding more than a pint of fine wine at a sitting, and a strong desire to preserve oneself, are the best aids to reaching a hundred.

One should not eat three pounds of pork at one meal after the age of 110, or marry a beautiful young princess after the age of 120.

In short, the general principles of longevity are supported by the evidence, and have not changed. The one qualification is that natural vitality, the character Fielding portrayed in Tom Jones, seems to give a better chance of reaching a hundred than the opposite principle of coddling oneself against the world outside.

29 January 1990

IMMIGRANTS ARE ALL RIGHT, BUT ONLY IF THEY PLAY CRICKET

D ecline and fall are sometimes followed by resurgence and recovery. That is happening to English cricket. When our team went to the West Indies, England were both the worst and the least enjoyable of the major Test Match sides. A series of captains had presided over a series of defeats. Mike Gatting's conduct in leading a team to South Africa had appeared to demoralize even further our leading professional cricketers. No one thought that the team under Graham Gooch stood a chance; there was talk of them losing all five matches, of a 'blackwash'.

They are now in the middle of the fourth Test. They won the first; the second was rained off; the West Indies were saved by rain and delaying tactics in the third; England fought back in their first innings of the fourth to come within 88 runs of a large West Indies score. Whatever now happens, this England side has proved itself the equal of the strongest team in the world, and in the early Tests, when injuries had not yet occurred, was unquestionably the better in performance.

However, there is one obvious point about the current England side. More than half of them are not English by immediate descent. Lamb and Smith were both born in South Africa. De Freitas, Small and Malcolm were born in the West Indies. Hussain comes from an Indian family. Without immigration none of them would have been playing for England at all.

What do the English make of this? Do we sit, watching the Test Match on Sky Television, drinking our Tetley's bitter in Northern public houses, and complain that England are winning because foreigners like Allan Lamb or black men like Gladstone Small – so touchingly named after our greatest Liberal statesman – have been allowed into the side? Would we prefer a purely English side, made of old English oak and thick as two short planks, rather than letting in these untrustworthy foreigners to win for us?

On the whole we do not. In the cricket field, where it really matters, we recognize that immigration brings in talent which we need and is of benefit to us. In cricket, even the English understand the difference between winning and losing, the difference between a bowler who can take West Indian wickets and one who will be plastered all over the ground, between a batsman like Allan Lamb who can score 119 off the West Indian attack and some earlier batsmen for whom double figures were a distant target, a glimmer of hope seldom attained against really fast bowling.

Cricket is the real world. We do not apply the same standards to the imaginary worlds of work or the economy. In yesterday's *The Independent on Sunday* there was a poll which displayed the full horror of British attitudes to immigration. The figures – if they are right – show that we are indeed a miserable people, worthily represented by politicians like Norman Tebbit and Gerald Kaufman, deeply prejudiced, deeply isolated, pathologically suspicious of strangers, a national example of the surly peasant who greets the hero with curses in Act I, beats him in Act II and turns him out into the snow and the wolves in Act III.

The survey was occasioned by the controversy over the proposed admission of a rather small number of Hong Kong Chinese. Of those asked, 65 per cent said the Government was wrong to allow 50,000 Chinese families to settle here, and only 25 per cent said it was right. But when they were asked whether Britain could absorb more of particular groups, the anti-immigration figures went higher than that. With regard to Indians and

Pakistanis, 84 per cent say no; West Indians, 83 per cent; Chinese, 77 per cent; Jews, 67 per cent; other Europeans, 60 per cent; white Commonwealth, 54 per cent.

There is certainly a case for the policy, which hardly anyone seriously challenges, of limiting the total of immigration. The inner-city problems are real, and so, to our discredit and sometimes to the discredit of immigrant groups, are the problems of race relations. But these figures are absurd. Even if one accepted that the general policy of immigration control meant that we could not absorb more of the largest ethnic groups, not because of their race but because they are already large, these figures also show an hysterical fear of people who are not now present in very large numbers and whose immigration could only lead to our national advantage.

It is absurd to suggest that Britain would suffer social problems from an increase in the numbers of white Commonwealth immigrants. They do not even present us with the problem of our racial fantasies and prejudices – no one thinks he is going to be mugged by a Canadian. The communities are small, the contribution they make to British life is remarkable. Only in the two specialized trades of newspaper proprietors and female impersonators could white Commonwealth immigration be regarded as a threat to local employment.

Citizens of the European community are another small group. They happen to have an absolute legal right to live and work here, yet 60 per cent of those answering the Numbers Market Research poll thought that we could not absorb more of them. This suggests, if the poll is correct, that 60 per cent of us are hysterical idiots. What is it they are saying? 'You cannot trust these Frenchies . . . that chap's grandfather was an Eyetie . . . looks like the Boche to me . . . in matters of commerce the fault of the Dutch is offering too little and asking too much.' From what warren of island prejudices is this foolishness derived?

Then what about the Jews? It does, I admit, add to the stink of Gerald Kaufman's opposition to the proposals for Hong Kong that the politics he is playing are the racial prejudice which always threatens the Jews. At least Norman Tebbit is not promoting anti-Tebbitism, except, I suppose, among all right-minded people. When I think of what Jewish scientists, scholars, musicians and businessmen have contributed to post-war British life – and how few of them there are – I am profoundly grateful for the early twentieth-century immigrations from Russian pogroms and the Nazi terror.

Then there are the Chinese. There is no more hard-working, peaceable or useful community in Britain. There is no case for supposing that another 50,000 Chinese families from Hong Kong, if they came, would be other than 50,000 additions to the general well-being of our society and to our economic capacity in a competitive world.

Leave alone all the other contributions of the West Indians and Asians, how would our hospitals be staffed without them? Last week I was talking to a group of Indians in Leicester. They were not rich, but they were self-disciplined, determined, family-minded and hard-working. They are already playing a major part in British industry and trade. Like our West Indian community, they are a young and energetic national asset.

I am not unsympathetic to the desire of the English to preserve their own culture, though that has been threatened by our architects more than by our immigrants. I understand the difficulty of national adjustment to world changes, which have come faster and been more penetrating than can easily be absorbed.

I know that the English are not the only xenophobic people in the world; one should talk to the Japanese. I know that it is difficult to balance a reasonable openness against the undoubted social problems of the immigrant slums of our inner cities. Yet when one reads this poll with its massive majorities for fear and prejudice, I can only feel what (expletive deleted) we English are. But then, of course, I come from an immigrant family myself.

9 April 1990

PUBLIC PAUPERS IN A WORLD OF PRIVATE PRINCES

I n 1945, we had a memorial service at Charterhouse School for the Rt Hon. and Most Reverend Cosmo Gordon Lang, DD, Archbishop of Canterbury and Primate of All England, who had been *ex officio* chairman of our governing body. He had indeed been a useful chairman. When there was a proposal to commandeer the school buildings for some military purpose in 1940, he telephoned his friend Anthony Eden and persuaded him to stop it.

I had to read the lesson. It was not for nothing that my mother had trained me in Shakespearian elocution, to breathe from the pit of one's stomach and produce the voice as though through the forehead. I made the most of 'O death where is thy sting? O grave where is thy victory?' From behind a pillar there came a muffled sob from one of the more sentimental members of the teaching staff, overcome by the pure, bell-like tones with which I pronounced the words of St Paul.

Archbishop Lang was the last of the prince bishops of the Church of England. He was the confidant of prime ministers – a close personal friend of Stanley Baldwin and at least a close aquaintance of Neville Chamberlain. He could well afford to play that role. When Britain went off the gold standard in 1931, his salary as archbishop was £15,000 a year, which he could have received – had he wished – in the form of about 3,800 ounces of

367

gold. That quantity of gold would have a current value of rather more than £750,000, a handsome salary even for an archbishop.

The price of gold has risen about fifty times since 1931, the retail price index about forty times and average earnings about a hundred times. In cost of living terms, the Archbishop's salary would, therefore, have been £600,000, and in comparative earnings terms, it would have been £1.5m. I would regard gold as the best measure of the real wealth his income conferred on the Archbishop.

Judged by the price of gold, Archbishop Runcie receives about 4 per cent of the real salary of his predecessor. He has not been reduced from prince to pauper, but he has certainly been reduced from prince to professor – and that is a substantial drop in income. It can, of course, be argued that the Christian clergy ought to be poor, that holy poverty has always been a Christian virtue, that the Apostles were not wealthy men, and that Archbishop Runcie's remuneration is, therefore, more fitting than Archbishop Lang's.

No doubt it is. I suspect, however, that the underpayment of the clergy in general is a weakness rather than a strength in the Church of England, where the clergy are not celibate and often have families to raise. Holy poverty for oneself is one thing; holy poverty for one's wife and children may be quite another. Yet the 96 per cent fall in the remuneration of the archbishop is only an extreme example of the general fall in the pay of the clergy and in the pay of state employees, particularly of senior state employees.

As against 1931, the Prime Minister, to start at the top, has had a salary cut of almost 80 per cent. Mrs Thatcher receives the pay that was thought appropriate in 1931 not for the Prime Minister, but for the Assistant Postmaster-General. The chairman of the BBC, Marmaduke Hussey, receives just over 20 per cent of the pay of John Whitley, the 1931 chairman, but is responsible for an undertaking that is probably forty times as large.

The Lord Chancellor is head of the legal profession. He was paid £10,000 in 1931, the equivalent of £500,000 now. He is still the highest-paid member of the Cabinet, but he has suffered an even larger cut than the Prime Minister, although not as large as the Archbishop of Canterbury.

Similar cuts have not taken place in cases where pay is determined by market value. Senior executives of large companies receive salaries ten or twenty times as large as those of the Prime Minister or the Lord Chancellor. It is state salaries that have been held behind. This can be seen most clearly in those professions that have both a private and a public sector. Successful commercial barristers earn up to ten times the pay of judges, while successful private consultants can earn a multiple of the pay of consultants in the National Health Service.

The most striking examples naturally come from the top jobs, but the differential between state and market pays has, in fact, devalued whole professions and occupations.

One is always impressed by the lifestyles of the professors of the prewar period, men such as Neville Keynes, Maynard Keynes's father, who was the Registrary of Cambridge University in the 1920s. He was not a rich man, but he lived a very comfortable life, in a substantial Cambridge house with servants, and sent his sons to Eton and Rugby. Registraries do not live like that now. Nor can they, because in constant terms they are paid only two-thirds as much.

This is not simply the consequence of the general narrowing of pay differentials. The gold measurement is one of purchasing power; average earnings have risen twice as much. In 1931, the Prime Minister was paid as much as seventy farmworkers, the chairman of the BBC as much as forty, the Archbishop of Canterbury as much as two hundred. Now the Prime Minister is the equal in pay of about eight farmworkers, the chairman of the BBC and the Archbishop of Canterbury of about four or five. The narrowing of differentials between high and low pay is not in question; the widening of differentials between state and market pay ought to be.

The consequences of the state being so poor a paymaster are almost all bad. The state undoubtedly loses the services of many able people. Nowadays one meets a large number of first-class ex-civil servants in jobs where they are paid the market rate, not to mention ex-teachers and ex-academics. Those who accept the state's rates of pay are exposed to unfair financial anxieties. From Cabinet ministers to hospital nurses, the state's employees lie awake at night, worrying about their mortgages. I am sure at least half the members of the present Cabinet have real financial worries – the rest having earning wives, earning husbands, or private wealth.

The state's industrial relations are notoriously worse than those of private business. The health service, education and the prison service are all areas of industrial bitterness. When one reads of a strike, or a strike threat, one almost assumes that it will be in the public sector. This bitterness also leads to low productivity. Every employer who underpays finds that he receives only the productivity he pays for.

The Government faces whole constituencies of resentment, which could quite possibly lead to its defeat at the next election. Those constituencies include the public-sector employees, and particularly public-sector professionals. The bitterness of academics towards Mrs Thatcher was shown by the rejection of the proposal for her honorary degree. But that bitterness is mirrored in most others sectors of public service save for those, such as the police, that have been specially favoured.

The Labour Party will not find it easy to solve this difficulty. If he becomes Prime Minister, Neil Kinnock will not start by putting his own salary up to £250,000 a year, although that is the minimum at which one could assess its market value. Labour will be universally expected to improve public-sector pay, but will be unable to do so without foregoing its plans to improve public services.

No doubt privatization is the logical answer. Market rates are the one rational way to assess pay levels. The smaller the public sector, the easier it would be to bring its pay up to the market level. The strange thing is that the underpaid public-sector community does not want to go private. Doctors, nurses, professors, teachers, civil servants do not like being paid below market levels, but they are solidly opposed to the one reform that would result in their being paid what they are worth.

25 June 1990

DON'T STOP AT THE DOG;
LET'S MUZZLE THE OWNER

'The Government cannot wash their hands of the problems associated with dogs,' Baroness Nicol told the House of Lords last Thursday. What are these problems? The greatest is thought to be that dogs do not use ordinary toilet facilities, but, like visitors to pop festivals, go to the bathroom in the streets. The secondary nuisance is that they bite people, or as Lord Mancroft rather unkindly put it, 'large and rather unpleasant dogs bite small and almost as unpleasant children'. It is estimated that dogs bite 8,000 postmen each year. The third concern is that dogs chase and kill other animals.

In order to protect the nation against dogs the House of Lords has passed an amendment to the Environmental Protection Bill, which would require every dog to be registered with the penalty of 'a fine not exceeding level two on the standard scale' for any owner who failed to do so. A registration tax of about £25 would be imposed to pay for this scheme, which would take 1,000 people to administer and provide employment for a further 1,000 dog wardens.

The Government is now considering this amendment. Three departments of state have already produced a consultative document, *Action on Dogs*, which considers various responses to the dog problems. Chris Patten, the Secretary of State for the Environment, is to be given powers under Part IV of the Environment Bill 'to include dog faeces within the duty of local authorities'.

The House of Lords seemed sympathetic to proposals that every dog should be labelled. Most peers would be satisfied with the dog wearing a collar and tag, as though dressed for entry to the Savoy Grill. Some peers wanted every dog to have an electronic implant, a minute glass device placed in the dog's ear. The Earl of Buchan told the House that this device also worked on carp.

In Japan, ancient carp – they live for a couple of centuries or more – have great financial value. One Japanese prime minister was accused of taking bribes in the form of valuable old carp, worth £100,000. Presumably, therefore, electronic implants in carp are designed to discourage burglary, rather than prevent them fouling the footpath.

Other proposals are that dogs of fierce breeds should be muzzled, or that dogs should be neutered. In the House of Lords, possibly owing to our high average age, we usually vote for proposals to keep down the human population; some peers seem in favour of extending this to dogs.

The ingenious suggestion was made that there should be a compulsory insurance of dogs against third party risk, and that neutered dogs should be insured at a lower rate. I am not sure I would trust a Rottweiler merely because he had been deprived of his doghood.

This great national scheme – registration, identity tags, 1,000 bureaucrats, 1,000 wardens, the criminal offence of not register-ing, the encouragement of neutering, the possibility of muzzles – has a familiar character. It combines all the elements of modern progressive legislation, on which all parties can unite. But why should the benefits of such a scheme be confined to dogs when there are many problems of human society which call for similar treatment?

Common observation does suggest that dogs foul the footpath more often than human beings or carp, although the hazards associated with bird droppings are even greater because they fly through the air. In the old days both men and women wore hats, which provided some protection. The droppings of a large bird, such as a Canada goose, are at least as large as those of a small dog, such as a Yorkshire terrier. Perhaps all Canada geese should be registered and muzzled, and Canada geese wardens should patrol St James's Park and the lake in the Buckingham Palace garden with nets to catch flying objects.

But even if dogs do more nuisance, there is no doubt human beings do more serious injury. For every child killed by a Rottweiler there are several killed by their own parents. If a case can be made for registering, tagging, neutering and muzzling dogs, an even stronger one can be made for registering, tagging, neutering and muzzling people.

The Government did, indeed, start down this road with its unfortunately impractical proposals for football hooligans. It should now take advantage of the work that has been done in dog control to reintroduce a comprehensive measure of human control. This could be made an amendment to the Environmental Protection Bill, since hooligans, and, indeed, human beings, are unquestionably a threat to the environment.

The first requirement is that all hooligans should register with their local authority. As it is difficult to determine who is most likely to be a hooligan, there could be exemptions for old age pensioners, children below school age and, perhaps, for pregnant and nursing mothers. Those failing to register would be liable, on summary conviction, to a fine not exceeding £10,000, or two years' imprisonment, or both. Those registering would pay an annual levy of £500 to meet the cost of administering the scheme and of the salaries of 100,000 hooligan wardens, who would patrol the streets in smart uniforms to prevent hooligans from committing offensive acts, or fouling the pavement.

After registration, every hooligan would have inserted in the lobe of his or her left ear a minute electronic device that would identify the hooligan with a registration number. Decrypting machines would be available at every local Hooligan Warden Centre, and wardens would carry hand-held decrypting devices that would identify hooligans when applied to the left ear. All hooligan registration numbers would be registered on a central computer in Aberystwyth.

Neutering and muzzling would only be applied in cases of

refusal to register, or in cases where actual hooligan conduct had been proved. Muzzling would, however, be required on a temporary basis for spectators at all sporting events. Wimbledon muzzles would be designed to allow the eating of strawberries, while muzzles at Ascot would, if appropriate, be decorated in the owners' colours.

Members of the Royal Family, defined as the descendants of King George III, would not normally be muzzled, unless they had relinquished their right to succession under the Act of Settlement for marrying a Roman Catholic. Peers of the realm and their eldest sons would wear a silk muzzle. In the case of bishops, the muzzle would be purple in colour; this concession would also apply to bishops of the Roman Catholic denomination, and to leaders of the Free Churches.

Home Office statistics show that the great majority of criminal offences, including hooligan offences, are committed by young adult males between the ages of fifteen and thirty. They suffer aggressive urges caused by an excess in the blood of the male sex hormone, testosterone. A research programme should be initiated to discover a safe chemical treatment to reduce hormone levels. If a satisfactofy chemical treatment could be developed, neutering could be reserved for persistent hooligans.

It might be thought difficult to recruit a sufficient number of trained hooligan wardens. This problem could be solved by deferring the vesting date until, say, 1 January 1992. There are a number of trained anti-hooligan operatives available in Eastern Europe. A crash programme in English for ex-members of the Stasi would enable them to supplement locally recruited hooligan wardens.

Let the dogs show the way. Nothing that is wild, or natural, or outside the law, should be free of its electronic tag, its warden or its muzzle. If we let the dogs walk freely in the streets we shall soon, in President Bush's eloquent phrase, be 'in deep do-do'.

9 July 1990

374

CRUEL SCHOOLING SYSTEM THAT LETS CHILDREN DOWN

A single case can often reveal the existence of a public scandal. I believe that the experience of Annis Garfield is such a case. It was reported in *The Daily Telegraph* last week and that was followed by an article by Mrs Garfield in Friday's *Daily Mail*.

Mrs Garfield wants to be a schoolteacher. Her educational qualifications are exceptional. She has a Cambridge degree in Classics; she has been an O-level examiner in English Literature for twelve years and an A-level examiner in Classical Studies for the last two years. She is a governor of her local comprehensive school. She has two children of her own, aged ten and twelve. She has been an all-round athlete. She comes from an academic family.

Since 1985 she has applied unsuccessfully to universities, polytechnics and colleges for a place on a course for the Postgraduate Certificate in Education. In many cases she was rejected without even having an interview. It cannot therefore be suggested that there is some defect in her personality which becomes apparent on interview and makes her unsuitable for teaching. In fact her personality, as it comes across in articles, is reminiscent of the individualist type of teacher whom pupils often remember with gratitude for the rest of their lives.

When she was given an interview it was made clear that the

objections to her were ideological. She is regarded as too old-fashioned, too much of a traditionalist. She was asked what she would teach in an English Literature class. She mentioned Keats and Coleridge, Jane Austen and Shakespeare.

She was rebuked for wanting to teach the classic English authors rather than contemporary American authors, or ethnic minority authors. She sums up her own philosophy of education in these words: 'I think children should be challenged. They should be disciplined. They should aspire to rise above the dully mediocre.' She also favours the traditional phonetic method of teaching English.

If she had run up against one intolerant admissions committee I do not think anybody ought to have been too worried. Individual intolerance, however ugly, is something everyone has to put up with. But she has been trying, with all her qualifications, to obtain a place on a teacher training course for five years and has been rejected by all the institutions she has applied to, often unseen. This has occurred in a period of teacher shortage, when teachers are being flown in from Germany and America to meet vacancies that cannot otherwise be filled. She has not been exposed merely to the capricious intolerance of an individual, but to the collective intolerance of an orthodoxy, the orthodoxy of a 'progressive educational establishment'.

If one criticizes this establishment one is bound to be accused of attacking teachers. That is not true. Many teachers are themselves critical of the British educational establishment, which they see as being out of touch with the real problems of the classroom, and, like most other establishments, predominately male, middle-class and middle-aged. In many cases teachers use the teaching method which they have found to work in practice; they do not always do what this establishment tells them. Yet the same self-renewing group of educationalists has controlled policy since the Sixties, and if the results are bad – and they are – that group must be held responsible.

That does not mean that we should now swing to a traditionalist orthodoxy. One establishment could easily be as bad as the other. My own philosophy of education is probably somewhere between Mrs Garfield's and the orthodoxy of the teacher-training establishment. I would be as horrified if teachers were denied places because they did not share traditionalist views as I am that Mrs Garfield was denied a place because she did hold them. But the rejection of an obviously well-qualified teacher on ideological grounds is outrageous, whether she is rejected for being a Marxist, or for having a Cambridge degree in Classics. A publicly funded teaching system has an absolute duty to be tolerant.

This case seems all the more irresponsible when one reads Martin Turner's study of 'sponsored reading failure'. He reports that a quarter of school-leavers find difficulty with reading and a third with writing. Only 50 per cent of British pupils at the age of sixteen have reached a level in mathematics equivalent to that attained by 96 per cent of Japanese sixteen-year-olds. A quarter, a third and a half of our school-leavers cannot read properly, cannot write properly and cannot figure properly. They have been shortchanged by the educational system; they will be unable to enjoy or prosper in life as well as they otherwise would; worst of all, Mr Turner gives strong reason to suppose that these low standards are falling, and have been falling throughout the Eighties.

He, too, finds that there is an orthodox educational philosophy which he regards as the main cause of these declining standards. 'This philosophy is characterized by its negatives: it is against instruction or "didactism", against testing, against reading schemes, against phonics, against dyslexia, against the notion of skills, against formal methods, against the notion that a child *ever* failed.' An educational philosophy which is opposed to instruction is against teaching.

What is certain is that parents, in the great majority, want the formal virtues and the testable results. Parents want their children to be able to read and write fluently, and they want them to reach the Japanese level of attainment in mathematics. Where parents have to pay for schools they insist that the schools produce these results, and independent schools which fail to do so have to close. In Australia, where there is a similar contrast between the methodology of state and independent schools, there has been a massive increase in independent school numbers: the independent share of the schooling market rose by 30 per cent between 1977 and 1989, to above a quarter.

Parents are naturally concerned about their children's futures. The quarter of children who cannot read properly are disqualified from most well-paid jobs; the half who cannot handle mathematics are disqualified from many well-paid jobs. An education which leaves a child disqualified for good employment is cruelly inadequate and unjust. It is particularly damaging for children from ethnic minorities; if you are black and illiterate your job prospects are grim.

I agree with Sir Claus Moser's proposal that there should now be a Royal Commission on British education. The statistics – which he is uniquely qualified to interpret – show how unacceptable the present results of British education are. The teaching profession is not being given the support or the prestige it deserves, at the primary, the secondary or the university level. Although much of the fault lies with a progressive orthodoxy, dating back to the received ideas of the Sixties, a decade of Conservative government has failed to halt, let alone to reverse, the decline.

If nothing further is done, a backlash is only too likely. Yet education is like lighting a fire in a grate. Without the flame of enthusiasm and encouragement the fire will not burn; that is the truth behind the progressive education movement. Without the grate of formal skills, some of them painful to acquire, the fire will rapidly die away, leaving only the smell of failure. That is the truth behind the traditionalist view. Our educational system should be broad enough to contain both views. But the present educational establishment has failed the nation and its children.

10 September 1990

THE GLORIOUS ETON
DAYS ARE NOT YET OVER

I n the past fifty years Britain has had ten prime ministers, who have held office for an average of five and a half years each, but have won only seven of the thirteen general elections they have contested. Three were educated at Eton, one each at Harrow and Haileybury, and five at grammar schools or schools of equivalent status.

No fewer than seven went to Oxford, none to Cambridge, one to Sandhurst, and two had no higher education. Of the Oxford prime ministers, two went to Christ Church, two to Balliol, and one each to University College, Jesus and Somerville.

One had been president and one librarian of the Oxford Union; two had been presidents of the Oxford University Conservative Association (OUCA); four had little political interest while they were at university. Statistically, Michael Heseltine's education record – Shrewsbury, Oxford, president of the union, president of OUCA – would have made him a favourite to succeed Mrs Thatcher. Douglas Hurd would have scored for being at Eton, but would have dropped points for having gone on to Cambridge. John Major shares only with James Callaghan the characteristic of not having spent time in higher education, though Churchill also became prime minister without going to Oxford.

That seventy per cent of British prime ministers in the past half century should have gone to the same university, and thirty per cent to the same school as well, does seem extraordinary. The leadership campaign rather suggested that this dominance might be a thing of the past. Certainly nobody held it against Douglas Hurd that he had not been to Oxford, but some people did hold it against him that he had been to Eton.

John Major benefited from his non-establishment image, and almost certainly gained votes from not having been to Oxbridge. Strangely enough, Douglas Hurd suffered more than Michael Heseltine from this type of social resentment. He was referred to as a grandee because his father had been a life peer, and he had been at Eton. Michael Heseltine is far richer than Douglas Hurd and has a much bigger house, but Shrewsbury does not have the same image as Eton, and it is no handicap to be an Old Salopian.

In the Cabinet, Eton and Oxford do not seem to be at the same disadvantage. Since Anthony Eden, Eton has been particularly successful at producing foreign secretaries: after Eden it gave us Macmillan, Douglas Home, Carrington and now Hurd – five foreign secretaries in forty years. It may well also have produced a future foreign secretary in William Waldegrave. The Eton style may make the British think of the lamp-post or the guillotine, but it still seems to be much appreciated by foreigners. Eton has two out of the twenty-two members of the present Cabinet – not a bad score for a single school.

Oxbridge remains as dominant in the Cabinet as it has been in the past fifty years among prime ministers. Strangely enough, Cambridge, with nine members of the Cabinet, has gone ahead of Oxford with only seven. Yet a combined total, from the two universities, of sixteen in the Cabinet of twenty-two proves that the Oxbridge dominance, at least of Conservative politics, continues. It seems likely that John Major's successor will again be an Oxbridge graduate, supposing that any member of the present Cabinet lasts long enough to succeed him.

There are two views about the Eton and Oxford influence on British politics. One is that it is a sign of social snobbery, that Oxbridge produces a favoured élite who find their way to the top because they start at the top, that less favoured candidates suffer injustice, and that the nation is ill-served. The other is that this type of education is justified because it continues to produce a supply of highly trained public servants.

The success for snobbery view cannot be maintained in the case of the most recent Oxford prime ministers, Harold Wilson, Ted Heath and Margaret Thatcher. They plainly were not grandees, or the children of grandees. All three made their way to Oxford by scholarships, none was born into a privileged position. They, just as much as John Major, are the result of meritocracy in action. They got to Oxford the same way they reached Downing Street, by tough competition against their contemporaries on their merits.

The same is true of most of the Oxbridge members of the new Cabinet. The one apparent exception is William Waldegrave, but he was a Fellow of All Souls, and has the most distinguished academic record of any Cabinet minister. You are not made a Fellow of All Souls because you went to Eton or because your father is an earl.

The character of Eton has changed too. It is now one of the most difficult schools to enter. Undoubtedly it used to contain a large member of sons of aristocratic families, some of whom were bright, and some of whom were not so bright. It is now a much less grand school in terms of many of the families that go there, but a much better school in terms of the academic standards expected of its students. It used to be the grammar schools that were competitive and Eton that was ornamental; Eton itself is now a very competitive school.

Michael Heseltine, Douglas Hurd and John Major are, all three, examples of competition in action. Michael Heseltine competed at Oxford, competed very successfully in business and has competed in politics. Douglas Hurd may look less competitive, but he won a scholarship to Eton, the Newcastle Scholarship while he was there, another scholarship to Trinity, Cambridge, became president of the Cambridge Union, gained a place in the Foreign Service, left because he was ambitious, and in due course became Home Secretary and then Foreign Secretary. Both Heseltine and Hurd, more clearly indeed than John Major, have shown their competitive determination at every stage of their lives.

The plausible reason people have for disliking Eton and Oxford is that they think they provide an easy route to the top. The truth is almost the exact opposite. Those who succeed at Eton and Oxbridge, or other competitive schools and good universities, have to do so on competitive merit. Rather than looking on these institutions as ladders of easy promotion, it would be more true to regard them as machines for selective competition, producing, as with Michael Heseltine, highly trained and motivated competitors.

If that is correct, then there will continue to be Eton and Oxford prime ministers in the future. I would be more worried, in fact, about Oxbridge than about Eton, though Eton undoubtedly suffers from an even more élitist image. Eton has transformed itself, but Oxbridge has not.

My impression is that other universities have been catching up in recent years with the quality of undergraduate teaching at Oxford; perhaps overtaking it. That happened to my old college, Balliol, which was the best undergraduate teaching college 100 years ago, and is now just one of several good ones. Students are well taught at London or Bristol or Edinburgh – which now has three members of the Cabinet. Well-taught students will always make their way in the world.

It is strange that the resentment against Eton and Oxbridge should have bubbled up now, just as it seemed to be becoming steadily less important. Oxbridge is genuinely open to talent. Eton has a highly competitive academic system. Both are providing an excellent education. Perhaps if the fellows of Eton want more prime ministers, they should now open their doors to young women. That may be where the future political opportunity really lies.

3 December 1990

A FAMILY WITH A HISTORY
OF UNSUITABLE FRIENDS

The Duchess of York shows a proper sense of royal history in having unsuitable friends. Junior members of the Royal Family have always had unsuitable friends, particularly the Princes of Wales. James I's son, Prince Henry, whose death brought the unfortunate Charles I to the throne, was a friend of Sir Walter Raleigh, that notorious womanizer, adventurer and seducer of ladies-in-waiting. George II's son, Frederick, who died in a tennis accident, was the friend of any enemy of his father, and even of poets from the middle class.

All George III's sons had unsuitable friends in large numbers, when they were not murdering their valets or designing Regent's Park. The friends included Regency dandies such as Beau Brummell. King Edward VII had gambling friends and banking friends and scores of women friends, some of whom lived in Paris. King Edward VIII had a dreary crew of toadies, with nicknames like 'Fruity', who spent their lives driving Wallis Simpson across France in fast cars. His set seemed to be modelled on the novels of Michael Arlen, and Mrs Simpson might well have been described in the same terms as Iris Storm, the heroine of *The Green Hat*. 'That lady was a fell lady.'

Even Princess Margaret has had some mildly unsuitable friends in her time, unsuitable not because they were Texan millionaires, but because they were artistic and unlikely to be seen shooting pheasants across the turnip fields of Norfolk, or wherever it is that pheasants go to be shot. The trouble nowadays is that the Prince of Wales does not have unsuitable friends, unless you regard architects as unsuitable as such and has therefore left the public responsibility of undesirable acquaintances of his sister-in-law.

This is, from the point of view of the tabloid newspapers, an arrangement which could be bettered. When princes have unsuitable friends, they are likely to include highly attractive women. I have never met Ms Koo Stark, though she spent her honeymoon in a hotel which was once my home, but she was admirably suited to the role. A beautiful woman who as they say, 'moves in royal circles', will make any tabloid editor spill his coffee as he orders his light brigade to go after her.

I have never met Ms Pamella Bordes either, which perhaps makes me a unique figure among those who have edited London journals in the past twenty years. She would have made an unextremely suitable unsuitable acquaintance for any young prince.

Royalty has always had the support of two groups. The first is a rather serious-minded set of advisers who regard the work of a court, the care of the monarchy, as a public duty. The patriotic courtier, who serves the monarch in order to serve the nation, goes back in history to the reign of King Alfred and beyond. Such people are still to be found in Buckingham Palace or at public ceremonies, inconspicuous, devoted and seldom, except by accident, photographed for the tabloid press.

The other group consists of those who do not take life so seriously. Some of them are no doubt bad people, selfish, idle, untrustworthy, self-indulgent. Many of them are too rich for their own good, and may be regarded as thoroughly silly. Some are good-natured and friendly people, with a gift for making life interesting and agreeable. Whichever they are, a royal family needs them. A court should not be an entirely serious place; a court without laughter and beautiful women lacks essential ingredients of civilization.

No doubt the tabloid press, with its commercial interest in everything the Royal Family does, makes this side of traditional royal life more difficult to conduct and more frequently embarrassing. People knew that Edward VII, like his forebear Charles II, was a greedy womanizer, but most of his philandering – though not all of it – was conducted behind a screen of discretion. The corpulent personage padded softly down the corridors of those country houses where the hostess felt honoured to entertain both the prince and his current mistress. Nowadays, as Lillie Langtry opened her bedroom door, the man from *The Sun* would be on the threshold offering her a large fee for an exclusive interview.

We cannot expect that this side of royal life, in all its range from innocent enjoyment to cynical excess, will ever be abolished. Royal personages are rich, well-fed, and free of most of the restrictions of ordinary life. They live in a world in some ways easier but in some ways much harder than the rest of us. When they are young it is customary for princes to kick over the traces. In history most of them have done so, though not all. Nowadays princesses may be expected to lead as lively a social life as the princes; young blood is likely to run as high in Windsor as it does in Wimbledon.

We should not take any of this too much to heart. I do not think that the Duchess of York ought to take paid holidays to Palm Beach, because I think Palm Beach is a rich, vulgar place full of rich, vulgar people. But for her to do so is at worst an error of taste, and not a grave matter. When she is as old as I am she will probably no longer want to go to Palm Beach, and will be happy to criticize the young people who do. 'In our day,' she may then say, 'we knew how to behave. What we did had a certain style.'

I am not moved by the fact that she is staying in the house of a millionaire who has had three wives. What are his three wives to me? Nor, for that matter, do I mind that Governor Clinton of Arkansas may have had an affair ten years ago with the then recently elected Miss America, though to judge by her photograph she may have been fortunate to win the title. It will not make him a better or a worse president of the United States, if he can get himself elected.

Nor do I believe for a moment that the Duchess's antics,

innocent as they seem to be, are doing any damage to the monarchy. The question of the future of the Crown is a non-question; it is all got up by the Press. The British people remain loyal to the Queen, whom they admire and like. The Queen does her job very well, and is extremely conscientious. So long as we can take her seriously, we do not have to take all the lesser members of the Royal Family equally seriously. Fortunately, the Prince of Wales has inherited the Queen's conscientious temperament.

Britain would not only lose a constitutional benefit, the great focus of national loyalty, if it lost the monarchy. It also would be a far less interesting country. Britain has not remained the top nation in many things, not in wealth, not in power, not even in cricket. We still have what is undeniably the top monarchy in the world, with the Emperor of Japan, I suppose, coming second. Other nations and other nations' newspapers are almost as interested in our monarchy as we are ourselves. Some apparently more so.

Anyone who has walked through the empty palaces of Versailles or Vienna knows how much of the life of a nation is drained away when a monarchy goes, how much of the colour and pageantry. If Windsor and Buckingham Palace were to be turned into bare museums, and Michael Heseltine stood against Roy Hattersley and David Steel for the titular office of President of the United Kingdom, Britain would be a sadder, a diminished place. Our politicians nowadays are not such great men that their appeal can challenge that of more than a thousand years of royal history.

20 January 1992

INDEX